PROJECTS IN LINGUISTICS

PROJECTS IN LINGUISTICS

A Practical Guide to Researching Language

ALISON WRAY
University of Wales, Swansea

KATE TROTT and AILEEN BLOOMER
University College of Ripon and York St. John, York

with

SHIRLEY REAY and CHRIS BUTLER

A member of the Hodder Headline Group
LONDON • NEW YORK • SYDNEY • AUCKLAND

First published in Great Britain 1998 by
Arnold, a member of the Hodder Headline Group
338 Euston Road, London NW1 3BH
http://www.arnoldpublishers.com

Co-published in the United States of America by
Oxford University Press Inc.,
198 Madison Avenue, New York NY10016

British Library Cataloguing in Publication Data
A catalogue record for this book is available from the British Library

Library of Congress Cataloging-in-Publication Data
A catalog record for this book is available from the Library of Congress

ISBN 0 340 65210 1 (pb)
ISBN 0 340 70002 5 (hb)

2 3 4 5 6 7 8 9 10

Production Editor: Rada Radojicic
Production Controller: Rose James
Cover Design: Dudles

Composition by Saxon Graphics Ltd, Derby
Printed and bound in Great Britain by J W Arrowsmith Ltd, Bristol

Contents

PART II   TECHNIQUES FOR COLLECTING DATA

PART III   TOOLS FOR DATA ANALYSIS AND PROJECT WRITING

Preface

Why we wrote this book

We wrote this book because you can't learn how to do good essays and research projects just by reading the subject textbooks. There is a lot of knowledge that a student is expected to somehow 'pick up': what good research looks like; how researchers express themselves; what is a good and bad place to start from. The alert student will gather some of this information piecemeal from tutorials, feedback on written work, talking to other students and so on; but there is usually no way of being sure that you have done all the right things until the work comes back marked.

From the marker's point of view, there are certain things that a piece of work can contain which will make it look credible. There are other things that, at best, give the impression that the student has no ability in or commitment to the subject, or, at worst, make it impossible to assess at all. Yet many of the things that can damn an essay or project are just to do with having the knack of how to write on that subject.

Who the book is for

The book is intended, primarily, for undergraduates taking linguistics or language studies as part or all of their degree programme, and who are expected to engage in research-type project work. However, those embarking on postgraduate research, particularly if they have not previously done data analysis in linguistics, will find the book a useful source of basic procedural information and references to key texts. Secondary- and high-school students engaged in project work should also find it approachable, even if it sometimes assumes more technical knowledge than they yet have.

What the book does

The book is arranged in three parts. Part One is divided into chapters covering some of the major sub-disciplines most commonly chosen by students for their projects. They do not always map onto a single undergraduate module or conventional sub-area of linguistics, because, in our experience, projects don't do this either. But it should not be too difficult to make the connections back to introductory textbooks or class notes. Within each of these chapters there is a brief review of introductory texts (see additional note below), a list of major journals and a brief account of the major research areas. There are also over 250 practical suggestions for projects. These are specifically aimed at the needs of the student who is required to engage with data of some kind, but who is not expecting to make an original contribution to the field (though some of the projects undoubtedly could lead to this if handled well). Part Two contains chapters on methodology, which provide techniques and guidance on how to set up and run research. The final part contains tools: guidance in practical procedures, and specific information that is often needed but not always easy to find.

But before all that, there is an introductory chapter intended to set the scene and help the reader orientate him- or herself. It is strongly recommended that this chapter is read before anything else.

What the book doesn't do

Although each of the project chapters contains an overview of the research that has been done in the area, this book is not intended to provide a full introduction to those areas. Rather than giving a great deal of primary information, already available in dedicated textbooks, we refer the reader to those textbooks. This not only keeps the book focused on its primary function, but also provides the reader with the beginnings of a bibliography. Because of its purpose, there are several areas of linguistics that are not covered at all. Furthermore, many of the projects that are proposed would not be suitable for a more rigorous (i.e. postgraduate or professional) research context. Rather, we have directed our attentions unashamedly towards generating ideas that students will find inspiring and encouraging, and have exploited the freedom from narrower research constraints which can still be enjoyed at this exploratory level.

A note on the textbook review tables

In Chapters 2 to 11 and 23, tables have been provided which attempt to capture the general nature of various textbooks in a way that will make it possible to pinpoint which are most likely to be useful. We have tried to include both the most recent books and also a selection of older ones, on the basis that some texts survive in the market for many years because they are particularly good, and that students often find that older books are more easily available in libraries. The level indicator is only a rough guide, and operates as follows: a book rated (1) is suitable for those reading about the subject for the first time, maybe at secondary and high-school or first-year undergraduate level. A book so rated should be easy to understand and not assume much prior knowledge, but may lack the depth and detail required for later undergraduate and for postgraduate level. At the other extreme, a book rated (4) may be quite dense and difficult to understand, using technical terms and assuming that the reader has a background in linguistics or a related field. As the purpose of this book is to provide ways for the student to build confidence in accessing information, understanding it and using it in practical projects, most of the books reviewed fall into the category 1 to 3. Unless otherwise stated, it should be assumed that a book covers most of the topics considered central to the field, and that they are covered in more depth in those books at a more advanced level (graded 3 or 4) than in those graded 1 or 2.

Acknowledgements

We should like to thank Chris Butler for providing the material for Chapters 19 and 23 and for his general support throughout the project. Shirley Reay not only wrote Chapter 4, but also made a major contribution to the overall planning of the book. We are also grateful to her for her many valuable comments on the finished typescript. Kathy Chilton provided a number of useful suggestions, particularly regarding Chapter 18, and Paul Meara made helpful comments on Chapters 2, 5 and 13. Our thanks are also due to the students from the University College of Ripon and York St. John, whose fascinating projects have inspired many of our suggestions.

Alison Wray, University of Wales, Swansea

Kate Trott, University College of Ripon and York St. John, York

Aileen Bloomer, University College of Ripon and York St. John, York

August, 1997

THE INTERNATIONAL PHONETIC ALPHABET (revised to 1993, corrected 1996)

CONSONANTS (PULMONIC)

	Bilabial	Labiodental	Dental	Alveolar	Postalveolar	Retroflex	Palatal	Velar	Uvular	Pharyngeal	Glottal
Plosive	p b			t d		ʈ ɖ	c ɟ	k ɡ	q ɢ		ʔ
Nasal	m	ɱ		n		ɳ	ɲ	ŋ	N		
Trill	ʙ			r					R		
Tap or Flap				ɾ		ɽ					
Fricative	ɸ β	f v	θ ð	s z	ʃ ʒ	ʂ ʐ	ç ʝ	x ɣ	χ ʁ	ħ ʕ	h ɦ
Lateral fricative				ɬ ɮ							
Approximant		ʋ		ɹ		ɻ	j	ɰ			
Lateral approximant				l		ɭ	ʎ	L			

Where symbols appear in pairs, the one to the right represents a voiced consonant. Shaded areas denote articulations judged impossible.

CONSONANTS (NON-PULMONIC)

Clicks		Voiced implosives		Ejectives	
ʘ	Bilabial	ɓ	Bilabial	ʼ	Examples:
ǀ	Dental	ɗ	Dental/alveolar	pʼ	Bilabial
ǃ	(Post)alveolar	ʄ	Palatal	tʼ	Dental/alveolar
ǂ	Palatoalveolar	ɠ	Velar	kʼ	Velar
ǁ	Alveolar lateral	ʛ	Uvular	sʼ	Alveolar fricative

OTHER SYMBOLS

ʍ Voiceless labial-velar fricative	ɕ ʑ Alveolo-palatal fricatives
w Voiced labial-velar approximant	ɺ Alveolar lateral flap
ɥ Voiced labial-palatal approximant	ɧ Simultaneous ʃ and x
ʜ Voiceless epiglottal fricative	
ʢ Voiced epiglottal fricative	Affricates and double articulations can be represented by two symbols joined by a tie bar if necessary.
ʡ Epiglottal plosive	k͡p t͡s

VOWELS

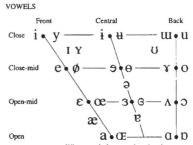

Where symbols appear in pairs, the one to the right represents a rounded vowel.

SUPRASEGMENTALS

ˈ	Primary stress
ˌ	Secondary stress ˌfoʊnəˈtɪʃən
ː	Long eː
ˑ	Half-long eˑ
˘	Extra-short ĕ
ǀ	Minor (foot) group
ǁ	Major (intonation) group
.	Syllable break ɹi.ækt
‿	Linking (absence of a break)

DIACRITICS

Diacritics may be placed above a symbol with a descender, e.g. ŋ̊

̥	Voiceless	n̥ d̥	̤	Breathy voiced	b̤ a̤	̪	Dental t̪ d̪
̬	Voiced	s̬ t̬	̰	Creaky voiced	b̰ a̰	̺	Apical t̺ d̺
ʰ	Aspirated	tʰ dʰ	̼	Linguolabial	t̼ d̼	̻	Laminal t̻ d̻
̹	More rounded	ɔ̹	ʷ	Labialized	tʷ dʷ	̃	Nasalized ẽ
̜	Less rounded	ɔ̜	ʲ	Palatalized	tʲ dʲ	ⁿ	Nasal release dⁿ
̟	Advanced	u̟	ˠ	Velarized	tˠ dˠ	ˡ	Lateral release dˡ
̠	Retracted	e̠	ˤ	Pharyngealized	tˤ dˤ	̚	No audible release d̚
̈	Centralized	ë	̃	Velarized or pharyngealized	ɫ		
̽	Mid-centralized	e̽	̝	Raised	e̝ (ɹ̝ = voiced alveolar fricative)		
̩	Syllabic	n̩	̞	Lowered	e̞ (β̞ = voiced bilabial approximant)		
̯	Non-syllabic	e̯	̘	Advanced Tongue Root	e̘		
˞	Rhoticity	ɚ a˞	̙	Retracted Tongue Root	e̙		

TONES AND WORD ACCENTS

LEVEL			CONTOUR		
e̋ or ˥	Extra high		ě or ˇ		Rising
é ˦	High		ê ˆ		Falling
ē ˧	Mid		e᷄ ˬ		High rising
è ˨	Low		e᷅ ˯		Low rising
ȅ ˩	Extra low		e᷈ ˜		Rising-falling
ꜜ	Downstep		↗		Global rise
ꜛ	Upstep		↘		Global fall

1

Introduction: Starting on the right foot

Choosing an area

In this book we are assuming that you are about to embark upon a data-based, dissertation-length project in an area of your choice. However, even if you are preparing an essay for a specific module, the book will be able to help you tailor it to your own requirements and preferences. In either case, the secret of good research is to know what it is practical to do and what it is wise to do, so here are some questions you can usefully ask yourself.

What can be researched?

There are plenty of questions that we can ask about language. But not all of them are suitable for a research project. For example, some questions cannot be answered for practical reasons, such as *how many words are there in all the languages in all the world?* Even if you could settle on an adequate definition of 'word' and 'language', you couldn't ever gather the information. A good research question is one that you can envisage finding an answer to. So, never just ask the question. Always imagine the possible answers and how you would find them out.

What shall I write about?

Obviously, try to choose an area that interests you, as this is an important aspect of doing good work. Remember that you will have to eat, sleep and breathe this project for at least a few weeks, if not several months, so do yourself the favour of choosing something you can live with. If you cannot think of a subject, glancing through the rest of this book may provide some inspiration. Alternatively, take half an hour with a cup of coffee and your old files and textbooks and simply remind yourself of the bits of linguistics that you found most interesting. Try to remember what it was about linguistics that fired your interest in the first place. Maybe your studies so far have not given you an opportunity to pursue some of the interests you brought with you, and now might be your chance to follow them up.

If you have other projects coming up over then next year or two, prepare the ground now. As you read, think, chat and write other pieces of work, jot down any thoughts, references, etc. in a book or file marked 'project ideas'. Then, when it comes to it, you'll have plenty of ideas to choose from.

What makes a good project?

- A good project is something that is going to be do-able within the bounds of the available facilities. To ensure this, plan through the stages very carefully, listing what you will need. For many students, it is even a problem getting access to a quiet room, let alone a patient during brain surgery!
- Be aware of what aspects of linguistics you are best at. You need to work to your strengths.
- Try to focus on something that is genuinely of interest in the field. The more you read, the better idea you will have about what is considered important.
- It is a good idea to base your work on something that someone else has done, either trying to replicate their results or changing one **variable** (see Chapter 23), such as the age or gender of the subjects.
- In looking for ideas, try to use sources that are as up-to-date as possible. There are some experiments and theories which are classics, but research mostly has a shortish shelf-life, and the main reason why students end up basing their work on an experiment or idea from the 1960s or 1970s is because they used a very old book from the library!

Who will supervise me?

Supervising student projects can be one of the most rewarding, or one of the most demoralizing, things that a university teacher has to do. You have the power to determine which! You will get most out of a supervisor who shares your interest in the subject, especially if he or she is personally research-active in it. It really is worth finding out what areas the available staff are most involved in; and don't just base your judgement on what they have taught you on previous courses, as they don't always get to teach their favourite subjects, especially in relatively small departments. Find out from the department's list of staff research interests who works in areas that interest you, and then arrange to see them. Most people love talking about their own research and will be delighted to have you take an interest.

What am I expected to do?

There are in-house rules for project writing and presentation. In some places they are uniform across the whole institution, in others they are subject-specific. If you have taken modules in more than one department, you may find that there are different protocols, so make sure you have the appropriate ones for each subject. In-house rules include things like:

- What the word limit is and how you calculate it. Do quotes, appendices and summary tables count? Are you allowed to go over or under the limit, and by how much? What happens if you don't stick to the limit? What happens if you submit your work late?
- What is the presentation format? Is it compulsory to word-process? Do you need to leave a right-hand as well as a left-hand margin? Should you write/print on one side of the paper or both? How many copies are you to submit? Does the work have to be bound, or in a certain type of folder? Even if there are no specific rules, put yourself in the place of the person marking not just your project but numerous others like it (possibly at 2 o'clock in the morning), and think about the following points. If comments are to be made *on* your work, it is not helpful to put each sheet in a separate plastic envelope. In some kinds of presentation files, the words at the right-hand edge of the reverse side of the paper cannot be read because of the file-grip mechanism, so you need to leave a margin. As a general rule, the smaller the package your work comes in the better – walking home with 40 ring binders is actually a physical impossibility.
- What is the preferred referencing system? A full description of the two most common ones (**Humane** and **Harvard**) can be found in Chapter 21.

Getting organized

How do I organize my time?

You have only limited time to achieve your goal. You want your work to be as good as possible, which means not rushing it, but also not wearing yourself out. You need to use your time well, and know when to stop. Only by planning can you really identify what needs doing, in what order, and how long it will take. If you don't have some idea of this, you are leaving a great deal to chance. One way to schedule things is to work backwards:

16th: DEADLINE

15th: add any handwritten bits (symbols, diagrams etc.); photocopy; take to the binder. (Note that while some types of binding can be done while you wait, others take longer. Check in advance, so that you can make allowances in your schedule)

14th: print final version (NB: *never* leave printing to the last day. You *know* why!!)

12th: draft-print 'final version' and read it **slowly** for typing errors, style, expression, accuracy in referencing and general sense; make any alterations

11th: write conclusion and final version of introduction

10th: finish chapter/section X

5th: finish chapter/section Y

It is important to honour your timetable. When you have achieved your goal, stop and rest. Getting ahead of your own schedule can be a good psychological step, but only if you don't slow down so much that you waste the time you gained. If you get wildly out with your timetable, rewrite it, taking into account any factors you overlooked last time, and making any necessary adjustments in what you hope to cover.

Making a plan

From the start, have a clear idea of what you are intending to cover and what you aren't. Write a list of chapter and/or section headings, and list what will go in each. Whenever you come across a useful idea or reference, note it in the appropriate place on your plan, so that you can find it when you need it. You can always change your plan later, but it's better to have one. It saves you doing all sorts of unnecessary work for chapters or sections that you haven't realized you won't need to write. Also, read the *'Before you write'* section of Chapter 25.

How to read and how to make notes

Avoid just reading things that might be relevant in some general way. Always know why you are reading something and what you hope to find out, and don't make notes that are not specific to your work. Rather than ending up with separate pages of notes for each book or article you read, make the notes under the headings for which they are appropriate in your work. So, any page of your notes will contain references to several different works. This means that you are more likely to recognize when two authors disagree. It also means that writing up can be done without wading through all the notes again. Always label a note or quote with the author's name, date of publication and page number, so you know where to find it again. If what you have written is a quote, put it in inverted commas; otherwise you may not remember later, and may think it is your own words. To present some-one else's words as your own is plagiarism (see Chapter 22). Copy accurately, especially spelling and punctuation.

Using resources

Where to look in libraries

Besides the linguistics section, remember to check other sections (e.g. education, sociology, philosophy, psychology) that may have relevant books. Check general reference books, including encyclopaedias of linguistics such as Bright (1992) and Asher (1994), current and past journals (lists of relevant titles are given in the project chapters later in this book), abstracting journals (see Chapter 24 for how to use them), bibliographies (these tell you who has written what in a given subject area), unpublished MA dissertations and Ph.D. theses, and archives of past undergraduate projects.

You can also use information from the World Wide Web. Note, however, that there is no quality control on the WWW, so information may be inaccurate or even positively (and deliberately) misleading.

Which libraries to use

Besides your own and any other local university or college libraries, remember to consider hospital and other institutional libraries and local archives. The local city or county library may also have useful books, and if you need inter-library loans, you may be charged less there than in your own institution. Major university libraries and public libraries in large cities may not let you borrow books, but you can arrange in advance to gain read-only access. National libraries, such as the British Library in London, normally require a special ticket, and you may need a letter of introduction from your institution confirming that you are engaged in research. The books of the British Library Lending Division are available via the inter-library loan system (ask your librarian for details).

Buying books

Apart from set textbooks, there may be other books that you want to buy, but this can get expensive. Choose carefully – best of all are books that will be of use to you again in the future. If there are books that you need your own copy of, but which you can't afford, negotiate with a friend to buy jointly. Exchange lists of the books you already have, too, so that you don't buy a book someone else could lend you. Use the second-hand market. If you keep books in good condition, they can often be resold, and one of last year's students may have a copy of what you want at a knock-down price.

Journals and how to use them

On the whole, the information in journals is more up-to-date than anything you will read in a book. Usefully, the work reported is often in a format not dissimilar to the way your project will look. Most institutions keep the latest issues of journals in one place, and then bind several issues together and put them on the stacks (shelves). Check the contents pages of journals for relevant-sounding titles and for authors who you know work in your field. Use the reference lists in journal articles as a quick way of finding other relevant material. If you want a copy of an article published in a journal your library does not keep, apply for it through the inter-library loan scheme. Identify likely articles by reading the summary in an abstracting journal (see Chapter 24). If you find a journal article difficult to understand, whether because of its style or the previous knowledge it assumes, start by reading the abstract, the introduction and the conclusion. These will present the main points and help you to orientate yourself. Then go back and read the rest of the article.

Using people

There are lots of people in the world who know things that you don't, so ask them. The golden rule is to ask sensible questions, so that you don't annoy people or waste their time. If you do your homework first, most people will be pleased to give you time and information.

Databases

Many valuable databases can be obtained on disk, CD-ROM and via the Internet. These include general corpora of English and other languages, and specific corpora such as the CHILDES database of child language (see Chapter 3). Chapter 19 gives guidance on how to obtain and use corpora. Databases have long been available in book form too, though. For example, you can find out the frequency with which different words occur in texts from word-frequency lists such as Johansson and Hofland (1989), Nation (1986), Hindmarsh (1980), Carroll *et al.* (1971), Kucera and Francis (1967) and West (1953).

Using dictionaries and glossaries

If you are unsure what a word or a technical term means, then look it up. Apart from general English-language dictionaries, there are a number of specialist linguistics dictionaries, including Crystal (1996), Trask (1993, 1995a) and Richards *et al.* (1992). Many books have glossaries at the back, e.g. Wardhaugh (1993), Fromkin and Rodman (1993) and Crystal (1997a), and Kuiper and Allan (1996) has chapter-specific glossaries in chapters 1, 4, 6 and 8.

Being a researcher

There are certain hallmarks of being a researcher, certain assumptions that are made, and ways in which the work is approached. Here are a few pointers.

What research looks like

Most research investigates a **hypothesis**. A hypothesis is a thoughtful guess about the way things might be. An experimental hypothesis makes predictions about the outcome of specific controlled events, and the outcomes actually achieved enable you to confirm or fail to confirm the hypothesis. Hypotheses are also used in non-experimental research. They enable you to identify in advance what contrasts or features you are looking for in your data, so that you can set up the data collection in an appropriate way. For example, in an observation study your hypothesis might be that a child will interact differently with adults than it does with other children. This gives you a focused goal, and reminds you to avoid having other differences between the two situations, such as what activities the child is engaged in. If your research is not built upon a hypothesis, there is a serious danger that you will not be able to explain what you have found out. Hypotheses are made in the light of **theories**. A theory is an explanation of something that can be observed. Theories are only of value to science if they are not self-fulfilling; that is, if we can imagine what we would observe if the theory was not true.

Because each piece of research builds on what has gone before, care has to be taken that the results at every stage are trustworthy. Thresholds are therefore maintained below which an observed phenomenon, however interesting, is not considered to be reliable. Normally the threshold relates to how consistently the phenomenon is found or how big the difference is between the pattern observed and one that you could get by chance. Statistical tests can tell you if a measurement is **significant** at an acceptable level of potential error. See Chapter 23 for a fuller explanation.

Much legitimate research involves re-running experiments and analyses done by others, challenging established theories with new data and so on. Because linguistics spans the sciences and the humanities, it deals with strikingly different kinds of intellectual material:

- Quantitative data, on which statistical tests can be done: experimental results, word counts, etc.

- Qualitative data: judgments, perceptions, insights, etc.
- Pure theory: models of internal processes which, though testable in terms of what language is like, are in essence non-experimental.

Using theory

All research should be theory- or model-based, and most research involves testing, by such means as experiment or observation, a prediction of the theory or model. Observational work, interviews, experiments and case studies must all be underpinned by some theory or model upon which they will shed light. The results can then be used to enter into a wider discussion. Your best chance of identifying a good focus for investigation is to begin with a model, rather than desperately searching for one after you've got your data. Remember that all the research you read about or hear about in lectures will have been designed to test some aspect of a model, so if you choose to base your work on someone else's experiments or observations, make sure you understand why they thought their investigation was interesting.

Theory-only projects

In some circumstances it may be possible to focus entirely on the critical evaluation or the development of a theory or model without collecting any data of your own. There are two basic reasons why you might embark on a theory-only project. First, you may want to write about an aspect of language that either is not amenable to testing or cannot usefully be investigated via data-collection (though either way it should still be possible to illustrate your points with linguistic examples). Areas of linguistic study where these criteria might apply in some circumstances include such subjects as the evolution or origin of language, philosophy of language or syntactic theory. Second, it may not be feasible to collect the sort of data that you require. In this case, you will be referring to data-based research, but it will be the published material of other researchers. Into this category might fall projects focusing on clinical linguistics, exotic languages, historical linguistics, and so on. Do not see theory-only projects as an escape route from empirical research – they are difficult to do well. Also, check that a non-empirical project is acceptable for your assessment.

If you are writing a theory-only project, begin with a clear overview of the literature. You should read around the area that interests you as extensively as is practical, because otherwise your arguments will be unsubstantiated. Identify a theory that interests you and which you feel is open for debate, then try to find an angle on it that will create interesting discussion. This could be done by looking at wider implications in some way. For example, a model of lexical retrieval for monolinguals could be discussed in the light of the needs and practices of multilinguals. Can the model cope with this easily or do lots of parts of the model need reorganizing? Or a model that represents the transition from thought to utterance could be explored from the viewpoint of human evolution: does it lend itself to there being a survival advantage at every stage of man's evolution? For further ideas on this, see Aitchison 1994: 222. Or if someone has proposed a model that accounts for the production of speech, how easily can it be applied to writing? Can it simply be reversed to account for comprehension? If it is a model of adult language, does it apply equally to children?

Draw diagrams to demonstrate how your model works. Diagrams should be explicit and should adequately illustrate the sequence of events that will produce the envisaged outcome. It should be possible to explain the predicted results if the structures are subject to breakdown or malfunction at any stage. Explain the ways in which your model differs in construction, process and outcome from others.

Setting up data-based research

Chapters 2 to 11 in this book explore the types of projects that you may be able to undertake. Different areas of research require different techniques, and these are described in Chapters 12 to 16. But before you start there are many general considerations, which we will look at now. It is very important that you read the next few pages, and that you remember to re-read them as you plan and carry out your project. What is said below is, of course, subject to modification in the light of what your own course requirements are, so don't forget to check with your own supervisor or tutor what you are expected to achieve, what methods or approaches are preferred and what equipment is available.

Making sure you know enough

Although it is best to choose a project that uses skills you already have, this may not be entirely possible. If you need additional skills, check whether there are tutors who can help, either directly, or through recommending self-study texts or other sources of assistance. You may feel that a tutor can give you an honest answer to the question 'Am I up to it?' See if there are courses you can opt for, or specific lectures you can attend, which could help. If you know well in advance what your project will be on, plan your courses to prepare you for it. Lecturers often remark that students could help themselves more during project work by looking back carefully at courses they have previously taken, perhaps digging out old lecture notes and reading lists and generally making use of established resources.

Getting subjects and informants

As linguistics is about human language, most projects need access to people. You may want to work with one person in some detail (for example, in a case study) or you may need to get a number of people to perform some task, either individually or as a group. Either way, you must be sure that appropriate people will be available. Here are some questions you need to consider. How will you persuade your subjects to give up their time? What will you tell them about the purpose of your study? You may feel that they will respond differently if they know what you are interested in, so you will need a cover story. If you need to record speakers without their knowledge, there are issues of ethics (see 'Safety and ethics' below). If you want to compare males with females, are you easily going to recruit the same number of each? If you are collecting your data in the vacation, who will you use? If you recruit willing members of your family, what will be the effect of their differences in age, education and so on.

Remember that your subjects are doing you a favour by participating. It is in your interests to keep them sweet, so be as efficient as you can in making arrangements, keeping to appointments and clearly explaining what you want them to do. Remember to thank them afterwards. Subjects may be interested to know, at a later date, how the study turned out.

Accessing and using equipment

Establish what you need and whether it is available. Do ask for help and advice from the technicians. Also, there may be postgraduates in your department or outside it who have experience in using the equipment. Even if your own department does not have what you need, another one may (the psychology department, the audio-visual unit, the computing department or an individual researcher). If you need special computer software there may be a fellow-student who will help you write it. If you have a clear idea of what a piece of equipment does then you may be able to think of an alternative (cheaper, simpler) way of achieving the same result.

Safety and ethics

If you are at all unsure about the safety aspect of your data collection, get advice. You will not be very popular if you kill one subject in three, and you should really aim to avoid even sending them away with a headache. (The headaches that you get are, however, par for the course.) As for ethics, whilst, for procedural reasons, you may not be able to tell a subject precisely what you are looking for, you should have the general consent of that individual to use the material you collect. It is best to avoid data that is in any way compromising to the subject (i.e. anything they would be ashamed to admit to in public), and if you *do* have anything of that nature, every care should be taken to retain total confidentiality as to its source, by not naming subjects or providing other clues that could associate them with it. There are legal requirements regarding the handling of certains types of personal data; these are summarized in Chapter 20. Many universities have an Ethics Committee, and certain types of research procedures need to be cleared there before they can be applied. Check with your supervisor whether there is such a committee, and whether it is relevant to your work.

Reducing the risk of it going wrong

Research that involves other people is sure to present all sorts of problems you haven't foreseen. If your questionnaire is ambiguous, your experimental stimuli are inappropriate or your tape recorder doesn't work, you can end up with data that is useless or even non-existent! Beware of the **observer's paradox**: it is often impossible to collect data without the subject knowing that you are doing so. Yet the presence of a tape recorder, experimental equipment or even simply you yourself may have an effect on the linguistic behaviour of the subject(s), so the data may not be representative of what would happen if no observation were taking place. Various techniques have been devised to help in interview situations at least: asking exciting or emotive questions can help concentrate a speaker's attention on the content of what they say, diverting their attention from the form of the language they use to express their ideas. In experiments, try to make any equipment as unobtrusive and unintimidating as possible and allow time for the subjects to get used to it and understand what it does.

By running a **pilot study** (experiments and questionnaires) or a rehearsal (recordings and interviews) you can identify many problems before you do the major part of the research. A pilot study is a trial run using a small number of people similar to those you will use as subjects. Even if you are doing an observational study, case study or a text analysis, you can have a 'dummy run' by taking a small piece of suitable data and working through it to check that you will be able to achieve your objectives. Try to make the pilot as representative as possible by taking it seriously. Gather the results and practise processing them, whether through the tables and statistics (multiply them by 10 or 20 if that helps the number-crunching) or through some process of interpretation. Ask the people who took part in the pilot or rehearsal to help you modify the procedures so that they will work better (would two short sessions be better than one long one? Were the instructions clear?). If it is an interview study, ask your pilot subjects to help you frame the questions or procedures better. Because of their advance knowledge of the procedures and stimuli or questions it is usually inappropriate to use pilot subjects again in the main study.

Ending up with manageable results

The biggest single error made by inexperienced researchers is not thinking about what the results will look like until they have them. It may seem as if the difficult part of the work is getting the data, but it isn't! There is nothing worse than sitting down with 40 hours of tape or 300 pieces of paper and thinking, 'What do I do with this lot?' Here are some tips. If you haven't got time to transcribe an hour's taped data from each person, don't collect it that way. If you are designing a questionnaire, make sure you know how to collate the full range of answers you may get (see Chapter 14). You also need to know what to do with a rogue result or an unhelpful respondent – can you identify in advance clear grounds for excluding such a case and no others? Check whether you are expected, as part of your assessment, to perform statistical tests on your results. If you are, or if you feel that it is appropriate to do so, work out in advance what test(s) you will use, and have a clear idea of how you will generate the values that go into them. Chapter 23 will help you.

Handling data and knowing how to interpret your results

Summarizing data (especially scores) into formats that are easy to digest and compare is essential if both you and your readers are to make sense of them. Clearly thought out and labelled tables can be very important for numerical or descriptive data. Remember to refer closely to the information in tables. Never simply let it 'speak for itself'; you need to demonstrate that you know both how the tables were devised and also how to interpret them, so be prepared to give worked examples of some of your results, plus detailed general discussion, before drawing broader conclusions. If you do not find the patterns you expected in your data, you still have a result. Consider why it has happened. Could the reason lie in your experimental design? Be prepared to evaluate your work critically and state how it could be improved in future.

   Numerical data may appear straightforward, but it is not difficult to end up not knowing what the numbers actually mean. Before you start, make sure you are able to state clearly what it will mean if result A is bigger than B, B is bigger than A, A and B are the same, and so on. Know where every figure will go in a table and which ones you will want to compare with which. Use Chapter 23 on statistics before you design your study, to ensure that you will have results you can process! Non-numerical data is often much more messy and difficult to draw firm conclusions from. You may know that a speaker tends to put up more resistance to an interruption by person A than by person B, but how can you quantify that? The questions that will be raised by your data analysis should be predictable from your background reading before you start. It is very unlikely that you are treading a particular research path for the first time, and so there will be answers to all your questions within the published literature, providing you have started from the same place as previous researchers and done similar things. So careful advance planning, with a clear vision of what results you might get, is the key to interpreting them later. Never simply start collecting data in the hope that you will find something interesting – you may, but you will not necessarily know what to do with it.

Drawing conclusions

In all cases, you will be aiming to draw some conclusion about an aspect of how language works or how people use or process language. At the very least you should be able to provide some speculations, on the basis of your data, about how phenomena of the type you have observed could come about. There is nothing wrong with reasoning through various possible arguments in your write-up, visibly discarding one model in favour of another: it gives the assessor a much clearer idea of how you have got to your final conclusion. You are likely to conclude, amongst other things, that a slightly different methodology might have worked better. Therefore, include a brief description of what you would do next time, either to improve the procedures or to further what you have achieved this time. This needn't be done in a self-deprecatory manner. Remember that one major purpose of research is to identify what to investigate next, and how.

Writing up

All write-ups require that you justify your work by providing contextualization in the form of a general literature review, and/or a description of any specific work, model or theory that your work is exploring, expanding or challenging. Aim for clarity and avoid empty statements. In linguistics, and especially in 'scientific' linguistics, it is a good idea to write under headings: this helps to keep everything in its place, saves words and makes the work much easier to read (see also Chapter 25). If you run an experiment, the general format of the write-up should be that of any scientific report, with headings such as *review of previous studies, aim, method, results, conclusions*. Other types of research will need different headings, and you can gain an idea of this from looking at how relevant journal papers are set out. Aim to sound like a 'proper academic'. For example, avoid being apologetic about your lack of knowledge or experience, or about things that have gone wrong. You have as much right as anyone to conduct research and everyone has to start somewhere. If something went awry, do what the top researchers do: just state what the problem was and how you think it could be avoided next time. You can also improve your academic style by modelling your expression on linguistics books and journals. Take careful note of comments about style in your essays and if you don't understand what you have done wrong, ask your tutor. Further guidance is given in Chapter 25 in this book.

Avoiding plagiarism

The threat of plagiarism is a source of great anxiety to lots of students who have never and will never plagiarize. On the other hand, unless care is taken with the way you write, you may inadvertently plagiarize. A definition of plagiarism and guidance on practical ways to avoid it, with a worked example, can be found in Chapter 22.

Being streetwise: keeping on the right side of your assessor

It pays to understand the psychology of your assessor. Getting in a pile of projects to mark does not always fill a university teacher with feelings of unqualified delight. It is in your interests to maximize the chance that your assessor has a smile on his or her face from the moment your project reaches the top of the pile to the moment that the grade is put onto the marksheet. The best way to achieve this is by writing outstanding work, but there are a few other tactics as well, that will make him or her feel that you have taken care to make your work easy to read. Obey the house-rules for presentation, word-counting and deadlines (see above) and express yourself with care (see Chapter 25). Label your work clearly, and if there is any danger of odd pages coming loose, label every page with your name and the page number. Do everything you can to indicate clearly the structure of your work, so that the assessor knows at every point what you are doing and why. Use a word-processor. If you have to write things in by hand (e.g. phonetic symbols), then remember to do it, and make them neat and legible. If your writing is terrible, get a friend to write them in for you.

As regards audio and video data, make the recording quality as good as possible (see Chapter 12 for hints). If you have recorded data over something else on an old tape, record some silence at the end of the data so that you do not confuse the assessor with unrelated material or deafen him or her with your favourite band. If the data is not at the beginning of the tape, wind it to the right place. The tape should be an edited one, containing only the data you have written about, along with, if sensible, a small amount of context. If you are referring to specific utterances on tape, put the examples onto tape in order, introduced with a reference number. Alternatively, provide a transcription of the data with counter numbers clearly marked, so that your assessor can fast-forward to the right place. Bear in mind, however, that counter numbers rarely correspond from machine to machine. Another method is to provide a list of what is on the tape, the length in minutes and seconds of each bit and some sort of brief description of the contents of each section, so that the assessor can work out where he or she is after a fast-forward. Remember to label the tape and the box with your name and the course or module number and the tape contents; and keep a copy of all data and of the project itself, in case it gets mislaid.

PART

I

AREAS OF STUDY AND PROJECT IDEAS

|2|

Psycholinguistics

Psycholinguistics is concerned with language and the brain. It asks questions like:

- How does the brain store all those words?
- How does it access them so quickly and efficiently most of the time, yet occasionally give us that *tip-of-the-tongue* condition?
- Why are we more likely to mishear something that is out of context?
- How do we know how to finish off a sentence that someone else starts?
- How similar are the processes of listening and reading?
- When the brain encounters a sentence it has never seen or heard before, does it have to look everything up in some vast dictionary and grammar store, or are there short-cuts that it can take to work out what it means?
- Does it process the words in the order in which it hears or sees them, or does it store up strings of words and then process them all at once?
- Why doesn't it take idioms like *he's one sandwich short of a picnic* literally?
- How does it know when someone has made a mistake in what they have said?
- What mechanisms operate during speech production to ensure that all the words come out in the right order and with the right intonation?
- What can the language of brain-damaged people tell us about how language-processing occurs?

Just imagine trying to teach a computer to speak and understand a language exactly like a human, and it becomes clear why we shouldn't take the answers to questions like these for granted.

To be a 'perfect psycholinguist' (if such a thing could exist), you would need to have a comprehensive understanding of the way the brain operates (neurology), the processes by which we perceive and interpret the world (psychology) and the variety of categories and intricate structures that are found in human language (linguistics). You would also need to have a laboratory full of up-to-date equipment suitable for both psychological and neurological experimentation, and know how to use it. For your experiments, you would need access to a never-ending supply of 'ordinary people' and various types of patients from neurological units. In practice, most researchers in psycholinguistics are restricted to working within one or two sub-areas. Some operate exclusively within a laboratory or other controlled environment, testing specific hypotheses in a manner parallel to the procedures of other sciences. Some work in a clinical environment, building up models of the normal functions of the brain by observing people whose language has for some reason gone wrong. Some try to relate issues in theoretical linguistics to possible models of how the brain might store and process information.

Textbooks and major journals

Psycholinguistics is a sub-discipline of both psychology and linguistics, and the slant within textbooks varies accordingly, so you are likely to encounter some rather different viewpoints and approaches. It is best to look at a range of different books to gain ideas for projects, and not to be put off by descriptions of work that you would not be equipped to even contemplate! Try to get an idea of the background of each writer and how he or she views psycholinguistics. What the books all have in common is an account of the most important models and empirical research findings. Table 2.1 reviews a selection of the books that you may find most useful. In Fig. 2.1 you will find the names of the journals most likely to contain research papers relevant to psycholinguistics.

Table 2.1 Useful texts for psycholinguists (see page xiv for key to levels)

Book	Level	Notes on Content/Style
Aitchison 1989, 1994	1–2	quirky approach and style but reliable
Caron 1992	3	reports experimental studies on normal adults only; useful theme-based approach
Clark and Clark 1977	3	breadth and depth of coverage; readable; key textbook despite its age
Eysenck and Keane 1995, chs. 12–14	3–4	written for psychologists; densely packed with good information; worth getting an overview from an easier book first
Foss and Hakes 1978	3	out of date on theory but approachable; helpful headings
Garman 1990	4	assumes knowledge of linguistics
Garnham 1985	3	nothing on acquisition, pathology or other 'descriptive' areas; focus on theories
Greene and Coulson 1995	2–3	concise, no-nonsense guide; summaries of experiments including procedures used

Book	Level	Notes on Content/Style
Harley 1995	3	wide coverage, aimed at psychologists; appendix on Connectionism
Kess 1992	2–3	psycholinguistic perspective on syntax, discourse and semantics, etc.
McNeill 1987	3	not suitable as an introduction, but gives useful perspectives on issues
Prideaux 1984	2–3	unique, practical compendium of do-able experiments, explaining their theoretical background and how to do them
Singer 1990	3	focus on psychology of discourse and sentence processing, including reviews of experimental work

Applied Psycholinguistics
Behavioral and Brain Sciences
Brain
Brain and Language
British Journal of Psychology
British Journal of Disorders of Communication
Child Development
Cognition
Cognitive Neuropsychology
Cognitive Psychology
Cognitive Science
Cortex
First Language
Journal of Child Language
Journal of Cognitive Neuroscience
Journal of Experimental Psychology: Human Perception and Performance
Journal of Memory and Language[a]
Journal of Neurolinguistics
Journal of Psycholinguistic Research
Journal of Psychology
Journal of Speech and Hearing Research
Journal of Verbal Learning and Verbal Behaviour[a]
Language and Speech
Language
Language and Cognitive Processes
Language and Communication
Linguistic Inquiry
Linguistics
Memory and Cognition
Neuropsychologia
Psychological Bulletin
Psychological Review
Quarterly Journal of Experimental Psychology

Fig 2.1 Major journals for research in psycholinguistics
[a] Same journal: *JVLVB* renamed as *JML*

Central themes and project ideas

There are two levels at which a project in psycholinguistics can operate.

- If you have some experience of experimental research and have access to specialist equipment and supervision, you can plan to replicate or adapt a published experiment. Find references to such experiments by reading the overviews recommended below, and going from there back to the original account, which will normally be in a journal. Only the original paper will give you sufficient detail of the procedures and analyses for you to plan your own work. Get advice at an early stage from your supervisor, and ensure that you have plenty of time for the planning, execution, analysis and writing up. General guidance on experimental work can be found in Chapter 13.

• If you are not experienced, if you have little call on equipment and/or if your supervisor has insufficient time or specialist knowledge to support you, you are not in a position to conduct research that is compatible with the complex procedures of the published work. However, there are plenty of projects that require less technical skill but which can still be used to shed light on the psychological processes of language. It is mostly projects of this sort that are suggested in the following sections.

Modularity

Following Fodor (1983), most psychologists believe that human cognition is modular. This means that it consists of a number of independent processors. If processors operate independently, then it should be possible to find people who have impairment of one, while the others function normally. As far as language is concerned, interest lies in establishing whether the processes responsible for the production and comprehension of speech and writing are four independent ones or not. For example, if you lose the ability to process *spoken* input, does that also mean that you will be unable to process *written* input? A model of processing consistent with this pattern might have the comprehension of written input mediated by an internal phonological representation of the input, so that all written input had to be turned into 'speech' before it could be decoded.

Although it seems as if it should be straightforward to establish these relationships through clinical case studies, this is not so, for several reasons. First, each process is complex and involves several stages, while any two processes might be partly independent and partly interdependent. Second, damage occurs in different places in different patients, making it difficult to adequately categorize any patient relative to any other. Third, there is likely to be more than one route to processing any one type of input, and damage may affect only one of them. Finally, two processes might be fundamentally independent but tend to both get damaged in many patients, because they operate out of adjacent areas of the brain.

You can gain an impression of these problems from Eysenck and Keane (1995: 285–7). Read more about modularity in Eysenck and Keane (1995: 14–16), Caplan (1987: 36–8, 180 ff.) and Harley (1995: 24–8). For a slightly different slant, emanating from the field of artificial intelligence, read Minsky (1988). Harley (1995: 282) briefly reviews evidence that speech input and speech output involve separate processors. Evidence against there being a specialized module from speech perception, as separate from other auditory perception processes, is weighed up in Eysenck and Keane (1995: 278).

PROJECTS

1. Investigate the hypothesis that some types of extraneous sound are more distracting to linguistic processing than others by giving a difficult linguistic task to three groups of subjects, one of which completes it with sound (a) in the background, one with sound (b) and one, control, group with no sound. Possible sounds include: a single prolonged tone, speech in English, speech in an unknown language, classical vocal music, classical instrumental music, vocal rock music, instrumental rock music or jazz. Don't try to have groups for all these kinds of sounds, as you will need enormous numbers of subjects and the statistics will get very complicated as you attempt to compare the performance of each group with each of the others. It would be better to run two simple experiments than one complicated one. Questions to address include: Why should extraneous noise be harder to filter out in some cases than others? What does that tell us about the way the brain shares its energies and attentions? What sort of model might be drawn up to represent the phenomena and explain the outcomes observed?

2. Compare memory for objects with memory for words. Give one group of subjects a set of household objects to memorize. Give a second group just a list of the names of the same objects to memorize. Hypothesis: it is easier to remember the names of objects than it is to remember the objects themselves. Null Hypothesis: it is equally easy or difficult to remember objects that you have seen as to remember the names of objects that you have seen written down. Account for your results in terms of a processing model. For example, does the process of memorizing an object involve naming it?

3. Assess the transferability of linguistic training to another task by giving one group of subjects training in strategies for memorizing random lists of words. Give a second group no training. Then ask both groups to memorize long lists of words and recall them. In a second test, give them long lists of numbers to recall. Hypothesis (a): the trained group will perform better in the words list than the untrained group; null hypothesis: training makes no difference. Hypothesis (b): the memorization of words and numbers require different skills, so any advantage for the trained group in word memorization will not hold for number memorization; alternative hypothesis: the trained group will perform better on both tests because memory training is transferable from one type of stimulus to another. Note that because, here, one prediction is built on another, it is easier to explain some result patterns than others. Consider the significance of an outcome where the untrained group performed better on: the word test; the number test; both.

Themes in comprehension

HOW WE UNDERSTAND THE SPOKEN WORD: THREE THEORIES

Three major theories have been put forward in recent years about how we process the spoken word. The interest lies in how we deduce the meaning so efficiently when the quality of the acoustic input is so variable, and how we work out so quickly what a word is – often after only the first two phonemes (Marslen-Wilson and Tyler 1980).

Motor theory

The listener recreates the motor movements associated with speaking the words, though not necessarily in a way that can be measured physically. This theory has been largely discredited now (Eysenck and Keane 1995: 280–1), but there is still the potential for testing it in projects.

Cohort theory

As soon as we hear a word begin, we 'flag up' all the words we know which have that sound at the beginning, creating a **word-initial cohort**. We then disqualify those which no longer fit when the next sound is heard, or which are unlikely because of the context. The cohort model is described in Eysenck and Keane (1995: 281–3), Harley (1995: 58–63), Garman (1990: 286–90), Caron (1992: 54–6) and most other introductory books on psycholinguistics. A more simple and graphic account of its basic operation is given in Aitchison (1994: 217–18). We also recommend reading the original paper by Marslen-Wilson and Tyler (1980).

TRACE theory

The TRACE model (McClelland and Elman 1986) derives from an approach to the modelling of psychological processes called **connectionism**, and entails the dynamic connection of **nodes** (processing units) creating the information pathways where they are most useful. When we hear a word beginning with a [tʰ], say, this excites the pathway for the phoneme /t/, and that in turn begins to excite the pathways to all the words beginning with /t/. The next sound in the word excites new nodes and pathways, and there is therefore a build-up of activation to those words that have all of the sounds heard so far. TRACE is described and evaluated in Eysenck and Keane (1995: 283–4) and Harley (1995: 56–8).

PROJECT

4. Ask as many friends and relations as you can to jot down examples of *slips of the ear*, that is, when they mishear something. Give them as much time as possible – at least several weeks – and make sure they remember to make a note of things at the time. Some genuine examples are: *The United Nations is thinking of withdrawing all the blueberries from the former*

Yugoslavia (Blue Berets – the UN Peacekeeping force); *Hormone treatment should be available for postmen or pausal women* (post-menopausal women); *I'm going on a trip to Cabbage World* (Cadbury World). Further examples and a taxonomy for them can be found in Garman (1990: 162–4).

Use the examples (don't forget to collect your own too!) to assess the models of lexical processing described above. Are there any examples of mishearings that do not begin with the same sounds? If so, how can the standard models of processing account for them?

HOW WE UNDERSTAND THE WRITTEN WORD: THREE THEORIES

Reading is a secondary linguistic skill. Whereas a child develops naturally the facility to speak and understand speech, reading and writing are learnt. They are an extremely recent innovation in mankind's development and still have little or no role in many parts of the world. Therefore, we should expect that the processes of reading and writing are overlaid on the much older processes of understanding and producing speech. However, evidence from some kinds of brain-damaged patients suggests that when we read, we do not always simply translate the words on the page into a phonological representation and access the meaning that way: rather, there appear to be short-cuts that do not involve the mediation of speech processes (see, for example, Eysenck and Keane 1995: 295–300).

Eysenck and Keane (1995: 288–9) review the advantages and disadvantages of five different approaches to the psycholinguistic study of reading processes. Amongst the issues that have been addressed recently in the research are: is the recognition of a word aided by the preceding context? (Rayner and Sereno 1994); are words identified by recognizing the component letters, or by overall wordshape? (see Eysenck and Keane 1995: 292).

Autonomous serial search model

Words in the brain are likened to books on a library shelf, with each word listed independently in three different access files (like library catalogues): orthographic, phonological and syntactic-semantic. The comprehension process is speeded up by the most frequent words being the first to be searched through. You can find out more about this model in Aitchison (1994: 212–13) and Harley (1995: 88–90).

Logogen model

Each word has a threshold of activation, which, when reached, triggers it to be recognized. The level of activation goes up when information is received about the letters in the word, or about the context in which the word occurs. Frequent words have a lower threshold and words that have been used already also have their threshold temporarily reduced, as they are more likely than usual to be needed again. Read about the logogen model in Morton (1979), Garnham (1985: 46–50), Caron (1992: 53–4), Harley (1995: 90–4), Garman (1990: 276 ff.) and Eysenck and Keane (1995: 211 ff.)

Interactive activation model

Based on connectionist principles, this is similar in nature to the TRACE model for speech comprehension (see earlier). Nodes and pathways are activated when we recognize parts of letters, whole letters and words. Thus, words beginning with *w* achieve an increased level of activation when the letter level has recognized that *w* is the initial letter. As the subsequent letters in the word are identified the activation is increased again for those words still consistent with the information, until the correct one can be chosen (often before all the letters have been processed). For a description and evaluation of this model, see Eysenck and Keane (1995: 292–4) and Harley (1995: 94–7). Coltheart *et al.* (1993) also review models of reading, based on clinical evidence.

PROJECTS

5. In order to test whether reading is mediated by phonological processing, present on a computer screen sentences that are (a) acceptable (e.g. *Chess appeals to clever boys*), (b) nonsense (e.g. *Trees blossom during knives*) and (c) nonsense, but that sound identical to acceptable ones (e.g. *Wardrobes and dressers differ in sighs*). Time subjects pressing one or other of two keys, according to whether the sentence makes sense or not. Hypothesis: sentences in set (c) will take longer to judge as nonsense than those in set (b). Alternative hypothesis: there is no phonological involvement in silent reading, so (b) and (c) will take the same amount of time to decode and respond to. In order to counter the problem of some sentences simply being intrinsically harder than others, have two groups of subjects, each of which has homophones where the other has the correct spelling, such that the second group would have *Wardrobes and dressers differ in size* in set (a) and *Chess appeals to clever buoys* in (c). In constructing the stimuli bear in mind that the position in the sentence of the homophone may make a difference to the speed of processing, because if the first three words are already nonsense you don't have to look any further. Compare your results with those of Baron (1973).

6. Base an experiment around that of Van Orden (1987). This involves measuring reaction times to questions such as: *is BREAD a FOOD?; is MELT a FOOD?; is MEET a FOOD?* For a brief description of the procedures, the results, a later replication and problems with the design, see Eysenck and Keane (1995: 294–5).

HOW WE UNDERSTAND SENTENCES

It is generally believed that there are differences in the way that we access the meaning of spoken and written words, but that the processes by which we achieve the comprehension of larger units (i.e. phrases, clauses, sentences) are common to both mediums (Eysenck and Keane 1995: 303). Speech and writing are therefore considered together in this section.

The nature of sentences and how they convey ideas is explored in Chapter 9 of this book, but here we consider what psycholinguistic research tells us about how we process them. As Eysenck and Keane (1995: 303 ff.) point out, we need to recognize that any given sentence displays a number of characteristics: it is potentially novel – that is, there is no guarantee that we will have come across it before; it has a grammatical structure; it has a literal meaning; and it has an intended meaning (which may be different; for more on this see **pragmatics** in Chapter 9 of this book).

The relative complexity of sentence types

According to an early theory of Chomsky's (1957; 1965), the more procedures a sentence has to go through from its surface structure to its underlying (deep) structure, the longer the decoding will take (the theory of **Derivational Complexity**). The passive, negative and the locking of two clauses together as main and dependent are among the **transformations** from and to the underlying form, which Chomsky claimed had to be carried out in real, measurable time. Psycholinguists attempted to test the hypothesis, by timing subjects' reactions in decoding tasks involving sentences of different transformational complexity, but failed to find consistent support for it. For further details of this, see Aitchison (1989: 183–94), Fodor *et al.* (1974) and Greene and Coulson (1995: 32 ff.). For an example of an early experiment, look at Slobin (1966).

Subsequent research has offered other models of how sentence parsing (decoding) is achieved. Clifton and Ferreira (1989: 79) provide a list of sentence types predicted to take longer to parse according to their model. Parsing models by Bever, Kimball, and Frazier and Fodor are described in Garnham (1985: 77–87). For a comprehensive description of model types, see Garman (1990, ch 6).

Lexical and structural ambiguity

There are potential lexical ambiguities in much of what we hear. Why do we not normally notice that, for example, *Have you got enough time for this?* could equally well be *Have you got enough thyme for this?* Researchers have wanted to establish whether all the possible interpretations of a phonetic string are available at first, and then eliminated, or whether one interpretation is assumed (possibly the most frequent) and the others remain unretrieved unless there is a problem making the chosen one fit the context. There are accounts of research into lexical ambiguity in Garnham (1985: 62–7), Aitchison (1994: 213–16) and Harley (1995: 289–97).

Ambiguity also occurs at the syntactic level. It entails two or more possible interpretations of the structure of a clause, as in *Hubert saw his grandmother riding on a horse.* Syntactic ambiguity is of interest because it can tell us how our grammatical and semantic processing interact. If we decode a whole clause grammatically before we try to interpret it, then we should not expect to find any evidence of the semantic context having resolved the disambiguation before the clause has ended. Evidence from experiments such as those of Tyler and Marslen-Wilson (1977) suggests that we do use semantic information to help us resolve syntactic ambiguity. For a brief description of this work, see Harley (1995: 298).

Garden-path sentences

Garden-path sentences are so called because they *lead us up the garden path* by misleading us about their construction. An example is *The ball bounced past the window burst.* They are significant because our problems in interpreting them as grammatical appear to depend on our decoding strategy. If we have already 'decided' that we know how the sentence is constructed before we reach the point where that structure becomes evidently false, this can prevent us recognizing the correct, and only grammatical, interpretation (*The ball which was bounced past the window burst*) even when the whole sentence has been heard. For a fuller description and references to experiments, see Kess (1992: 129 ff.). Eysenck and Keane (1995: 304–5) take a wider and more critical view of Frazier and Rayner's (1982) model for the garden-path phenomenon and how it relates to the resolution of ambiguity in general. A review and challenge to garden-path theory along with four experiments can be found in Ni *et al.* (1996). For additional general information, use Malmkjaer (1991: 368–75) and Pinker (1994: 212–17). Garden-path sentences are also briefly discussed in Chapter 9 of this book.

Inferencing

To what extent is our understanding of stretches of language helped by inferences that we make, that 'bridge the gap' between what is explicitly stated and what we might need to know in order to create an adequate picture of the situation? Two theories exist in opposition: the **constructionist** view is that we make a large number of inferences when we hear or read a sentence – enough to create a coherent picture, and to make it possible to understand many facts that have simply never been stated. The **minimalist** view is that we make very few inferences. Eysenck and Keane (1995: 308–12) examine both views and review the research that has attempted to test their relative merits. Graesser *et al.* (1994), for example, propose that the extent to which you draw inferences depends largely on why you are reading or listening to the text.

A useful account of much other research into the processing of sentences is given in Eysenck and Keane (1995, ch. 13), where you can also find a description and evaluation of Rayner and Pollatsek's (1989) integrated model of reading (326–9).

PROJECTS

7. In many cases, one reading of a lexically or structurally ambiguous sentence makes more sense in the context than the other reading. But there are also cases where context does not disambiguate them. Do informants still tend to think of one of the two available readings first? One theory suggests that the more frequent meaning will be accessed first (see Garman 1990: 255–7, Harley 1995: 71–3).

   Construct some sentences that contain ambiguity, but where the two readings seem equally likely (e.g. lexical: *Everyone enjoyed the port*; structural: *Marmaduke had a conversation with a postman riding on a horse; I saw the man with the telescope*). Randomize the order of the sentences and record them onto a tape, ensuring that there is nothing in the way they are read that favours one interpretation over the other. Interview informants individually. Tell them in advance that the stimuli are ambiguous – they will soon work it out anyway – play them one sentence at a time and ask them which interpretation they registered first. Hypothesis: informants will all tend to think of the same reading first. Null hypothesis: both readings are equally likely to be recognized first, if there is no context to aid the interpretation. If the hypothesis is supported, attempt to explain what it is about the preferred interpretation that has given it that status.

8. To test the Derivational Complexity Theory, present a passage on computer screen, and then pose true–false comprehension questions. Write active and passive versions of each question, and give each of two groups of subjects a mixture. Time their responses to the questions (have them press one computer key for 'true' and another for 'false'). Hypothesis: passive questions will take longer to respond to than their corresponding active.

   Because any given question is framed in the passive to one group and the active in the other, you are controlling for some questions being inherently more difficult than others. Remember that some passive sentences are easier to identify as such than others, because pragmatics precludes the possibility of seeing the grammatical subject as the actor (e.g. *The walls were painted by the handyman*). For more details of this, see Slobin (1966) or Greene and Coulson (1995: 32–4). In order to avoid complications regarding the balance of actives and passives in the original passage, make sure the whole passage is in the active. A low-tech alternative is to read the questions out and time the subjects' verbal 'true/false' response. Do this by recording the entire question–answer session, and timing the period from the beginning of the question to their answer (remembering to always read the questions at the same speed!).

9. Sachs (1967) predicted that when we listen to spoken input for meaning, we discard the information about its form after decoding it. She tested this by asking subjects whether or not they had heard certain sentences in a passage: some sentences had been in it, and of those which had not, some were paraphrases of what had been in it (e.g. passive where the original was active), while others were different in meaning. Her results indicated that '[the] original sentence which is perceived is rapidly forgotten, and the

memory then is for the information contained in the sentence' (Sachs 1967: 422). Replicate her experiment, perhaps with some modifications, and see if your results agree with hers. There are brief reports of the experiment in Slobin (1979: 55–6) and Garnham (1985: 139).

Themes in production

PRODUCING SPEECH

In order to speak a word, we have to take the idea that we have in mind to a store of words, find and retrieve a match, activate the instructions about how to pronounce it, and pass those instructions to the articulators (tongue, larynx, and so on). To produce a whole utterance there must be forward planning to ensure the words are articulated in the right order, with the correct intonation, and so on. We can investigate these processes in three ways: by experimentation, by the analysis of speech errors in normal individuals, and by the observation of the problems encountered by certain types of aphasic patients.

Experimental data: an example

It is not at all easy to investigate the process of speech production experimentally, because we normally only have access to the final product. One question that has been addressed, however, is: when we retrieve a word, do we have information about both its meaning and its sound at the same time, or first one and then the other? Levelt *et al.* (1991) found that subjects who were naming pictures were not put off if a semantically related word was presented late on in the retrieval process; this suggests that by that late stage the retrieval had passed through the semantic stage and was being dealt with phonologically, ready for the word to be spoken. For other details of this experiment and follow-up ones, see Eysenck and Keane (1995: 338).

Speech errors and tip of the tongue

Inadvertent errors in the speech of normal people can provide indications of how we access individual words and how we plan the larger units of our utterances. Garrett (e.g. 1976) studied speech errors in some depth (see Caplan 1987: 273–4; Harley 1995: 260–6), and found:

- more errors with content words than other words, including semantic substitutions, words swapping places (e.g. *he is planting the garden in the flowers*), and the transposition of sounds between words (e.g. *shinking sips* for *sinking ships*). Where an affix gets separated from its root (e.g. *He is schooling to go* for *He is going to school*) it is the affix that stays in place and the content word that moves.
- prepositions occasionally undergo semantic substitution.
- there is always a phrase boundary between the two words in a word swap.

- there is rarely a phrase boundary between the two words in a sound swap.

For an examination of a whole range of speech errors, see Garman (1990: 151–62). Fromkin (1973) provides an easy introduction to slips of the tongue and Cutler (1982) investigates them in more depth. A short assessment of the processes involved is given in Eysenck and Keane (1995: 336–7). For some examples, see Crystal (1997a: 265). Besides errors as such, research has looked at general dysfluencies, including pauses, in the production of speech and writing. For a review of the findings on pauses, see Harley (1995: 244–50).

General accounts of the tip-of-the-tongue phenomenon can be found in Aitchison (1994: ch.12) and Garman (1990: 170–1); for discussion contextualized in other theories, see Eysenck and Keane (1995: 335 ff.). An experiment designed to elicit the tip-of-the-tongue phenomenon in experimental conditions is reported in Brown and McNeill (1966). The experiment is briefly described in Harley (1995: 246–7), Garman (1990: 170) and most other introductory texts.

Aphasia

Many descriptions exist of speech errors and word-finding difficulties in aphasics, and, clearly, models of normal processing need to be able to account for the phenomenon. Amongst the word-level symptoms that manifest themselves in various forms of aphasia are:

- an inability to access content words: this is like an extreme form of the tip-of-the-tongue phenomenon. For an example of typical output see Eysenck and Keane (1995: 340).
- making up non-existent words (**neologisms**): see Harley (1995: 270).
- semantic errors: substitution of a word with a similar or associated meaning. For examples, see Aitchison (1994: e.g. 21–2).
- phonological errors: problems with sequencing the sounds, or the persistent use of a wrong sound over several attempts. For examples see Aitchison (1994: e.g. 21–2).
- more problems with verbs than nouns (Malmkjaer 1991: 18).

Broca's aphasics often have agrammatism, consisting of problems putting words into sentences so that they 'look as though they are being output one at a time' (Harley 1995: 267), and also particular difficulties with the elements that carry the grammatical structure, such as function words (e.g. prepositions) and word endings. Wernicke's aphasics, who produce long strings that seem as though they should be meaningful but actually are incomprehensible, have better access to the grammatical words than to content words. For brief information about the major symptoms of aphasia, see Eysenck and Keane (1995: 339–41) and Harley (1995: 266–76). A general consideration of how aphasia contributes to research into normal processing, and many examples of aphasic speech, can be found in

Aitchison (1994). For a detailed introduction to aphasia see Garman (1990, ch. 8), Caplan (1987) or Lesser (1989).

PROJECTS

10. The Brown and McNeill (1966) tip-of-the-tongue experiment is reasonably easy to replicate. You may want to modify it in various ways. Reading their account may give you ideas for an experiment of a different design that elicits the same phenomenon.

11. Write a case history of one aphasic patient, include examples of spontaneous speech, recitations of well-known rhymes or lists (e.g. days of the week), specific naming tasks, and so on. Are all of these tasks equally easy or difficult? If not, what may be causing the differences? If you have the opportunity to conduct a longitudinal study, log the patient's improvement or deterioration. What strategies does the patient have for coping with his or her problems? How do carers and others deal with them? Do teaching or therapy have any long-term effect?

12. Challenge one or more models of language processing (in general) or lexical retrieval (in particular) to adequately explain the patterns of word-loss described in the aphasia literature. Use a resource like Eysenck and Keane (1995) or Harley (1995) to find a suitable model.

13. Find a person with word-finding difficulties and catalogue: words consistently accessible; words occasionally accessible; words never accessible, and words said in error for other words. Look for semantic and syntactic patterns to these sets and use this to test hypotheses such as: concrete nouns are more easily accessed than abstract ones; function words (*and, by, of, yet*, etc.) are very difficult to access; word substitutions are always in the same word class (noun for noun, verb for verb, etc.); personal names are more difficult to access than generic nouns (e.g. *John* is harder to access than '*boy*'). Are whole sets of semantically linked words lost at once?

Each case is different and the patterns you find will depend on the precise symptoms of the individual, so don't prejudge. Use the information to examine one or more models of lexical storage and access (see above).

14. Elicit speech errors by recording subjects when tired or drunk, or when reading a technical passage as if for a video voiceover. Sort the errors into types and use them to evaluate a model of reading and/or speech production.

15. Collect speech errors over a long period of time, or use commercially available audio- or videotaped compilations of out-takes from TV or radio. Rather than just listing your examples, use them to challenge or support models of speech production. In categorizing and analysing your data, consider questions such as: What was said? What was intended? How soon did the speaker spot the problem? Why at that particular point? Did the listener spot the problem? Why/how? What did the speaker do? What did the listener do? Was there an actual, or potential, breakdown in communication? What is the phonetic/articulatory relationship between what was said and what was intended, and what happened in the phonological environment, e.g. did any assimilation match the intended or the actual output?

READING AND WRITING

To read words we must recognize their shape and/or letters, and have some way of relating them to meaning. Mostly we can also link them with a phonological form, though it is certainly possible to know a word without knowing how to say it. In order to write a word, we need to first select it from the mental lexicon and then access information about how it is spelled. Interesting questions arise about whether speakers of different languages have different processing systems, because in languages with a good grapheme–phoneme correspondence, such as Spanish, it is possible to move between pronunciation and spelling via simple 'rules' (see Harley 1995: 117 for references to research into this), whereas English has words that are not pronounced as they are spelled (e.g. *knight*; *Leicester*). These require a word-specific listing. Yet our ability to pronounce non-words like *blenk* shows that we have the grapheme–phoneme pathway as well.

Slips of the pen
As we might expect if our model of writing parallels that for reading, as described earlier, there is evidence that errors in writing can occur at letter-part, whole-letter and word level. Garman (1990: 165–7) describes slips at all these levels. For many more examples, and a fuller examination of what they can tell us, see Hotopf (1983). There has been little research on errors in the writing of longer units – perhaps because we are more likely to spot them as they are happening and to repair them at an early stage. However, Hotopf (1983) examines a sizeable collection of data.

PROJECTS

16. Adapt the Sachs experiment (see above) for written input. Use one of the current models of processing (such as those reviewed in Eysenck and Keane 1995) to predict in what ways changing the medium may change the outcome of the experiment. Are your predictions borne out?

17. Replicate the experiment reported by Kaufer *et al.* (1986), in which writers were asked to think aloud as they composed text and the location of their pauses was noted. It was found that experienced writers operated in larger units than inexperienced ones. For a brief description of this experiment see Eysenck and Keane (1995: 342–3).

18. Get subjects to type a passage as fast as possible onto computer without being able to see the screen (it is best if they are fairly fast typists). As they can't see what they've put in, they will be unable to go back and correct. Analyse the errors, first separating out those that are to do with adjacent keys. Are there transpositions across words, across phrase boundaries, etc.? Relate your findings to those from research into slips of the pen and dysgraphia (see below).

19. Replicate or adapt Griffiths's (1986) experiment where subjects copied a written passage while observers noted where they paused to look back to the original. He found that pausing was not random, but tended to happen at syntactic (constituent) boundaries. The methodology could be adapted for copying onto a computer.

Dyslexia and dysgraphia

Dyslexia in common parlance actually refers to **developmental dyslexia** and **developmental dysgraphia**: disabilities that some children of normal intelligence have in learning to read and write, and which can persist into adulthood if not remedied. There are several reasons why developmental dyslexia and dysgraphia are still not understood:

- until recently, children with severe dyslexia were misdiagnosed as stupid or lazy.
- bright, resourceful and/or highly motivated dyslexics often find ways of compensating for their difficulties, and indeed may not always realize that they are dyslexic.
- the terms 'dyslexia' and 'dysgraphia' do not describe single phenomena. They are used of an array of symptoms, and a given individual may have only some of them. These symptoms may indicate different levels of severity in a single brain dysfunction, or may be caused by different things.

To find out more about developmental dyslexia, see Crystal (1997a: 275–7), Ellis (1993), Snowling (1987) and Olson (1994). Miles and Miles (1983) provides a simple and accessible practical guide to defining and identifying dyslexia, and also suggests ways in which dyslexic children can be given practical help. There are references to further reading and also to readers, workbooks and materials suitable for use with dyslexic children. Addresses of associations dealing with dyslexia are listed. Harley (1995: 133–6) assesses the similarities and differences between developmental and acquired dyslexia. Cromer (1991: 289–97) describes the writing problems of (developmentally) dysphasic children.

There exist also **acquired dyslexia** and **dysgraphia**, however. These affect individuals previously able to read and write, but who lose some or all of that ability after a brain injury. Acquired dyslexia can take different forms, suggesting breakdowns at different stages of the reading process. It is not always easy to tell what the nature of the problem is. If a dyslexic patient reads the word *daughter* as *sister*, how are we to tell whether the correct word was found in the lexicon but the wrong one was selected at the pronunciation stage, or whether the error had already been made much earlier, so that it was *sister* that was looked up and (correctly) pronounced?

Several types of acquired dyslexia have been identified, including:

- **surface dyslexia**: irregular words are read phonetically, suggesting that, when reading at least, sufferers do not have access to their lexicon (which would supply information about the peculiarities of the pronunciation), and have to use a phonological route to reading.
- **phonological dyslexia**: non-words (e.g. *blobe*) cannot be read aloud, but words known to the patient can be correctly read, including ones with irregular pronunciation. This indicates that reading is only achievable via the lexicon, which, of course, does not contain any item that hasn't been encountered before. There are also problems reading function words.
- **deep dyslexia**: non-words and function words cannot be read aloud, and there are semantic errors, such as *flower* for *rose*. As in phonological dyslexia, there appears to be no ability to use a phonological route in reading, but there is evidently also a problem in ensuring that it is the target word that is assigned a pronunciation.

All of these dyslexias have other symptoms associated with them too. For examples of the sorts of problems that acquired dyslexia can present, and how models of processing attempt to account for them, see Crystal (1997a: 274), Eysenck and Keane (1995: 296–300) and, for considerably more depth, Harley (1995: 111–17) and Coltheart *et al.* (1987). For models of reading based on clinical evidence see Coltheart *et al.* (1993), and for a model founded in the connectionist approach, Plaut and Shallice (1993).

Acquired dysgraphia manifests different symptoms, amongst which are semantic errors (e.g. writing *sun* when asked to write *sky*, and *chair* for *desk*), homophone errors (e.g. writing *sought* for *sort* and *scene* for *seen*), phonetic spelling (e.g. *flud* for *flood*, *neffue* for *nephew*) and the inability to write unknown or non-words. For more information about these examples, and the way they relate to a model of how we write words, see Eysenck and Keane (1995: 348–9). There are further examples of acquired dysgraphia in Crystal (1997a: 275).

PROJECT

20. Analyse data from a dyslexic child (or adult) before, during and after remedial help. Gauge the extent to which the problem has been solved, poor skills have been directly improved and/or alternative strategies have been developed to compensate for an immutable deficit. Incorporate your assessment into a model of reading, to explain what differences in the processing procedures appear to have been achieved in order to improve the outcome. Before you embark on this, make sure that there are no procedural problems with collecting and holding the data – some institutions may not allow it on confidentiality grounds, but a friendly parent may have no objections to your studying their child's old school-books, and a dyslexic adult may be very willing to provide you with relevant data. Also check whether your own university has ethics procedures (see Chapter 1).

The units of normal processing

A number of researchers, including Pawley and Syder (1983), Sinclair (1991) and Wray (1990, 1992a) have suggested that language comprehension and production can be at least partially achieved using 'a large number of semi-preconstructed phrases that constitute single choices, even though they appear to be analyzable into sections' (Sinclair 1991: 110). Amongst those noted by Pawley and Syder is: *NP be-TENSE sorry to keep-TENSE you waiting*, which generates many sentences all to the same pattern, including: *I'm sorry to keep you waiting; I'm so sorry to have kept you waiting; Mr X is sorry to keep you waiting all this time* (Pawley and Syder 1983: 210).

These constructions, and others that are more fixed such as *What in the world* and *The thing is*, are variously called **sentence frames, (routine) formulae, chunks, schemata, templates, sentence builders** and **lexical phrases**. They may be advantageous as regards processing resources (Wray 1990, 1992a) and/or language learning (Nattinger and DeCarrico 1992). If quite lengthy phrases or clauses can be stored and accessed like single lexical items, there are important implications for models of how we process sentences, and certain predictions can be made about patterns in speech errors.

PROJECT

21. Record someone recounting the same experience several times to different people (and maybe several weeks apart) to see if the same structures and expressions are used to describe the same events on separate occasions. Consider the implications of 'preferred' ways of saying things, for a standard model of language processing.

Language and thought

Since the work of Sapir and Whorf, there has been much interest in the question of whether we 'simply' express thoughts through our language, or whether the way our language operates has an effect upon the way we think. Out of this have come two hypotheses, the stronger **linguistic determinism** – the way we think is determined by our language so that we are, as Sapir put it, 'at the mercy of our language' – and the weaker **linguistic relativity**: we are more likely to interpret the world in a certain way because of our 'language habits' (see Slobin 1979: 175). The theme was taken up by

George Orwell who, in an essay at the back of his novel *Nineteen Eighty-Four*, explains how a new version of English, *Newspeak*, will prevent subversive thought by containing no words capable of expressing it. For direct access to Whorf's ideas, see Carroll (1956). Slobin (1979: 174–85) explores in some detail the implications and predictions of the Sapir-Whorf hypotheses. For a critical appraisal of the debate see Pinker (1994, ch. 3); Pinker concludes that the Sapir-Whorf position is unsustainable, and that thought is independent of language.

PROJECTS

22. A counsellor was recently heard to say in a radio interview, 'Before we talked about problems we didn't think about them.' This might imply that if there was no counselling culture, many of the problems it deals with would not exist. Survey the views of counsellors, clients and people who have never used a counsellor to explore the hypotheses that talking about something (a) changes the way you perceive it, (b) can create a problem in your mind that didn't exist before, and/or (c) gives you words to express thoughts and feelings you already have. Link this to the Sapir-Whorf hypotheses of linguistic determinism and linguistic relativity.

23. Someone who does not eat meat is called a *vegetarian*, someone who eats no animal products at all is called a *vegan* and someone allergic to gluten is referred to as a *coeliac*, but there is no commonly used term for a person who avoids red meat or dairy products, and no clear way to differentiate between vegetarians who do and do not eat fish. Compile a list of common dietary preferences, and conduct a survey to find out how people commonly refer to them. What level of consistency is there? Does it matter if there is no agreed terminology for things, provided we can find some way of talking about them? Would there be any advantage for our ability to conceptualize and communicate if there were agreed words for all of these different preferences and conditions?

OTHER PROJECT IDEAS

24. Design your own model to show how different components of language processing interact. Are the words selected first and then made into a sentence, or is the sentence planned first and then words slotted into it? At what point are the sounds selected? Are they selected as *phonemes* and then given an allophonic identity at a later stage, or is all the phonetic information selected at once? Evaluate the model against published data or other models.

25. Take a psycholinguistic perspective on some other area of linguistics that you know well, such as phonetic sequencing, the production and/or comprehension of intonation, the construction and/or comprehension of sentences, functional approaches to language production/comprehension, the storage of idioms and so on. Draw up a model or use one from the literature, and then take a detailed look at what the model needs to deal with in

the course of constructing or understanding an utterance. Remember that it will be your detailed knowledge of this other area of linguistic theory that will justify the model you produce.

26. Investigate experimentally the hypothesis that science students will perform less well on a difficult linguistic task than humanities students. Justifications for this hypothesis might be, for example, that: any individual is either mathematical or linguistic, and people select careers that reflect their strengths; scientists do not get as much practice in language tasks; scientists are less confident in language tasks. If the results do not support the hypothesis, suggest reasons why.

27. Run an experiment separately on two groups. In both cases tell them to write down as many words beginning with, say, 'm' as they can think of in two minutes (you can make this harder by specifying that they must be nouns and/or more than three letters long). Then go through the same procedure again (using a different letter), but before they start, tell one group that an average score on this test is 10 words, and tell the other group that it is 35 words. Hypothesis (a): when people feel pressured into attaining high standards they will perform less well. Hypothesis (b): when people feel pressured into attaining high standards they will perform better. Null hypothesis: putting pressure onto people does not significantly reduce or increase their ability to access items in the lexicon.

    Use the results of the first task as a control (see Chapter 13), to check that the two groups are capable of performing to similar levels in identical conditions. Then you can have confidence that any differences in the second task are relevant to your hypotheses.

28. Monitor the progress of two aphasic individuals considered by the experts to have broadly similar symptoms and prognoses, but one of whom gets more help (speech therapy, family involvement and so on) than the other. Use this to examine the role of practice, motivation and the need to communicate in the recovery of speech.

For further project ideas, see Prideaux (1984), Clark and Clark (1977) and Greene and Coulson (1995).

3

First-language acquisition and development

Research in first-language acquisition and development addresses the central question of why and how children succeed in acquiring language. To establish this, researchers focus on the acquisition of rules and structures, including grammar, vocabulary and the sound system, and also on how children gain knowledge about how to use language appropriately in different situations. Questions of current interest include:

- What do children bring to the process of acquisition?
- Are there general patterns (**language universals**) for the acquisition of all human languages?
- How crucial is the role of the language the child hears around it, both from carers and other children?
- To what extent do children vary in their language acquisition and usage and why?
- How long does language acquisition take?
- Is there a 'critical period', or finite age range, within which acquisition must take place, if it is to occur at all?
- To what extent should the acquisition of literacy be seen as part of the overall language acquisition and development process? In what respects are the processes of oral and written language acquisition similar?
- How does language acquisition proceed in bilingual or multilingual children?
- Do the processes at work in second- or foreign-language acquisition in adults resemble the processes of first-language acquisition?

Approaches to research

Many of the above questions are addressed by studying the structure and meaning of the language produced by children at different ages or stages of development. This has made it possible to construct a generalized profile of the stages of language acquisition, and to make detailed comparisons of the child's language and the adult model. Study of the **variation** between children focuses on the *rate* at which aspects of language are acquired and the *route* of development. The term 'route', here, can refer to the order in which language rules are acquired and also the strategies used to acquire them. Research into how language comes to be used in ways appropriate to **social context, gender** and **social group** includes an examination of the mechanisms by which situation-sensitive usage is acquired, and the relevance of adult role models. **Cross-linguistic** and **cross-cultural comparisons** of the acquisition process provide a broader baseline for hypotheses about innate language abilities and universals. Studies of different types of **language disability** and **abnormal delay** in acquisition, whether due to internal or external causes, tell us about normal processes by indicating what it looks like when various individual components go wrong.

Terminology

Acquisition is often used to refer to the learning of language structures or rules, especially those of grammar, phonology and so on. (Note that within the context of second-language acquisition research, the term 'acquisition' can have a slightly different meaning – see Chapter 5). **Development** often refers to the child's *use* of the acquired language rules and structures in a widening variety of language contexts.

Textbooks and major journals

Table 3.1 Useful texts for first-language acquisition (see page xiv for key to levels)

Book	Level	Notes on Content/Style
Aitchison 1989	1	cryptic chapter headings – not good for quick and easy reference
Bennett-Kastor 1988	3	focuses on methodology; few illustrative samples of child speech
Cruttenden 1979	2–3	incl. reading and writing
Crystal 1986	1	'parent's guide'
Crystal 1987	1–2	aimed at teachers and therapeutic professionals; incl. writing and education-related issues
Crystal 1995, section 23	1	includes language disability
Crystal 1997a, part VII	1	excellent resource for basic information and many illustrations
Crystal, *et al* 1989	3–4	language disability, incl. practical techniques for analysis & assessment (e.g. LARSP)

Book	Level	Notes on Content/Style
Elliot 1981	3	narrow but detailed coverage; incl. parental language, social class, context, bilingualism; experimental studies in ch. 6
Fletcher 1985	3–4	single case-study, useful as a model for similar studies and for example data
Fletcher and Garman 1986	3–4	each chapter by a different specialist in the field; first edition (1979) has different chapters in it
Fletcher and MacWhinney 1995	4	incl. non-normal development; methodology; theoretical and social issues
Foster 1990	3	incl. pragmatic and conversational development; little on variation
Freeborn *et al.* 1993, chs. 5 and 6	1	covers: speech *vs.* writing; data-based focus on acquisition in individual children; some of data is available on tape
Fromkin and Rodman 1993, ch. 10	1	does not cover variation in child language
Garton and Pratt 1989	2–3	concise on oral development; incl. theories of acquisition, metalinguistic knowledge; strong on literacy development
Goodluck 1991	4	Chomskyan perspective; little on communicative competence, variation or literacy
Harris 1993	2	focuses on children's reading and writing, incl. schoolwork
Ingram 1989	4	incl. history of child language studies; little on communicative competence, literacy or variation
Kress 1994	3	focuses on children's reading and writing, incl. meaning, development of genres, errors, and social perspectives; worked examples
Lightbown and Spada 1993	2	useful for comparison of first and second language acquisition
Montgomery 1995, chs. 1 and 2	1–2	focuses on Hallidayan functional approach; incl. data and project ideas
Perera 1984	3	focuses on children's reading and writing
Romaine 1984	2–3	focus on variation between children; literacy as communicative competence; methodology
Stilwell Peccei 1994	1	does not link easily with published studies and theories; incl. project ideas
Tough 1976	1–2	useful for the worked examples and picture stories (which may need updating)

British Journal of Developmental Psychology	*Journal of Psycholinguistic Research*
Child Development	*Journal of Reading Behaviour*
Cognition	*Journal of Speech and Hearing Research*
Developmental Psychology	*Journal of Verbal Learning and Verbal Behavior*
Journal of Child Language	*Language*
Journal of Educational Psychology	*Language Acquisition*
Journal of Experimental Child Psychology	*Language and Society*
Journal of Experimental Psychology	*Merril-Palmer Quarterly*
	Psychological Review

Fig 3.1 Major journals for research in child language

The CHILDES database

The **Child Language Data Exchange System (CHILDES)** is a computer-based collection of corpora accumulated by individuals and groups of researchers, and available through the Internet. It is briefly described in Crystal (1995, 1997a). Fletcher and MacWhinney's (1995, section 5) up-to-date overview of the computational analysis of child utterances focuses on the range of resources available through CHILDES. If you want good quality data and have not got the resources to collect it yourself, you can use data from here instead. Data collected for one type of analysis can often be used for a quite different one, provided that the transcription has included sufficient detail.

Things to think about

- Focus on an aspect of child language that enables you to capitalize on the core skills and knowledge that you are most competent and interested in.
- Make sure you have a general overview of the main stages of language acquisition and development, so that you know roughly what to expect and look out for, and where it fits into the broader picture.
- Engaging in an analysis of your data from within an established theoretical framework, drawn from such areas as syntax, semantics or phonology, is important in assuring that you avoid simply listing examples; you should be identifying patterns and commenting on their significance.
- Children do not possess adult competence in language use. Child language has its own rules which may not closely resemble those of adult language, so be careful in identifying things as 'wrong' or 'ungrammatical' – in the child's system they may be correct.
- Remember that child language can include writing, which may be studied in its own right or compared with the spoken language of children.

- Although the preschool years manifest most development, some structures and skills of oral language, such as passives and relative clauses, appear in this period. Intonation patterns are also still developing (see Cruttenden 1979), and broader aspects of communicative competence can also provide a rewarding focus with older children.

Working with children

Since the Children Act of 1989, and as a result of general attempts to offer greater protection for children, it is no longer as easy as it was to get access to child subjects at school or through youth organizations. None the less, these remain a good way of contacting a large number of children from a wide variety of backgrounds and ages.

- If you want to operate from within a school, write formally to headteachers, stating clearly what your work will involve and also ways in which the children might benefit, and bearing in mind that you will be intruding on their valuable school time. Indicate as clearly as you can what extra work, if any, may be involved for the staff. A headteacher may well want to meet you in advance of making a decision. If you can, take a flexible approach, and maybe even look for ways of linking your work to an ongoing class project. If you can afford to help out during your visits this may help to make your involvement more welcome. You will probably also need to seek parental approval, as, in the eyes of the law, children are not old enough to decide what is in their best interests.
- Children do not necessarily behave in a similar way to adult subjects. Children you know already may well wonder why you are engaging in different types of activity with them and be unable to focus on them as a result of this curiosity.
- When planning activities, be aware that children have a shorter attention span than adults. It is also worth showing planned activities to teachers or parents in advance, to check that the materials are pitched at an appropriate level.
- If using pictures or other types of stimulus to generate language use, make a pilot run with these to check that children at particular ages can make sense of the images; using drawn images with unusual shading, for example, can distract children and lead to a series of 'off the point' questions and comments.
- To avoid some children feeling 'left out', and to ensure good relations with the school you are working in, you may need to be prepared to run activities with some children whose data you do not plan to use.
- Children are often far more curious than adults about recording equipment. Not only may they be distracted or inhibited by it, they may want to play with it during your data collection exercise!

- Children tend to move around far more than adult subjects. Can you set up your audio or video-recording equipment to cope with this?
- Parents and teachers may be keen that the children cannot be identified from your recording, and protecting their anonymity is obviously much more difficult with video than audio data. Be sensitive to the justifiable concerns of adult carers about the potential for videos to fall into the wrong hands. Also be aware that some teachers may be nervous of their teaching being videoed.
- School environments can be very noisy and prone to unexpected disruption. The time available between breaks may prove rather shorter than you expect.
- It can be very hard to distinguish between different child voices in audio recordings, even when you know the children quite well. This is especially true when several are interacting. It can even be difficult to tell girls apart from boys. Using a video recorder and getting children to introduce themselves on audio tapes at the start of activities are two ways of reducing the risk of later problems, but most important is to keep careful notes at the time.
- If your work involves an assessment of children's social class or background, be aware that children are not always able to supply reliable information themselves, school records are not always very up-to-date and schools and parents might be cautious about releasing such data. Furthermore, socio-economic categorizations based on parental occupations are not always appropriate or accurate.

For further information about research procedures, see Chapters 12 to 16.

Central themes and project ideas

There is a huge range of possible project areas within the field of child language, because many aspects of language can be studied at different stages of development. What is provided below is a selection of areas and ideas taken from some of the main branches of research within child language, including studies of prelinguistic development; the development of core structures such as grammar and phonology; broader aspects of communicative competence, such as conversation and joke-telling; literacy development; and variation in child language.

Longitudinal case studies

Many linguists have undertaken and published case studies of their own children, or of a few specially selected children. The emphasis for most has been on finding out more about 'normative' development. Roger Brown conducted a longitudinal study of three children, Adam, Eve and Sarah

(Brown 1973). This work is a primary source of information on analyses and indices of development, such as a child's Mean Length of Utterance (MLU) and stages of grammatical morpheme development. Paul Fletcher studied his daughter, Sophie (Fletcher 1985), providing a 'profile' of her development in areas including syntax and phonology at strategic points in her early life. Michael Halliday studied his son Nigel's early vocalizations and transition into early multiword utterances from a functional perspective (Halliday 1975). His proposed 'developmental functions of language' provide one key framework for the analysis of early utterance meaning.

Conducting a longitudinal case study requires commitment over a considerable period, not just from you but also from the child and its family, so keep them sweet! If you know you have a project coming up, and you think you might want to write a study of this sort, talk to a potential supervisor early on about starting to collect the data. It is better to collect something you end up not using than to wish later that you had planned ahead.

PROJECTS

29. Follow the progress of two children of the same age, one of whom is an only child and one of whom is the youngest in a larger family. Do they develop language features at the same rate and in the same order? Remember to look not only at formal structures but also at general comprehensibility and at interactional strategies. Compare your findings with those of similar published studies. How might their profiles of development have been determined by differences in their everyday communication needs? If possible, use children from a similar social background, and also of the same sex, as some research has suggested that males and females have different speeds of development and/or communicational strategies.

30. Record a child every few weeks as he/she learns to read. Do the skills develop gradually and/or is there a sudden transition from being a non-reader to being a reader? You might try asking the child for his or her own thoughts on what reading is, what it is for and how it is achieved.

Pre-linguistic development

Are children working on their language development before they can produce their first word? In recent years many researchers have addressed this question, examining aspects of prelinguistic (i.e. birth to one-word) development. Halliday (1975) studied prelinguistic utterances for evidence of growing patterns of meaning and function in his son's utterances. He looked for the same sound strings or 'proto-words' being used consistently to refer to the same things. Other researchers, such as Stark (1986), have focused on how prelinguistic sound-making, such as cooing and babbling, lays the foundation for phonological and intonational development.

A good overview of prelinguistic development is provided by Foster (1990, chs. 2 and 3), and Fletcher and MacWhinney (1995) contains recent key articles on various related themes by Locke, Kent and Miolo, and Menn and Stoel-Gammon. Prelinguistic speech comprehension has been studied by Hirsh-Pasek and Golinkoff (1996).

PROJECT

31. Video a prelinguistic child with its mother. Show the recording to the mother and ask her which of the baby's noises and gestures she believes are intentional communication. Analyse these, looking for patterns and for indications that they are the precursors of language. Include a commentary on any difficulties you encounter with this. Remember to relate your findings to those of other studies, and/or to profiles of normative ages and stages of development.

Over- and under-extension: lexical and semantic development

Young children often use words in a way which suggests they have a different understanding of them compared to adult usage. They may use a word to refer to too wide a category of things, such as 'apple' to refer to all fruit that are round – this is known as **over-extension**. Conversely, they may use a word to refer to too small a category of things, such as using the word 'dog' only for the family's pet dog and not for the next-door neighbour's – **under-extension**. This is a rich field for possible projects, since nearly all children, irrespective of their native language, go through periods of apparent over-extension of words (under-extension is less well-documented). Several researchers have proposed explanations for this behaviour. One key contributor is Eve Clark, whose early proposal, the **Semantic Feature Hypothesis**, is still perhaps the most influential of all (see Clark and Clark 1977). Other competing theories of work meaning are reviewed in Dromi (1987), and an update of Clark's ideas appears in Clark (1993). Gleitman and Landau (1994) contains a valuable collection of papers reviewing recent work on lexical acquisition.

PROJECT

32. Collect examples of over-extension in a child's speech, taking care to keep notes of precisely what was being referred to. How easy is it to identify the perceptual boundaries that the child might be operating with, when it assigns the same name to several things? What support is there for the hypothesis that the child's view is the same as the adult's, but it just doesn't have enough words for everything it wants to talk about? (You could get insight into this by seeing how easily the child adopts a new word that breaks up the set). Aitchison (1994, ch. 15) will give you some preliminary pointers to what over-extension may entail.

Children's morphology

One of the best known studies in this area is Jean Berko-Gleason's 'wug' study, of which simple summaries are given in Aitchison (1989, ch. 6) and Fromkin and Rodman (1993, ch. 10). The study demonstrated that children have an internalized rule for the plural, because they were able to give the correct phonological form for made-up words (for which they could therefore never have heard a plural before).

Children often make apparent errors in the way they form past tenses, comparative adjectives and plurals, often going though a phase of using a regular ending where the adult form is irregular. Since this is a very common phenomenon, it makes it an accessible and popular project area.

PROJECT

33. Draw up an inventory of morphological errors in a child's language production. Categorize each according to whether it is an irregular form for a regular one, a regular form for an irregular one or an irregular form for a different irregular one. Also ascertain which word classes the errors occur in: verbs (are all tenses represented?), nouns, adjectives (e.g. *the bestest* for *the best*), etc. If the balance is unequal, look for reasons, both within child language development and within the target language that the child is aiming for. Compare your findings with those reported in the published literature.

Development of phonology and intonation

One very productive approach to the language of under-fives especially is to study apparent 'mispronunciations'. These can appear to be idiosyncratic mistakes but, as with inflectional errors, many children display similar patterns, and these are considered to be part of normative development unless they persist too long. Excellent summaries of the patterns of mispronunciation, which make useful analytical frameworks, can be found in Clark and Clark (1977, ch. 10) and de Villiers and de Villiers (1978). Smith (1973) is acknowledged as a key source study.

On intonation, Cruttenden (1974) is still a fascinating source; he used recordings of the football results, studying children's ability to predict the second part of the result on the basis of the intonation used in the first. Seven-year-olds were found to be poor at predicting whether the second part of the score was higher, lower or a draw, whereas by 10 children were generally far more skilled. Adults usually have few problems with such predictions. Such work suggests that, whilst intonation is one of the first aspects of language which children focus on and start to master, it is also one of the last to be 'perfected'. Other sources on intonation include Cruttenden (1979, ch. 2) and papers in Fletcher and Garman (1986, especially ch. 8).

PROJECTS

34. Replicate Cruttenden's study and compare your results with his. If there are differences, what might account for them?

35. Analyse the consistent 'mispronunciations' in words that you elicit from a two- to three-year-old child.

   - Identify the phonological processes (substitution, assimilation, syllabic structure) that characterize these mispronunciations (see Clark and Clark 1977 and de Villiers and de Villiers 1978 for systematic coverage of these).
   - Look at the articulations of particular developing phonemes in different phonotactic contexts (word initial, word medial, word final, connected speech, etc.), and compare the patterns of consonants with those given in Crystal (1997a: 242). As Crystal's caption indicates, there is substantial variation in the speed of the acquisition of consonants. There can also, however, be some difficulty in being sure of whether the child has or has not fully mastered a consonant. Drawing on the experience gained from your analysis, explore various possible reasons why this problem might be encountered by linguists.

Comprehension of complex grammatical structures

There are numerous such studies, the best known of which is probably that of Carol Chomsky. Chomsky probed children's comprehension of structures such as active and passive sentences by asking them to perform actions with puppets. Her study also investigated other structures, such as the use of the verbs 'ask', 'tell' and 'promise', in an attempt to shed light on why these features are acquired later than other aspects of language. See Chomsky (1969; also summarized in Garton and Pratt 1989, ch. 4).

PROJECT

36. Taking careful note of Chomsky's procedures and stimuli, devise an experiment of your own along similar lines. Make it close enough for your results to be compared with hers. How do you account for any differences? Write also about the procedural difficulties inherent in this kind of experiment.

Children's metalinguistic awareness

Research in this area has focused on:

   - children's awareness of what a word, sound and sentence, etc. is, and at what age or stage of awareness each type of structure emerges (e.g. Clark's work, described in Garton and Pratt 1989, ch. 7).

- the role of language games and nursery rhymes in promoting metalinguistic awareness (e.g. work by Bryant *et al.* reviewed in Garton and Pratt 1989: 136).
- the link between metalinguistic awareness and the development of literacy. See Garton and Pratt (1989, ch. 7) for summaries of example studies and further references, and Gombert (1992) for more advanced coverage.
- children's appreciation of verbal jokes and puns. This skill is very much part of a child's broader developing communicative competence, and can be an entertaining area in which to run projects. For children to understand jokes and puns, they often need to understand 'sense relations' such as synonymy and polysemy. This may also be linked to a milestone in cognitive development which Piaget proposed that children reach at around the age of 7 (see **generic epistemology** in Richards, Platt and Platt 1992: 155).

PROJECT

37. Following the established research practice, test children's surface and deep understanding of humour by telling them jokes, monitoring the reaction and then asking the children to explain why the joke was funny or why it was a joke. Crystal (1986: 185 ff.) provides very introductory information on this 'playing with language', and Trott (1996) gives a more detailed overview. Some source studies include Fowles and Glanz (1977) and Shultz and Horibe (1974).

Colour terms

This is an interesting and relatively little-studied aspect of child language development. It can be studied as part of overall lexical and semantic development. For introductory information see Crystal (1986: 99 ff.) and, for a fuller summary, Trott (1996: 26–30).

PROJECTS

38. Keep a note of the order in which a child acquires colour terms, and what objects the child labels with them. Compare your results with the findings of Berlin and Kay (1969), regarding the order in which languages add colour terms to their inventory (for a brief summary of this see Crystal 1997a: 106).

39. Some children go through a stage of using colour terms liberally but apparently quite haphazardly. If you have access to such a child, make a careful study of this phenomenon: does the child simply not know which colour name is which, is it operating 'over-extension' (see earlier) of the colour names it knows, or has it failed to grasp the notion of colour-naming at all, so that it doesn't realize what property of an object is being referred to when it is called *red*?

40. If you have access to a child who is bilingual, compare the order in which the colours are correctly learned and used in each language. To do this you will need to understand both languages yourself, or have help from someone who does. It does not matter if the colour terms develop in one language before the other, but include in your account a consideration of what effect knowing (some) colour names in one language might have on learning the colour terminology of the other.

41. Compare colour-term acquisition in two monolingual children acquiring different languages. Use children of the same gender, and whose background and day-to-day experience are as similar as possible. As in project 40, make suitable provision if you do not know both languages yourself. Compare your results with normative development as reported in the literature. Are there any linguistic or social reasons that you can identify to account for any differences between your two subjects, or your subjects and the reports in the literature?

42. Test a small number of children who have not yet mastered their colour names by playing a sorting game with them, in which they have to put like colours together. Do they choose to put together different shades of blue, separately from shades of green, etc.? Use your findings to address the question of whether children have the colour concepts *before* the words appear (cf. Berlin and Kay 1969, but also Pinker 1994: 62 and 65–6), or whether, as with most words, they have to learn the boundaries of meaning by experience (see 'under-' and 'over-extension' above).

43. Are there differences between males' and females' uses of colour terminology? Use a paint chart with the names of the colours removed, and ask, say, three boys and three girls aged about 8 or 9, to give each colour an appropriate name. Do both sexes find this task equally easy? What sort of wider vocabulary (e.g. names for things in the physical world) is drawn upon to meet the shortfall in established colour names? Do girls know more of the secondary colour names (such as vermilion, maroon and ochre) than boys? Warning: be sensitive to the possibility that children will become confused and/or bored if they are bombarded with too many colours for which they do not have names.

Carer language (or child-directed speech)

The role of carer language, or **child-directed speech**, has been a hotly debated issue in child language ever since Noam Chomsky declared adult language to be a 'degenerate' model from which children could never learn all the rules of their language. A key researcher has been Catherine Snow (e.g. Snow 1986). Of interest are the properties of carer language, and the extent to which it is necessary, or at least beneficial, to the child's language development. However, it is not easy to establish such a causal link. One approach has been to compare language acquisition in cultures where carers use no special language register with that in cultures where such a register has been identified. Famous studies of this nature are by Ochs in Western Samoa and Schieffelin in Papua New Guinea (see Romaine 1984, ch. 6 for a description of these).

PROJECTS

44. If you are fluent in two languages associated with different cultures, observe the carer talk used with a child from each. Look for special vocabulary, intonation features, repetition, simplified structures (e.g. short sentences) and the overall amount of verbal communication offered by the carer. You may find the work of Heath (1983) useful. This studied middle-class white and lower-class black and white communities in the United States, giving an insight into how children are socialized, through the influence of adults, into particular expectations and norms of language usage.

45. Do fathers as well as mothers use the special features of carer language? Using Berko-Gleason (1975) as a starting point, gather your own data from a family where you can record both parents in one-to-one interaction with the child. If feasible and appropriate, extend this to study the carer talk of an older sibling. As carers may be inhibited to behave normally when someone else is listening, be prepared to run the tape for quite a long time. Alternatively, explore the possibility of leaving the machine running while you leave, or even using a baby intercom to listen in during your absence.

46. Observe one or more young children playing with dolls. Do they use features of carer language? See Romaine (1984, ch. 6) for studies.

47. If you can find a pair of mixed sex twins, record the carer talk that goes on with each individually, and the two together. Wells' Bristol Survey found evidence that parents talked more to boys during some activities, and more to girls during others (see, for example, Wells 1986b).

Conversational development

This field tends to overlap with that of the role of carer language (see above), since it is generally acknowledged that children first learn from carers how to participate in conversations. McTear (1985) and Foster (1990) provide coverage of conversational development. Garton and Pratt (1989, ch. 6) summarize some research (largely from the Bristol Survey) into the differences in conversation that children encounter when making the transition from home to school.

PROJECT

48. Compare the conversational skills of two or more children of either different ages, or of the same age but different gender, social background, or family size, etc. Are there indications that any differences you find are genuinely to do with the *development* of conversation skills, as opposed to more permanent differences in style and/or personality? One type of data that might be particularly interesting is children's telephone conversation skills.

See also project number 62.

Sources of variation in child language

Since the early 1980s there has been growing interest in the variation between children in their rate and route of acquisition. This has developed in part as a reaction to the tendency for child language researchers to focus on the 'average' or 'normal' child, as though all children develop identically. Researchers have started to consider a range of sources of variation in terms of how they might influence children's long-term language development and how they could affect the way that children behave as subjects in fieldwork projects. A considerable amount of key research on sources of variation stems from the Bristol Language Survey (see Wells 1981, 1985 and 1986a and b). A useful introduction is provided by Wells (1986b). Romaine (1984, especially chs. 4 and 6) provides coverage on social class, gender, peer group, school and family. Coates (1993, ch. 7) and Swann (1992) also give excellent coverage on gender.

PROJECT

49. Using a detailed child's picture book (e.g. from the *First Thousand Words* series), test children of the same age, who contrast on one of the variation criteria listed above, on their range of vocabulary. For example, you could test a boy and girl, or two girls from different backgrounds, or two boys, one of whom is in full-time preschool education while the other is not. How easy is it to gain a clear picture of any differences? You could also write about any limitations that you consider intrinsic to collecting data in this way.

Literacy development

For introductory coverage, see the textbook review earlier in this chapter. Read more specifically about research in this area in Garton and Pratt (1989, chs. 7 to 10), Perera (1979, 1986) and Smith (1986). For information on dyslexia, see Chapter 2 of this book.

OTHER PROJECT IDEAS

50. Conduct an observation study of how children interact with each other when they are engaged in activities at home or at school. Example: how they use language co-operatively in playing a game or undertaking a classroom task.

51. Observe the differences between parental and teacher strategies in telling stories with children or in controlling children.

52. Make a study of children's command of language *register*: how does they way that they talk to each other differ from the way they talk to the teacher?

53. Do a cross-sectional study of children at different stages of their development, aimed at creating a general picture of sequences of development. (Note that this entails the assumption that child A will behave like child B when it is child B's age, so no account is taken of variation between individuals.)

54. Get children of different ages to retell a story they have just heard or seen on video. Compare their ability to sequence the events and create a recognizable narrative structure. Use a story they have not come across before, as children are very good memorizers!

55. Conduct a case study of a child with a particular disability affecting language (such as a hearing impairment, stuttering or autism). Remember, however, that the demands on yourself, your informant and on parents or teachers may be greater than when working with a normal child. You will need to do a lot of research on the disability in question even before you start the case study, and for this research you may find that 'mainstream' linguistic textbooks are not very helpful. Additionally, you may find that relevant books on the subject are quite technical, or that the approach to language is different from the one you are familiar with from your previous studies.

56. Run an experimental study of comprehension, perhaps repeated over a period of time. For example, you could test subjects' comprehension of dimensional adjectives by showing them a set of five illustrated cards and asking them *show me the picture where the fence is taller than the tree*. (See Cruttenden 1979, section 4.5.1 for a summary of, and references to, studies on dimensional adjectives.)

|4|

Conversation analysis

SHIRLEY REAY

Conversation Analysis (CA) is a technique developed relatively recently for examining and exploring spoken language. Work in the area has focused on spontaneous talk which takes place in naturally occurring social situations, and also on talk in various 'institutional' settings, such as courtrooms, doctors' surgeries and news interviews, where the interaction is more agenda-driven. Despite the term 'conversation', it is also possible, though less common, to work on the speech of a single individual, by focusing on, for example, after-dinner speeches, testimonies made by alcoholics at AA meetings, or telephone answering-machine messages.

Through CA it has been possible to find common observable rules and procedures by which participants organize and manage their conversation behaviour (for example, who gets to speak next, when and how they get to speak, and so on). In other words, having isolated a set of basic features which constitute the 'machinery of conversation' (such as turn-taking, interruption and simple overlapping talk), it begins to become possible to see how some of these features vary from one context to another. Clearly, amongst other things, this makes CA useful for investigating how people alter their language behaviour according to who they are talking to and in what kind of setting.

Unlike other topics which are covered by chapters in this book, CA is not really a field of linguistics in its own right. First, it actually springs from a branch of ethnomethodology which is an area of sociological study. Second, it could more accurately be described as a method for analysing spoken language. CA uses either audio or video recordings of talk, which are carefully orthographically transcribed (see Chapter 18) to preserve as much detail as possible of the nature of the original.

Questions that CA addresses directly include:

- In what ways can talk be seen to be structured?

- How do participants make sense of each other's talk?
- How does a participant know when to start speaking after a previous speaker?
- How do two (or more) participants who begin speaking at the same time work out who will get the turn?
- How do speakers construct their turns to make sure that their listener understands them (known as **recipient design**)?
- How do speakers display understanding of the last speaker's turn?
- How do speakers who for some reason need to hold the floor for longer than is 'usual' (for example, in order to tell a story) signal this to their listeners?
- How do speakers indicate that they have not finished what they wish to say and that the other speaker(s) should not begin a new turn (known as **turn holding**)?
- How do speakers manage agreement and disagreement?
- How do participants move from one topic of conversation to another?
- How do participants deal with having to repair their own utterances or those of someone else?
- How do speakers bring a conversation to a close?
- What role do non-lexical or quasi-lexical items such as *er, mm hm* and laughter play in the participants' construction of meaning?
- How are pauses used and interpreted in conversation?
- How do speakers signal to their listeners that they are expecting them or inviting them to laugh at what they've said?

Once one has an answer to these fundamental questions about the structure of conversation, there are many more issues that can be addressed, such as the extent to which conversational behaviour varies in different settings (such as courtrooms and doctors' surgeries), how children develop their awareness of the management of conversation in others and how they acquire it for themselves, to what extent conversational behaviour varies between same-sex and mixed-sex conversations, and whether the patterns identified in CA research for English hold good for other languages too.

Textbooks

CA is a fairly specific approach to analysing spoken language, and not all books you come across will be central to CA itself. While it is certainly a good idea to familiarize yourself with the broader picture, it is also important to make sure that you have a clear understanding of CA as a model; so take note of which of the books in Table 4.1 fall within and which outside CA.

Table 4.1 Useful texts for conversation analysis (see page xiv for key to levels)

Book	Level	Notes on Content/Style
Aijmer 1996	3	Not specifically CA, but covers thanking, apologizing, requesting, offering, etc.
Atkinson and Heritage 1984	3–4	prominent researchers write about: agreement and disagreement; topic organization; talk and non-vocal activities, etc.
Beattie 1983	3–4	not specifically CA, but practical guidance on what to look for in transcriptions and some project ideas
Coulmas 1981	3	common, routine conversation situations
Drew 1994	2	brief history and outline of major issues
Drew and Heritage 1992	3–4	papers on: native/non-native understanding of subtext; how views polarize in interviews and discussions, etc.
Eggins and Slade 1997	3	relationship between CA and discourse analysis; negotiation and confrontation, humour, storytelling, gossip etc.
Heritage 1989	3	laughter, topic organization, preference organization, etc.; institutional conversation, e.g. classroom, courts, medical contexts
Langford 1994	1–2	practical guide, building step by step to full analysis; facilitates transcription practice, using tape of data (write to: Dr. D. Langford, UCRYSJ, Lord Mayor's Walk, York, YO3 7EX, UK.)
Levinson 1983, ch. 6	2–3	brief background and overview; relationship between CA and discourse analysis
Nofsinger 1991	2	also covers aspects of pragmatics
Psathas 1995	3	development of CA and its 'philosophy'; how CA is done and what can be included and interpreted: helpful for avoiding subjective data interpretations; appendix of standard transcription symbols
Sacks 1995	3–4	transcripts of original lectures: key to establishment of the CA field; useful background reading
Schiffrin 1987	3	discourse markers, e.g. *well, you know, oh*
Schiffrin 1994, ch. 7	3–4	includes (pp. 279–80) exercises that could inspire project ideas

Book	Level	Notes on Content/Style
Stubbs 1993	3	includes procedural/conceptual issues in collecting conversation data
Taylor and Cameron 1987	4	previous knowledge assumed; different approaches to analysis; interpretation and accountability
Wardhaugh 1985	2	not specifically on CA, but covers conversation generally, including theories of interaction (Grice, Searle)

Major journals

There are no major journals that deal exclusively with CA. Those listed in Fig. 4.1, however, carry articles on CA as part of their wider coverage.

British Journal of Social Psychology
Communication Monographs
Discourse Processes
Human Studies
International Journal of the Sociology of Language
Journal of Communication
Journal of Pragmatics
Language
Language and Communication
Language in Society
Language and Speech
Linguistics
Research on Language and Social Interaction
Semiotica
Speech and Language: Advances in Basic Research and Practice
Text

Fig 4.1 Major journals for research in conversation analysis

Central themes and project ideas

In any project that focuses on conversation you will need to transcribe your data accurately and according to current practice in the field. For guidance on how to do this, see Chapter 18 in this book. If you want to use a computer corpus, you may find help on what you can do with spoken data in this regard in Leech *et al.* (1995). You will also need a full grasp of the basic features of conversation: turn-taking, transition relevance points, interruption strategies, topic management, minimal response tokens and so on. Use the books recommended above to gain confidence in identifying these features and in using the terminology. Only then will you be in a position to examine your own data.

Scripted versus non-scripted conversation

It is almost always possible to tell, within a few seconds of turning on the radio or TV, whether the conversation you are listening to is scripted or not. It is extremely difficult, in fact, for an actor to sound entirely 'natural' when speaking from a script. There are a number of reasons for this, including:

- the way a script is constructed: many of the features we associate with conversation are simply not found there
- the purpose of a script: there is an external audience which needs to hear the words and be given sufficient contextualization to understand what is going on
- the non-spontaneity of a script: much of what makes spontaneous speech sound the way it does is that it is constructed at the time, while scripted speech is not. This affects the interaction between speakers too. In a script, each actor knows precisely when the next person will speak, whether there will be an interruption and if so, who will win the turn, and so on. This is entirely unlike most natural conversation, where these 'battles' have to be fought out at the time.

Some directors make a point of not using written scripts, but plan the 'route' of the conversation with the actors and allow them to ad lib until they have settled on a comfortable expression of the ideas.

PROJECTS

57. Compare a scripted conversation from a radio play or TV soap with a real one on a similar subject and taking place in a similar environment, perhaps from a fly-on-the-wall documentary. Write about the differences in the appearance of your two transcriptions, and compare the way in which turns are taken and relinquished and topics are managed, and how those present contribute verbally outside their own turn.

58. Ask some acting friends to learn an extract from a play and to experiment with different ways of performing it so that it sounds as natural as possible. Allow them to try changing the words, improvising, and so on. Record their 'performances' and transcribe them. Ask some independent 'judges' to rate the recordings for naturalness. What characterizes the versions that are judged most natural? How might scriptwriters help the actors to perform more naturally? Include a commentary on the problems that arise in attempting to define and quantify *naturalness* in conversation.

59. Take a stretch from a film or play which seems more naturalistic than most in its conversation, if possible one of those whose script has been developed out of improvisation. Assess what it is that gives it the appearance of naturalness, and identify the ways in which it is still not like real conversation. Are these 'shortfalls' intentional or accidental? In either case, why might they be unavoidable? Good places to look for improvised or semi-improvised dialogue are the films of Mike Leigh and some Woody Allen films. The comedians French and Saunders also sometimes improvise around a previously written script.

Radio and TV interviews

Since interviews tend to have a fairly predictable question-and-answer format, they can be an interesting opportunity to observe other aspects of conversational behaviour. Beattie (1982a, b) looks at James Callaghan and Margaret Thatcher in political interviews and analyses how often they interrupt the interviewer and how often they themselves are interrupted. There turned out to be some interesting patterns of turn-taking violations. You can read more about research into interviewing in the papers in Drew and Heritage (1992).

PROJECTS

60. Collect three or so conversations with the same political figure or personality, each conducted by a different interviewer. Compare not only the interviewing styles themselves, but also the ways in which these draw different conversational behaviour out of the interviewee. Perhaps he or she is more argumentative in one interview than another, or interrupts more, or takes longer turns.

61. Drawing on a live radio news and current affairs programme such as the BBC's *Today* on Radio 4, compare the way in which a chosen presenter copes with interviewing (a) a seasoned interviewee such as a politician, (b) a specific 'expert' who has been thrust into the media as a spokesperson for a current news item, and (c) a member of the public who probably has no experience of public speaking and no expertise to offer, but who has a 'bystander' or 'aggrieved-victim' story to tell. How does the interviewer's management of conversational features vary in terms of such matters as aggression, insistence on pursuing a theme, putting words in the interviewee's mouth, and in opening and closing the whole event?

The development of children's conversational skills

How do children learn about conversation? Whilst carers appear to impose conversational structure, especially turn-taking, on their interactions with the baby as soon as it is born (Crystal 1997a: 241), the conversation habits of a five-year-old, full of loud interruptions or shy silences, and largely devoid of attempts to draw extended turns out of others, indicate that some aspects of adult conversational patterns are learnt quite late. Foster

(1990) gives a useful rundown of past research into aspects of turn-taking, overlap, cohesion and repairs in child language. McTear (1985) is entirely dedicated to the topic of children's conversation, and is therefore an invaluable source of information for work in this area.

PROJECTS

62. Record a child just before he or she first enrols at nursery or school, and again a few days and a few weeks afterwards. Use your data to test the hypothesis that being for the first time with children and one or more teachers in a relatively structured environment will have a marked effect on the child's conversational behaviour. Look for evidence of newly learned skills in such areas as turn-taking, competing for a turn and listening. Aim to choose a child who has not had much experience of being with other children before, and avoid using one who is too young to have the general language skills that will support the conversational behaviour. You may have to make more than one recording for each time-window, in case your subject happens to be tired, uncommunicative or in any other way unrepresentative of normal on one occasion. Useful reading relevant to this would be Garton and Pratt (1989, ch. 6).

63. Set up a group discussion between some 12-year-olds, and another, on the same subject, between some 18-year-olds. Compare the interaction to ascertain whether the major conversational skills of adulthood have already been fully acquired by the age of 12.

Conversation and gender

Over recent years there has been a lot of research into the different ways in which women and men use language. Some of the most noticeable contrasts seem to lie in conversational behaviour. You can find references to this research, and some additional project suggestions, in Chapter 11 of this book.

PROJECTS

64. Record a group of female friends in conversation and see to what extent their overlapping talk is, as Coates (1996: 128) suggests, non-competitive. Compare this with a conversation between a group of females who do not know each other. Is non-competitiveness a function of being female or of familiarity? What does the literature say about the overlap behaviour of men in similar circumstances, and how compatible is that with your conclusions about the women?

65. Investigate **topic survival**: Fishman's (1978) research looked at how often, in mixed-sex conversations, topics were allowed to 'follow through' when women introduced them compared with when men did. Gather your own data from a group of friends. Do you find any difference? If so, are topics relinquished by the introducer (e.g. not followed through forcefully enough) or quashed by others? If there is no difference, are your speakers in any sense more 'equal' than in most male–female groups? You can gain a brief impression of Fishman's study in Graddol and Swann (1989: 75).

Language, power and hierarchy

Various studies have been done over the years to investigate how different structures of spoken language typify particular work occupations and roles (Heritage 1989, papers in Drew and Heritage 1992). Heath (1992) has considered the doctor–patient relationship. Others (such as O'Barr and Atkins 1980, West 1984) have looked at how the power distribution associated with gender and with social hierarchy may affect participant talk.

PROJECTS

66. Gain permission to collect data in an institution where the power relationships are quite clear-cut. This may not be easy, as the conversations in which power is most obviously wielded (in an office, say) are likely to be the most sensitive. Shadowing a head teacher in a primary school might be easier to arrange, but even so, his or her conversations with the staff will have to be treated as highly confidential.

67. Transcribe scenes from TV soap opera, comedy or drama set in a hierarchically organized environment such as an office or police station. How do the characters express the role relationships within the bounds of what is feasible in scripted speech (see earlier)?

68. Ask some children to play at being various authority figures. Does their conversational behaviour (such as length of turns, interruptions and management of overlaps) demonstrate the features we would expect in the 'real world'? Is their depiction subtle enough to be accurate, or is their understanding of the language of power relationships no more than a crude caricature?

69. Arrange to record the phone calls and/or visits in person to a complaints department dealing with members of the public. How does the conversational behaviour of different complainants affect the strategies adopted by the official?

OTHER PROJECT IDEAS

70. Record some telephone conversations. Do all of the same rules of normal conversational exchange apply in these circumstances? Look for indications of strategies being adopted or extended to compensate for others that are not possible on the phone. You can read about research in this area in Houtkoop-Steenstra (1991) and Hopper (1991).

71. Persuade a friend to have his or her palm read, and get permission for the session to be recorded (some palmists permit it as a matter of course). Analyse the interaction as a way of ascertaining how new information and new topics are introduced (by the palmist or the client), and how they are picked up and carried forward by the other party. What sort of power relationship is in evidence?

72. In some training courses for counsellors, recordings are made for teaching purposes. See if you can gain permission to use these to investigate the conversational strategies of counsellors, such as the ways in which they learn to introduce new topics, when and how they interject, and how they express agreement and disagreement. How do their strategies, and other characteristics of the conversations such as the length of turns, compare with those described in the literature as characteristic of ordinary two-way conversation? Compare beginners with more experienced trainees, or record the same individuals at different points in the course. Interview the trainers about the goals of their type of counselling, how these are reflected in the management of the conversation with a client, and what role they believe such management to play in the success of the counselling process. Remember that even training sessions in counselling are confidential, and you must exercise the utmost discretion in your use of such material.

73. Compare the conversation during an evangelical Bible Study meeting with the informal conversations between the same people before and after it. How different is the interactional behaviour of different individuals in the two contexts? Are there different authority hierarchies (for example, in the matter of who does the organizing or who has the final word)?

|5|

Second-language acquisition

There is considerable interest in the processes by which we succeed or fail in learning a second (or third, fourth, etc.) language. The insights we can gain from research into this area can tell us more about the nature of language, how the brain stores it and how language learning takes place. Research into second-language acquisition asks questions like:

- Is classroom learning a valid way to gain communicative language skills?
- Is there a fundamental difference between being taught a language and picking it up from the environment?
- Which language-teaching methods work best?
- Is second-language acquisition intrinsically the same as or different from first-language acquisition?
- Why are some adults more successful at language learning than others?
- Are children inherently better at language learning, and if so, why?
- Is there an age beyond which the 'natural' language-learning mechanisms no longer function effectively?
- Does residence abroad make a qualitative difference to language skills?
- How can we accurately gauge the knowledge of learners?
- Are there any consistent patterns in the order in which learners master language features?
- How successful are immersion programmes?
- How successful are self-teach courses?

Terminology

In your reading around this area, you need to be aware that the same terms may be used by different authors with slightly different meanings. Here is some of most common terminology.

The **mother tongue (MT)** is the language acquired in early childhood from parents, and spoken in the home environment; it is normally synonymous with **first language (L1)**. Although these terms may seem easy to define at first glance, there are many situations where it might be difficult to identify which language deserves either or both of these labels: for example, when each parent speaks a different language, when two or more languages are commonly used in the family or immediate community, when the child is regularly exposed to a second language outside the home, or when the child (or adult) is more comfortable with and fluent in a language learnt later, and/or has forgotten his or her earliest acquired language. It is worth remembering that such situations are by no means uncommon – in world terms, monolingualism is not the norm.

Foreign-language (FL) learning occurs when the language is taught in the L1 environment, often through the medium of L1, such as when French children learn English at school in France. A **foreign language** 'plays no major role in the community' (Ellis 1994: 12). **Second-language learning** occurs where the language being taught is that of the host community, such as in the case of Chileans arriving in Britain and learning English either informally or in classes. The term **second language (L2)** is also used in a more general way, as a cover term for second and foreign language; it may also be used for a third or fourth language. The term **second-language acquisition** is used to refer to both acquisition and learning (in Krashen's sense – see below), and you will find this abbreviated to **SLA, 2LA** and **L2A**. There are many situations in the world where the distinction between **foreign-** and **second-language learning** is not so clear-cut, especially where the language being learnt has some sort of special political or social status or significance, as is the case, for example, with English in India or South Africa.

Several acronyms relate to the English language. **EFL** and **ESL** refer to English as a Foreign and as a Second Language respectively. The terms **TEFL** (Teaching English as a Foreign Language) and **TESL** (Teaching English as a Second Language) have been replaced in the last few years with the term **TESOL** (Teaching English to Speakers of Other Languages).

Acquisition *vs.* **learning** is a distinction made by Stephen Krashen at the beginning of the 1980s, but no longer used by most writers, because of the problems inherent in demonstrating the difference independently of the underlying definitions. In Krashen's terms, **acquisition** is the subconscious assimilation of the language without any awareness of knowing rules. This is how the child gains its first language, and what children and adults may be capable of achieving for a second language, if exposed to it in a natural way and enabled to pick it up subconsciously. **Learning** is a conscious process, achieved particularly through formal study, and resulting in an explicit knowledge of rules.

Bilingualism has shown itself to be a difficult term to define, because there are so many different linguistic situations for which there is no other name available. For different writers the term can imply equal fluency and ability in two languages, any (however minimal) ability in one language together with fluency in another language, the ability to switch easily between two languages in speech, or the ability to understand more than one language, though not necessarily the ability to speak both. Baker (1993) gives a clear indication of the range of definitions that are generally used.

Language skills are normally defined as the skills of listening, speaking, reading and writing. Some formal classroom activities will encourage the learner to focus on one or two of the skills, others focus on integrating the skills within a communication activity.

Textbooks and major journals

Table 5.1 Useful texts for second-language acquisition (see page xiv for key to levels)

Book	Level	Notes on Content/Style
Bachman 1990; Bachman and Palmer 1996	3	approaches to language testing, aimed at teachers
Carroll and Hall 1985	3–4	language testing, incl. sample tests and stats.
Cook 1993	3–4	general issues; Chomskyan perspective
Cook 1996	3	major issues in theory of language teaching, including historical perspective
Ehrmann 1996	3	overview; emphasis on what makes language learning difficult
Ellis 1994	3	lengthy account (800 pages) of work in the field; ch. 1 summarizes the rest, so use that to pinpoint what you need from elsewhere
Heaton 1988	2–3	language testing, incl. sample tests and stats.
Lightbown and Spada 1993	1–2	first and second language acquisition compared; focus on implications for teaching; comparison of layman's beliefs with research findings
McNamara 1996	3	approaches to language testing, aimed at teachers
Scrivener 1994	1–2	focus on teaching; overview of techniques

AILA Review	*Language Learning*
Applied Linguistics	*Language Teaching Abstracts*
Applied Psycholinguistics	*Modern English Teacher*
English Language Teaching (ELT) Journal	*Modern Language Journal*
Interlanguage Studies Bulletin[a]	*Practical English Teacher*
IRAL	*Second Language Research*[a]
Journal of Applied Linguistics	*Studies in Second Language*
Journal of Psycholinguistic Research	*Acquisition*
Language in Society	*TESOL Quarterly*

Fig 5.1 Major journals for research in second-language acquisition

[a] same journal: name changed from *ISB* to *SLR*

Things to think about

- Language learning is a slow process, and you may not have a long enough time period to conduct a study that involves steady progress.
- 'Think-aloud reporting' is a technique whereby the researcher asks learners to verbalize their thinking processes as they complete a task. You can find out more about this in Wenden (1987) or the collection of papers edited by Faerch and Kasper (1987). Ellis (1994: 674) briefly notes some of the problems associated with this type of self-report data.
- Think carefully about which language you will use in your dealings with subjects. Tempting as it is to use the language *you* know best, bear in mind that this may cause difficulties for non-native speakers. If using a questionnaire it may be better, in some circumstances, to use the native language of the subjects. However, be careful not to make assumptions about what language that is, or their level of literacy in it.
- For more on the potential pitfalls of SLA research, see Seliger and Shohamy (1989).

Central themes and project ideas

Developmental sequences and the process of acquisition

Is there a fundamental difference between the processes of first- and second-language acquisition? It is well documented that children acquire certain morphological features of L1 (such as verb endings, and plural and possessive forms) in a fairly consistent order (e.g. Brown 1973, de Villiers and de Villiers 1973). Many studies have looked for a similar order of acquisition in the second language. For an overview of this research, see Ellis (1994, ch. 3), Lightbown and Spada (1993: 57–67) and most other introductory texts.

PROJECTS

74. Ask for access to the work of some language learners over, say, the last two years. Look for evidence of the successful and unsuccessful incorporation of, say, verb forms into their free writing (a) immediately after the form has been taught, (b) several weeks after and (c) several months after. If they are learning English, compare the order of acquisition with that given by Ellis (1994), Lightbown and Spada (1993) or some other authoritative source. If they are learning another language, find out if similar sequences have been identified (there are references to work on German in Ellis 1994: 103 ff.). Remember that a single example of a form being used correctly is not necessarily evidence that the learner has mastered it.

75. Interview one or more teachers about their approach to teaching, say, verb forms, the plural or the possessive. Are they aware of the research into the order of acquisition? For help with the possible answers to this, look at Ellis (1994, ch. 15) and Alderson (1997), who both explore the possibilities that SLA research is of no, of some, or of paramount importance for the teachers' presentation of the language in the classroom.

Comparison of L1 and L2 acquisition

Research into the similarities and differences between L1 and L2 acquisition goes further than just the developmental sequences described above. Much has been written about the learning environment, the quantity and quality of the input, the expectations and the actual output, the attitude and tolerance level of the listener to errors and dysfluency, the time period over which the language is learned and so on. A number of ideas could be developed from reading about **universal grammar** in more detail in, for example, White (1989), or Cook (1993, ch. 9).

PROJECT

76. Compare carer-talk (**motherese**) addressed to an L1 learner, with foreigner-talk. What are the similarities and what are the differences? Compare them for: range of vocabulary, use of any special words, the complexity (or absence of it) of the grammar, any non-adult or non-standard grammatical forms, pronunciation, intonation, volume range and so on.

Language-learning targets

Many people leave school saying that they 'know' another language – meaning that they can just about buy a postcard or a glass of beer using it. For others, knowing another language would mean that they could speak and write fluently about a wide range of subjects, and could follow the speech and writing of others with no difficulty. In other contexts it might mean being able to discuss the rules of grammar in great detail, whether or not that knowledge could be applied in comprehension or production. If we want to include all native speakers within the group who do 'know' the language, what constraints does that put upon the definition? What sorts of targets or goals do learners have?

PROJECTS

77. Use evidence from errors in the speech or writing of advanced non-native speakers to identify some of the more subtle aspects of full competence in a language. Pawley and Syder (1983) may give you some ideas.

78. Compare the views of some learners and their teacher (interviewed separately), about what 'knowing' a language means. If the responses do not fully correspond, consider what implications this might have for the success of the teaching and learning process in that class. Remember to consider the effect on some people of consistently failing to meet the goal they have set themselves.

79. Monitor the range of input encountered by one or more intermediate learners, looking at (a) variation between native speakers (within a group or family, national and international) and (b) contemporary change (for example, in the vocabulary and expressions of adolescents). How do learners handle such variation?

80. By careful observation of your own day, or by 'shadowing' a foreign student, compile guidelines for what English a foreign student most needs for successful communication in your school or university environment. Variations on this, if you have access to the appropriate environment, include: a nurse or doctor in a hospital, a businessman visiting in order to make a formal presentation about a product or service he hopes to sell, and so on. You may find it valuable to engage in some role play with a friend, to explore some of the finer points of these scenarios. Munby (1978) may provide some insights.

81. Carry out a survey of English-language teaching schools and units, to see how they go about testing the level of their students at entry. Are they satisfied with the accuracy of the tests. (i.e. do they have to redistribute the students across ability levels a week later, because the tests did not correctly sort them into groups)? A critical evaluation of entry tests is given in Wesche *et al.* (1996).

Grammar-based and communication-based teaching

Some teachers work on the assumption that without a thorough grounding in the grammar, semantics and phonology of the target language of English, the student cannot be expected to know and use the language. Their lessons will therefore focus on teaching grammatical structures, introducing lists of new vocabulary and correcting the students' pronunciation. Such an approach to language learning is widespread in many countries of the world, and it contrasts with approaches that focus primarily on communicative competence. In the latter, students are expected to use the language to interact (e.g. in role plays) and to share real information. There will be fewer activities which involve the more mechanical manipulations of language forms that appear in a structurally based lesson. The Natural Approach (Stephen Krashen), Suggestopaedia (Georgi Lozanov), Community Language Learning (Charles A. Curran), Language from Within (Beverly Galyean) and Total Physical Response (James Asher) have all been developed as alternatives to 'formal' teaching, and each makes substantive claims for its own validity.

PROJECTS

82. Cook (1996: 37 and 63) considers explicit teaching and the learning of the formal components of the language and suggests comparing a range of textbooks to see the different ways in which the language can be made explicit. You could do this for English or for another language which you know, or you could look for variation across different languages within a single published series, such as Linguaphone, Hugo, Teach Yourself or one of the BBC series.

83. Accumulate several different beginners' courses for a language, and persuade subjects to spend a set number of hours over a week studying the language, using the course material you assign to them. At the end of the week, interview the subjects as a group and individually, to find out, for example, how easy, interesting or useful they found the approach, whether they think they learnt anything, and whether they would feel motivated to carry on.

84. Make a single visit to each of several language classes (with different teachers) and assess each on a continuum for formal grammar instruction, communicative activities, use of L1 to explain things, and so on. Supplement this information with interviews with the teacher and a couple of students from each class. Ask them what they felt the balance was in the lesson you observed, as a way of assessing the correspondence between their views and yours (consider the significance of a mismatch). Check whether the teaching content and/or approach is laid down by the institution, and if so, whether it is what the teacher would use by choice. To what extent can this, or any teaching, be labelled as fully 'communicative' or 'grammar-driven', and why? Classroom observation is difficult to do well, and you may find Spada and Fröhlich (1995) useful in developing your approach.

85. Make several visits to one language class where there is at least some explanation of grammatical detail given in L1. Make a note of all the sentences that contain technical terms (recording the lesson will make this easier). List a selection of the sentences (don't just list the words out of context, as that makes the test much more difficult), and ask the class to write down what each one means. Use the scores to assess the extent to which the teacher is communicating the grammatical information, and consider whether it is a prerequisite for learning a grammatical point that you understand all the techical terms used to describe it.

86. Interview a group of learners about their goals in studying the language (such as what they will use it for). Widen this into a discussion of whether teachers need to be aware of what the learner expects or dreams of, and what they can do about it if they do. In a separate interview with the teacher, find out what he/she *thinks* they want the language for. Assess the extent to which the learners' goals map onto the style and approach of the teaching they are receiving and the sort of work they are being asked to produce.

Vocabulary acquisition

A wide range of studies has been carried out on the processes and the significance for overall learning of vocabulary acquisition. Amongst the questions that have been addressed are: Does it help or hinder learning if you present vocabulary out of context? Does it help learning if you teach the key vocabulary *before* you read a new passage, or should you let the learners read it first, and then have the new words explained? How many words do you need to know in order to function adequately in a language (for example, to hold a conversation, read a newspaper or follow a TV drama). Should you teach or learn words with related meanings together (such as opposites, synonyms, members of a set), or is that confusing? When can you say that you 'know' a word? What is the best way to memorize words? How can you test how many words a learner knows? Does it matter which words you learn first? How can you tell how difficult a passage is going to be for a learner to read? Answers to these, and many other questions, are considered in Nation's (1990) review of the research.

PROJECTS

87. Interview learners about their attitude and practical approach to vocabulary learning. Use this information to evaluate critically assumptions made in the research, and make suggestions for how teachers might help learners more.

88. Using data from willing 'guinea pigs', write a critical evaluation of the Linkword learning system developed by Mike Gruneberg (see, for example, 1987), now also available on CD-ROM (Gruneberg 1997). You can read more about the use of mnemonic techniques in vocabulary learning in Nation (1990: 166 ff.).

89. Get a class of language learners to memorize a set of words (and their translations) from a language they do not know. Test them and identify the most successful learners. Get them to tell the class what their techniques are. Go through the same process again, with a new set of words, telling the poorer performers to try one of the successful techniques. Compare the performances across the two tests to see if adopting the 'successful' techniques has had an effect. Widen this into a discussion of the usefulness of teaching learning *techniques* as well as the language itself.

90. Use one of the tests at the back of Nation (1990) as the basis for your own investigation. Alternatively, if you have very high competence in another language, try producing one or more of the tests in that language, and chronicle the problems you encounter.

Different concepts expressed in different languages

German has two words that both translate into English as *but*. In translating the sentence *Jane went to the pictures but I stayed at home*, the German word *aber* would be used for *but*. However, in the sentence *Jane didn't go to the pictures but stayed at home*, the word *sondern* would be used. In Welsh (and many other languages) there is no single pair of words for *yes* and *no* – you need to know what the verb is, what tense it is in and where it comes in the sentence before you can choose the right word. Researchers have been interested in investigating whether such differences between languages make them more difficult to learn, or whether all humans share an underlying sensitivity to differences in meaning, even if not all languages show them.

PROJECT

91. With the help of a bilingual informant, identify words in one language that do not have simple corresponding translations (words relating to culture, religion and food are often good candidates). Get a group of subjects who do not know the foreign language to learn the words on this list, plus, interspersed, a balancing number of words which *do* have a direct translation. Compare their success in remembering the words: is it easier to learn a word that you can 'hook' directly onto an L1 word?

The learner's approach and experience

What makes a successful language learner? Ellis and Sinclair (1989) look at this question, and you can gain an overview of work in the field from Richards and Lockhart (1994: 63–6). Stevick (1989) presents seven case studies of language learners, each of whom has a different approach. Bailey and Nunan (1996) provides a collection of papers on teaching methodology, but from the perspective of the learners and teachers rather than the theorists. One of the most influential studies of the 1970s was that of the *Good Language Learner*, conducted by Naiman, Fröhlich, Stern and Todesco, and their book has recently been republished (Naiman *et al.* 1978/1995). It is a classic account of the strategies used by successful foreign-language learners, and it could form the basis for a good replication study.

PROJECT

92. Do a case-study of a good language learner, and see how easily (if at all) he or she fits into one of Stevick's or Naiman *et al.*'s categories, by carefully identifying and categorizing his or her approach to different aspects of the learning process.

Interlanguage, error analysis and contrastive analysis

Interlanguage, a term coined by Selinker (1972), is used fairly loosely by many to mean, variously, what the learner can do at any given point after beginning L2 but before perfecting it, the total profile of all the learner's performance stages from beginning L2 to perfecting it, the underlying knowledge which produces the imperfect performance, and a system essentially the same for all learners, featuring rules and patterns consistently found at any given stage, irrespective of the L1 and the learning method (see also Ellis 1994: 710). In Selinker's original definition, interlanguage is the result of having to use a learning system that is not language-specific, and its features result from a combination of **language transfer** (elements of L1 are incorrectly imposed onto L2); **overgeneralization** (using an L2 rule in inappropriate conditions); **transfer of training** (an artefact of the teacher's style, creating an apparent rule where there is none); **learning strategies** (choices made by the learner to achieve short-term learning goals, such as simplifying the verb system); and **communication strategies** (a focus on getting the message across, even at the expense of total accuracy) (Cook 1993: 18–19).

Error analysis was for many years the standard approach to identifying the features of an interlanguage. **Contrastive analysis** takes direct account of how the L1 and L2 differ in their expression of an idea or their construction of a grammatical relationship, and predicts certain errors directly emanating from using the L1 patterns in L2. For an account of error analysis, see Cook (1993: 19 ff.) and Ellis (1994, ch. 2). Swan and Smith (1987) is useful for finding out what major types of interference can be expected from learners of English with different first languages.

PROJECTS

93. Compare the errors made in English by native speakers of two or more languages that you know in such areas as vocabulary use, grammatical forms and pronunciation. Do they make substantially different errors? Are you able to account for the errors in terms of features of the L1? Do the patterns correspond with those documented in Swan and Smith (1987)?

94. Collect and sort the corrections made by a teacher in class: which errors are allowed to pass? Interview the teacher to find out why and in what circumstances they choose to focus on certain errors and not others.

Language assessment and testing

There are almost as many forms of language test as there are approaches to language learning, because it would not be fair for students drilled in grammar and translation to be tested only on their communicative skills, and vice versa. In actual fact, it is often the tail that wags the dog, and much classroom practice is determined by the testing methods used in the external examinations.

PROJECTS

95. Find two classes of equivalent level, working towards roughly equivalent exams for different examining boards or agencies. Is it possible to identify any strong patterns in the teaching that reflect the customary exam format? What effects might such restrictions have upon balanced learning? If you can, find out what motivates the different examining agencies to present their tests in the way they do (it may not be all to do with language-related considerations at all: perhaps, for example, some sorts of answers are quicker to mark than others).

96. Explore some of the formal and communicative tests of English for speakers of other languages (for example, those produced by the University of Cambridge), asking how far they are genuine tests of language ability. Ask experienced teachers for their opinions about how easy it would be for a candidate to learn how to pass the exams while lacking aspects of the ability in that language that is assumed to go with such a performance.

97. Get hold of some tests for foreign learners of English (as above) and give them to native speakers to do. You could use people with different levels of education, and of different ages, including children. How do they perform? What would the implications be of (a) consistently very high scores and (b) a range of scores, some of which are below those of non-native speakers? What account should be taken of age and level of general education in *non*-native speakers?

Bilinguals, multilinguals and polyglots

Bilingualism is an enormous area of research in its own right. Most of the work, however, does not directly relate to the acquisition of the languages, so we shall not cover it here. However, there does exist work on how already knowing more than one language affects your subsequent learning of languages. Many *polyglots* (speakers of several languages) say that language learning gets easier the more of them you learn, because you get the hang of how to do it and can make generalizations and predictions based on your previous experience of what languages can do. Yet many learners experience interference between their foreign languages. Why that happens is perhaps a question for the psycholinguist, but how it affects the learning experience is a question relevant to SLA research.

PROJECTS

98. Interview a group of polyglots and childhood bilinguals. Are their experiences of interference between the languages (in retrieving words, say), the same or different? Use your findings to construct a model of how the different people might store their languages in the brain, and access them. Compare your models to those described by Cook (1993: 8–10)

99. Devise an experiment that will elicit cross-language interference. For example, you might get subjects to translate words alternately, and at speed, into their L2 and L3, and see how often they come out with the right word in the wrong language. How do your findings relate to the predictions that the models described in Cook (1993: 8–10) would make?

Foreign language teaching policy

Among the objectives for action proposed for the year 1996 by the European Commission in its White Paper on Education and Training was that citizens should 'develop proficiency in three European languages'. In its Fourth General Objective, the Paper states:

> It is desirable for foreign languages learning to start at pre-school level. It seems essential for such teaching to be placed on an established footing in primary education, with the learning of a second Community foreign language starting in secondary school. It could even be argued that secondary school pupils should study certain subjects in the first foreign language learned.
>
> (*White Paper on Education and Training: Teaching and Learning – Towards the Learning Society* Part Two, IV. Fourth General Objective – Proficiency in three Community languages)

While many European countries already have the educational culture and prerequisites to meet this objective, Britain's foreign-language-teaching provision in schools will need considerable upgrading to achieve it. Yet as long ago as the early 1960s there were calls in Britain for better language provision, leading to an experiment in teaching French from the age of 8. The report by Burstall *et al.* (1974) on the outcomes of this project stated, 'Pupils taught French from the age of 8 do not subsequently reveal any "substantial" gains in achievement' (Burstall *et al.* 1974: 243). The result was that pre-secondary French-teaching was largely abandoned.

Halsall (1968) compared French teaching in Holland, England and Flemish-speaking Belgium. She concluded that 'there was . . ., on average, a real inferiority in the standards achieved for French in the English secondary modern school at the 3rd and 4th year levels' (p. 89). A useful source of insight into the factors that might account for this (such as motivation, amount and type of input and attitudes at home) is Clark (1987, ch. 5), which documents practice and attitudes towards foreign-language teaching and learning in Scottish schools. For a study of French teaching in eight European countries see Carroll (1975). Dickson and Cumming (1996) provides a compendium of information profiling the language background and the policy on foreign-language-teaching provision in 25 European countries – a valuable reference source if you want to focus on principle and practice.

A few schools have experimented with teaching a curriculum subject such as history or geography through the medium of French or another language, with impressive results. For specific accounts of such attempts, see Hawkins and Perren 1978, chs. 2 to 5).

PROJECTS

100. Interview a group of native English-speaking, and non-native overseas students about their language learning experiences in school. How much time was given to the language? How much homework did they get? How much support did they get from home? What did they think they would use the language for? Make sure you are comparing like with like: visiting students are by definition motivated to try out their (above-average?) English, so at least compare them with home students who are studying a foreign language.

101. Interview school students and try to ascertain what motivates them to choose to study one or another foreign language. Have they dropped a language, and if so, why? What do their parents think of language learning? If you have access to individuals from more than one country, incorporate a comparison.

102. Hawkins (1987, ch. 3) poses the question 'why French?', and explores the complex issue of how French came to be, and has remained, the first foreign language offered in most British schools. You could:

   • re-examine his arguments in the light of subsequent political change
   • consider the validity of teaching French in a multi-ethnic school, and the advantages and disadvantages of teaching, say, an Asian language to all pupils instead
   • make a strategic plan for supplanting French with another language, considering the implications (and time scale) for: which language you choose, what happens to all the French teachers, where the new teachers will come from, the possible effects on culture and balances of power within and beyond Europe and so on. Rees (1989: especially 85–91) is a valuable source of information about attitudes to, and the feasibility of, offering a wider range of languages in schools.

103. Make a study of foreign-language teaching in the former Eastern-bloc countries since the collapse of communism. Focus on the marginalization of Russian as the first foreign language (outside Russia) and of other East European languages (inside Russia), and the rapid introduction of English. How has this been achieved? Are the standards achieved in English comparable with those previously achieved for Russian or other languages? You could try making contact with teachers of English in these countries via the Internet, or via a TESOL unit which is involved in training overseas.

104. Investigate the history and current status of Welsh teaching in Wales, Irish teaching in Ireland, or the teaching of another indigenous minority language. If possible, visit some schools and interview teachers and

pupils with the minority and the majority language as their mother-tongue. If you can't travel that far, write to them, or make Internet links.

Effect of the year abroad

Students who are sent abroad for a year's study expect and are expected to improve their language skills in the host language, but there has been surprisingly little research into the nature and amount of improvement achieved. Milton and Meara (1995) review some studies and report their own, in which the greatest improvement was made by those with the poorest skills at the outset. Students who were already competent benefited much less, if at all, linguistically.

PROJECT

105. Record an interview with an overseas exchange student at the beginning of his or her visit, and again some time later. In both interviews talk about the same subject so that it is easier to compare the two performances. Choose a subject about which he or she already has some knowledge at the time of the first interview. Analyse the language of the two interviews for fluency, breadth of vocabulary, variety of grammatical structures, length of conversational turn, idiomaticity, ability to make jokes and witticisms and so on, and list the types of error and their frequency. Use this data to assess the general improvement of the student during the stay. You could also ask him or her in the second interview what he or she feels about the level of improvement, and how it seems to have been achieved (for example, by socializing, studying or watching TV). In the light of Milton and Meara's findings, this study may work best with an individual who is not highly competent on arrival.

Role of the social and political status of English as L2

English occupies an extraordinary and complex position in the modern world. Its precise status varies in different places and is subject to constant change. It is not always easy to see who or what has elevated it to its position and what maintains it: the culture? policy? Crystal (1995) has a section entitled 'World English' in which he considers the different international varieties of English and asks whether the English language is under threat or is a threat to other languages, and Crystal (1997b) is dedicated to this subject. Hartmann (1996) contains a range of papers on aspects of the role and status of English in the European Union, including its use as a *lingua franca*, the adoption of English loan words into other languages, and the phenomenon of bilingualism with English in different EU countries. For a history of English-language teaching, which indicates how the status of English has been reflected in the changing demand for it abroad, see Howatt (1984).

PROJECTS

106. How has the current language situation arisen in a particular country of your choice? South Africa, India, Hong Kong and China would make interesting case studies. You need to think carefully about how you will gain the necessary information. A government office or embassy will give the official reasoning, but you may want to discuss the issues with citizens of that country as well.

107. Explore the reasons why English language is, or is not, on the school syllabus in a particular country. This type of project could simply take a historical perspective and explain how the country in question has reached the situation in which it now finds itself; or you could attempt to predict what language provision will be most appropriate for the country in the near future.

OTHER PROJECT IDEAS

108. Conduct some tests, or interview teachers, or both, to investigate whether girls are better at learning foreign languages than boys.

109. Through observation of non-native speakers in real interaction, analyse how the learner's social behaviour in the learning situation correlates with his or her overall achievement, fluency and/or accuracy.

110. Consider, in a theory-based project, to what extent learning Orwell's Newspeak (described in an essay at the back of his novel *Nineteen Eighty-Four*) would be the same as, and different from, learning an L2.

111. Compare three beginners in a foreign language: one in a regular class, one working with an individual tutor (contact could be made via a local Home Tutor scheme) and one teaching him or herself. Apart from monitoring and comparing their progress (remember to devise tests that do not favour one or the other's approach), consider what advantages and disadvantages each method of learning has, as regards changes in motivation, commitment and interest, availability of feedback, accuracy of what is learnt, number of hours put in and how regularly, and so on.

112. Use the various accounts of successful learning in Stevick (1989) as the basis for a critical appraisal of a model of how languages are learned.

For further inspiration, read Ellis (1994, ch. 1), and follow up an idea that interests you by finding his more detailed account elsewhere in the book.

|6|

Style in texts

When we read we react not only to the message contained in the text, but also, albeit subconsciously, to the language which conveys it. This fact provides the linguist's justification for analysing in detail the language used in texts. Literary texts, in particular, are crafted to have messages that are not immediately obvious to the reader. Part of the characterization of a literary text is that it functions at different linguistic levels to produce a complex overall effect, reinforcing or subtly refining the meaning expressed.

In this chapter we shall consider projects that focus on the lexical, syntactic and structural choices made by writers. If you are doing work in **text analysis, discourse analysis** or **stylistics**, you may find information and ideas here to help you.

The sorts of questions addressed by research in this field include:

- do different types of text have discernibly different styles?
- what is the effect on the reader of a piece *not* being in the style normally associated with it?
- does changing the style of writing change the message, and if so, in what way?
- have stylistic conventions changed over the years?
- would men and women write about the same subject differently?
- is it possible to have 'styleless' writing?
- can a stylistic analysis reliably determine the authorship of a text when that is in doubt?
- what makes some texts easier to read than others? Can would-be writers use the study of style to help them learn to produce texts that are more readable?
- how do poets exploit style to create an effect?

Textbooks and major journals

Table 6.1 Useful texts for style (see page xiv for key to levels)

Book	Level	Notes on Content/Style
Bloor and Bloor 1995	2	useful for terminology and concepts
Caldas-Coulthard and Coulthard 1996	4	power of language in social contexts; Critical Discourse Analysis approach
Carter 1987	2	semantics and lexicon
Carter 1982, Carter and Simpson 1989	3	examples of analysis of literary and non-literary texts
Carter and Nash 1990	2	worked example analyses and practice texts
Chiaro 1992	3	verbal wit and humour
Cook 1992	3	advertisements
Crystal 1995, 1997a	1	useful for terminology and concepts
Cummings and Simmons 1983	2	useful for terminology and concepts
Freeborn 1996	2	useful for terminology and concepts; authentic texts; worked examples
Gray 1984	2	useful for terminology and concepts
Leech 1969	2	sound patterns
Leech and Short 1981	2	fiction; collection of texts for further study
Nash 1985	2	verbal wit and humour
Nash 1990	3	popular fiction
Talbot 1995	3	popular fiction
Trask 1995b	2	useful for terminology and concepts
Wales 1989	2	useful for terminology and concepts

Communications	*Linguistic Enquiry*
Journal of Linguistics	*Poetics Today*
Journal of Pragmatics	*Prose Studies*
Language and Communication	*Style*
Language and Style	*Word*

Fig 6.1 Major journals for research in style

Finding and approaching a text

Almost any type of text can form the basis of a project, and finding the right one may seem as big and time-consuming a job as the analysis itself! Here are some questions to help you focus your interests:

- are you interested in a particular *type* of text, such as advertising texts, legal texts, the language of charity appeals or political flyers?
- do you read newspapers and take an interest in the language of the reporting journalist?
- would you like to do something useful with all the junk mail that comes through your letter box?
- have you ever wondered what makes a romantic novel recognizable as such?
- would your favourite soap opera make an interesting subject for analysis?

Find several examples of the type of text on which you wish to work so that you can start a preliminary analysis before taking the final decision about exactly which one(s) to concentrate on. Once you have decided on a type of text, decide whether you want to work on one single example in great detail or a comparison of two or more apparently similar texts. You could look at two newspaper reports of the same incident and analyse how the language reflects the ideological standpoints of the writers. You could examine one widely recognized text form, such as the sonnet, the essay or a national newspaper's letters page, birth announcements or obituaries to identify the characteristic features.

Central themes and project ideas

A text can be examined at many different levels, and you do not necessarily need to deal with them all in one project. Whatever level(s) of analysis you do choose, though, you need to be familiar with the theoretical frameworks currently used and the type of work which has already been done in the field.

Interpersonal function

Why was the text written in the first place? Sometimes this will be obvious, but quite often, particularly in advertising and in propaganda, the superficial aim of the text disguises a deeper message. For example, an advertisement that appears to be explaining how little servicing a particular car requires is, of course, actually trying to sell the car. A newspaper report of an event and an entry about the same event in a personal diary will read quite differently because they are written for different audiences. Cook

(1992) gives you some idea of how to approach advertisements as samples of individual texts, as well as indicating some of the more generic features of advertising. For ideas on how to tackle the analysis of propaganda, see Chilton (1985).

PROJECTS

113. Choose a specific brand-name product and compare the way in which it is advertised in different places. You will find most variation where there is fierce competition between brands and the product is not in itself geared to a niche market. A good example is high-street banking. Compare advertisements in a range of magazines and newspapers and in the bank's own publicity leaflets, considering the ways in which the same product is described differently for different readers. Remember to target adult comics, ethnic publications, religious newspapers and exclusive magazines aimed at the well-off, as well as best-selling magazines and newspapers. You may want to compare advertisements in publications from different countries.

114. A political leaflet from the Spartacist League in July 1997 talks of 'a thousand Orangemen . . . flaunt[ing] the bloody Union Jack in the face of the oppressed Catholics of Northern Ireland'. Collect leaflets from different sides in some major political conflict and compare their use of language in accounts of the same event or issue. Also use newspapers and journals, including those with international circulation such as *Time* and *New Statesman*. Remember to consider the collusion of the reader in deliberately choosing to read one publication rather than another, because he or she knows or senses what ideology each will reflect.

115. Using the public library archives, compare the coverage of an event (such as an election or a disaster) 30 or 50 years ago with the coverage of a similar event much more recently. Look not only at the reports during the day or two after it, but also the coverage in the longer term. One comparison might be the disaster in 1966 in Aberfan, Wales and the shootings in Dunblane, Scotland in 1996, both of which resulted in the death of many children in their school building. How have styles of reporting changed, and how are the changes best characterized linguistically?

116. Compare descriptions of a specific hotel as found in a holiday brochure, a guide book, a diary and on a postcard home. Carter and Nash (1990: 206 ff.) use this area as a basis for one of their practical exercises at the end of the book. Earlier on (p. 35 ff.) they analyse descriptions of places in a range of publications produced for different purposes, and use this to tease out characteristics of literary, as opposed to non-literary, language.

117. For a piece of household equipment (such as a hi-fi, microwave, personal computer or boiler) compare the description in the manual with the one in the sales literature that is trying to persuade you to buy the item, and, if appropriate, with the technical description for the engineer or installer.

118. Compare the style in which recipes for the same dish are written in a range of cookery books.

119. Look at estate agents' descriptions of various houses, considering the stylistic characteristics of detailed descriptions that are intended to persuade the reader to buy the property.

120. Perhaps using historical material, examine the subtleties of propaganda, where the intention is to present a one-sided account as if it was the whole truth.

Sound patterns

In some texts the sound patterns created by the writer are clearly the most important feature. Although we associate rhyme, alliteration, assonance and consonance with poetry, advertisers also frequently use such devices as a way of making a slogan more memorable. Whether you are describing a Shakespeare sonnet or a soap-powder advert, the formal description of the phonetic patterns will use the same approach and terminology. Stress and intonation are also often used to great effect.

Nursery rhymes often follow strong metrical patterns, the heavily stressed rhythms making them easier to memorize. *Twinkle twinkle little star* is a good example of a nursery rhyme with a particularly strong metrical rhythm. In *Three Blind Mice*, on the other hand, we see reflected the wider potential of the stress-timed pattern of everyday English speech, with different numbers of unstressed syllables packed in between equally spaced stressed ones. **Iambs, dactyls** and other metrical patterns and rhyme schemes are explained in most of the introductory books on literary stylistics (such as Leech 1969) or in the dictionaries of literary terms (such as Gray 1984). Cummings and Simmons (1983) show a detailed analysis of sound patterning in poetry and prose by Hopkins, Dylan Thomas, Birney, Frost and Arnold. Freeborn (1996) also gives some examples of sound patterning in a range of verse and prose texts, including Chaucer's *Canterbury Tales*, *Remember* by Christina Rossetti and Dylan Thomas's *Under Milk Wood*.

A writer may use onomatopoeia: the choice of words could imitate the noise of walking through crisp leaves in the forest in autumn or the sound of a snake slithering through the grass, for example. These effects can be captured in analysis by using phonetic or phonemic transcription to highlight common sound features that may be obscured by the complex spelling system of English. Indeed, even more general assonance and rhyme in a text benefits from this treatment: the words *all, haunch, lawn, broad, floor, more, pour, sure* appear to have little in common when spelled, yet a phonemic transcription reveals that, in many varieties of English, they all contain the same vowel.

PROJECTS

121. Look at the work of one or more poets (such as Gerard Manley Hopkins or Benjamin Zephaniah) to see what makes their work sound so different from that of other poets.

122. Focus on an advertising campaign that uses sound. For example, Perrier used a play on the word *eau* (French for *water*) to illustrate occasions when their product could be consumed, including: *S/eau lunch* (with a picture of a snail), *A reau at the regatta* (during the Henley regatta), and *Eau, I say* (during Wimbledon, where one commentator was known to exclaim 'Oh, I say' to a good shot). This last example demonstrates very clearly what is often called **intertextuality**: our interpretation of any one text may require a knowledge of other texts or situations. A new twist to this intertextuality came from a 'piggy-back' advertising campaign (where one advertiser exploits the idea of another) by Nestlé-Rowntree. An advertisement for Polo mints used the slogan *The mint with the heaule* with a picture of the mints looking like the bubbles in a glass of *Perrier*.

123. Record some political speeches at election time or at the annual party conferences, or consider party political slogans. Examine specifically the sound patterning that is used and how it reinforces the meaning.

Lexical choice

To work in this area you need to be familiar with the field of semantics. Carter (1987) provides a good introduction to areas such as connotation and denotation, and to semantic relationships like synonymy, antonymy and hyponymy. Crystal (1995) has a whole section on the lexicon and English vocabulary, including discussions on 'loaded vocabulary' (p. 170) and 'doublespeak' (p. 176).

A lexical analysis of style will ask: Why have these particular words been chosen and not others, and what are the connotations of the chosen words? For example, if *white* is mentioned, is it being used simply to indicate the colour of a physical object, or also to imply a sense of purity? (If the latter, there is a heavy cultural dependency, as white has different symbolism in different parts of the world).

In newspaper reporting the lexical choice of the journalist can indicate the ideological standpoint from which she or he is writing. Is a gunman described as a *terrorist*, a *guerrilla* or a *freedom-fighter*? Was a victim *shot by a marksman* or *picked off by a sniper*? In fiction, the author's perspective and opinion of characters is often indicated through the choice of nouns, verbs and adjectives with positive or negative connotations. Consider this description of Zoltan Kaparthy's dancing, in the musical *My Fair Lady*: *Oozing charm from ev'ry pore, he oiled his way around the floor.*

Carter and Nash (1990) focus on how individual characters are presented in Galsworthy's *The Man of Property* by analysing the way a dinner-party conversation is narrated. In an essay at the end of his novel *Nineteen Eighty-Four* George Orwell explains in some detail how lexical choice can be manipulated as a tool of political and personal repression.

In chapter 8 of Freeborn (1996) you can find a discussion of the notion of 'styleless prose', or that style which the semiologist Roland Barthes described as 'neutral writing'. He uses parts of Orwell's *Animal Farm*, Seth's *A Suitable Boy* and Camus' *The Outsider* to explore this from a grammatical and lexical perspective, and concludes that while the stylistic details can differ greatly from one text to another, there is style in all texts.

PROJECTS

124. Compare two translations of the same original text. By making different choices, the translators can create distinctly different texts. You can do a study of this sort even if you don't understand the original language: it is possible to compare the implications of the lexical and syntactic choices made by two translators of the same original text without any reference to that original – providing you don't want to make any judgement about which version is 'better'. To gain an idea of how two translations might differ, look at Leech and Short (1981: 352), where two translations of the first paragraph of Kafka's *The Trial* are juxtaposed.

125. Compare the way that writers get different effects from the same word. Choose something that is neutral enough to carry positive or negative connotations, e.g. *family; rain; compromise*.

126. Are the words used in a given text largely of Latin or of Anglo-Saxon origin? Books on the history of the English language (see Chapter 10 for references) will give you some insights into the significance of this distinction as well as how to spot the difference. Are the words in a text morphologically simple or complex, and what is the effect of this on the reader? Freeborn (1996) considers the effect of lexical choice by looking at different versions of part of the Sermon on the Mount from the Bible, and by looking at two translations of an extract from *The Swiss Family Robinson*. He also compares three versions of the first verses of St John's Gospel from different periods.

127. Find two or more texts on the same subject and see how *few* words they have in common, and how they cover the same ideas in different words. For example, compare a poetical and a prose description of a tiger.

128. Find examples of words that have a particular meaning and resonance in advertising. Examples are *crispy*, which is used as a desirable attribute for processed food that is high in fat, and *creamy* which is intended to give the impression of a luxury product (soup, soap, etc). Try replacing the words with others that have a similar meaning (e.g. for these examples, *crisp, hard*, etc. and *thick, viscous*, etc.). Work out the boundaries of the words' use – which products are and are not so described – and, by interviewing informants, assess the precise connotations and images that the words create.

Grammatical structure

Specific effects can be achieved by using short sentences with a simple clause and phrase structure on the one hand, and long and complex sentences with many embedded clauses and phrases on the other. A structure may be repeated for effect, while a passive construction may enable the agent to remain unnamed. Useful guidance on basic clause and phrase structure can be found in Bloor and Bloor (1995) and in Freeborn (1995). You can find out how to apply this knowledge to text analysis in Freeborn (1996) as well as in Carter (1982), Fairclough (1989) and Fowler (1991). You should also read Chapter 9 in this book.

Questions you can ask when approaching text analysis from this angle include:

- Are the sentences of equal length and complexity throughout the text?
- Is the clause structure always unmarked, or have particular elements sometimes been emphasized by being placed at the beginning of the sentence or deliberately held back until the end?
- Have any structural patterns been created by cohesive devices such as repetition or ellipsis, anaphoric or cataphoric reference?
- Are any of these then deliberately broken to create a particular effect? Creating and then destroying a structural pattern is a technique employed by many writers to highlight a particular point, as this extract from *Yes Prime Minister* (Lynn and Jay 1987: 107) illustrates:

The Times is read by the people who run the country.
The Daily Mirror is read by the people who think they run the country.
The Guardian is read by the people who think they ought to run the country.
The Morning Star is read by the people who think the country ought to be run by another country.
The Independent is read by the people who don't know who runs the country but are sure they are doing it wrong.
The Daily Mail is read by the wives of the people who run the country.
The Financial Times is read by the people who own the country.
The Daily Express is read by the people who think the country ought to be run as it used to be run.
The Daily Telegraph is read by the people who still think it is their country.
And the Sun's readers don't care who runs the country providing she has big tits.

PROJECTS

129. Reading schemes for young children are often graded in terms of the structures used in the text. Examine the books in such a scheme. How precise is the grading? What effect does the limiting of available structures have on the flow of the text?

130. There are many simplified versions of classic texts for learners of English as a Foreign Language. How has the original text been modified in terms of structure? Ask some native and non-native speakers of English to compare the two and say which they prefer and why.

131. Compare old and recent versions of the Bible or a church liturgy. What differences are there in the grammar and form – or are the changes all lexical? Have the changes made the text more accessible?

132. Are business letters today written following the same conventions as, say, in the 1930s?

Authorship

Stylistic studies have been used to ascertain the authorship of disputed texts. These days, they are supported by computer analyses. Such research can help establish whether a newly found sixteenth-century play is by Shakespeare, but it can equally well be used forensically, to compare a ransom note with written material known to be by a given suspect. For general information about how these investigations are carried out, see Crystal (1997a: 68–9). Much more detail about the procedures involved, and how the techniques can be applied, is given in Farringdon (1996).

PROJECT

133. Show a selection of short newspaper pieces to informants and ask them to judge whether they were written by men or women. Get them to identify what it is that helped them decide. Does the accuracy or otherwise of their judgements indicate that these apparent pointers are reliable?

Ideology and power

A recent significant development in text analysis has been the investigation of how language is used to exercise power over people in subtle ways. This research goes under the name of **critical discourse analysis (CDA)**. In CDA, the approach is unashamedly political, and aims to uncover implicit ideology in apparently innocuous language. You can read about this work in Caldas-Coulthard and Coulthard (1996), Fairclough (1995), Fowler (1991),

Kress (1990) and Meinhof and Richardson (1994), amongst others. A critique of CDA, with practical proposals, based on corpus analysis, for making it a more water-tight pursuit, is given by Stubbs (1997).

PROJECTS

134. Stubbs (1995) presents the following distributions from his corpus research:

little girl or *girls*: 146   *little boy* or *boys*: 91
small girl or *girls*:   8   *small boy* or *boys*: 46   (p. 383)

He examined the collocations of *little, small, big* and *large* and concludes that *little* tends to have a connotation of *cute and likeable* or else 'it can convey that a speaker's attitude is patronising or perjorative' (p. 385). In other words, *little* has 'strong cultural connotations' (Stubbs 1997: 113) which give it certain associative attributes and which then, through the collocational patterns, apply these attributes differentially to males and females.

Use a corpus (see Chapter 19 for how to do this) to make your own search for the collocations of a word that you suspect may have gender- or race-specific, or other (for example, negative) weightings. You are aiming to see whether the words occurring within, say, a ten-word stretch either side tend to have particular associations that have resonance for our contemporary culture and/or politics. Some you might try are: *handsome, pert, jolly, communist, feminist* and *clever*.

135. A project focusing on lexical choice in newspaper reports was suggested earlier. A CDA approach to journalistic writing would look at a wider range of stylistic devices in different newspapers and link these to their implicit ideologies. Fruitful topics might be reports on:

● the Gaza Strip in pro- and anti-Israeli publications
● socio-economic issues or the rights of the disabled in charity and more militant publications
● race issues in an extreme right-wing publication and in newspapers written for and by ethnic minority groups
● human-rights issues as reported by Amnesty International, broadsheets and tabloids
● the portrayal of women in men's and women's popular magazines and in feminist publications.

136. Focus on environmental or humanitarian issues to see how language can be used to empower or disempower people. The journal *New Internationalist* often provides a different political perspective from that of the daily newspapers. How is this achieved linguistically? The nuclear-power industry and world poverty are two useful focuses for such a study.

|7|

Sociolinguistics

Sociolinguistics studies the relationship between language and society. Trudgill provides a good summary of some aspects of its coverage:

> Whenever we speak, we cannot avoid giving our listeners clues about our origins and the sort of person we are. Our accent and our speech generally show where we come from, and what sort of background we have. We may even give some indication of certain of our ideas and attitudes, and all of this information can be used by the people we are speaking with to help them formulate an opinion about us.
>
> These two aspects of language behaviour are very important from a social point of view: first, the function of language in establishing social relationships; and, second, the role played by language in conveying information about the speaker. (Trudgill 1995: 2)

Sociolinguistics has become a thriving area within linguistics since the 1960s and there are now numerous sub-areas within it. It would be impossible to summarize them all in a single chapter, but you will gain a feel for the subject here, and should follow up leads in the books recommended below. In addition, remember the chapters in this book on language and gender, accents and dialects and conversation analysis, all of which border on and link into this area. Chapters 14, 15 and 16 are also important reading before you embark on a project in sociolinguistics.

There are many questions which sociolinguistics addresses. Some main themes and questions include:

- How do accents and dialects develop?
- Is there a link between a speaker's use of regional accents or dialects and his or her social characteristics (for example, age, gender, social background and ethnicity)?
- What is the relationship between 'standard' and 'non-standard' accents and dialects?

- How do we decide what is a dialect or accent and what is a language?
- What do people's attitudes towards accents, dialects and other aspects of language use tell us, and why are some accents, dialects or languages, and their speakers, perceived in particular ways? How accurate are these perceptions when compared with other types of evidence?
- How does language change across time and geographical areas?
- How and why does language vary from one social context (situation) to another?
- What happens when languages come into contact, or when speakers of a country need to use more than one language on a regular basis (bilingualism or multilingualism)?
- How do 'pidgins' and 'creoles' come into existence; are they more like dialects or languages; and why has it taken so long for them to be studied in depth?
- Why do speakers sometimes change their accent, dialect or even the language spoken when in conversation with others, and what sorts of changes do they make?
- How do speakers signal their identity in the language they use, and why do people who live in specific communities sometimes speak in a similar way?
- What is the link between language and disadvantage (for example, the language of minority groups) or language and power?

Terminology and central concepts

There are a number of terms which it is useful to understand before approaching textbooks and project areas.

An essential characteristic of language is **variation**, which linguists have studied with increasing interest and breadth. While some approaches within linguistics (such as Chomsky's) expressly do not focus on *variation* in language, but rather on its structural properties and rules (linked to 'linguistic competence'), *socio*linguistics studies how speakers use language *appropriately*, in terms of what Dell Hymes first called **communicative competence**: 'when to speak, when not and as to what to talk about with whom, when, where, in what manner' (Hymes 1971: 277). In other words, sociolinguists stress that language varies not only in the sense that words can be combined together to form an infinite number of sentences or longer discourses, but also **systematically** according to a range of factors such as age, sex, background of speaker and the situation or social context where the language is used.

Within sociolinguistics there is a division into **micro** and **macro** research. **Microlinguistic** studies 'typically focus on very specific linguistic items or individual differences' in language use, and look for 'wide-ranging linguistic and/or social implications (e.g. the distribution of *singing* and *singin'*)' (Wardhaugh 1992: 17). They often involve the detailed study of interpersonal communication. **Macrolinguistic** studies, on the other hand, 'examine large amounts of language data to draw broad conclusions about group relationships' (Wardhaugh 1992: 17) and relate these to social factors. Aspects of bilingualism, multilingualism and language planning are issues which often fall under this heading.

The roots of sociolinguistics lie in the work of key figures such as William Labov, often referred to as the 'father of sociolinguistics', who conducted studies in **modern (urban) dialectology**. Coates (1993) suggests that 'there are many sociolinguists who consider studies of social variation in grammar and phonology [i.e. accent and dialect studies following Labov's methodology] to be *sociolinguistics proper*' (p. 106). However, sociolinguistics has diversified considerably since Labov's early studies in the 1960s. Some of the techniques used in sociolinguistics for collecting data (such as questionnaires and interviews) stem from the older field of **traditional dialectology (rural dialectology** or **dialect geography)**. However, traditional dialectology largely ignored social variation; few young or female informants were used, and town-dwellers were excluded, since their dialect was thought to be too new or inconsistent to reflect the older forms of 'pure' dialect which researchers assumed existed. Language change was to some extent the enemy of traditional dialectologists rather than their focus, since it 'muddied the waters' in their search for older forms. For comparisons of modern (urban) dialectology and early sociolinguistics with traditional dialectology, see Chambers and Trudgill (1980, chs. 2 and 4) and Coates (1993, chs. 3 and 4.)

Textbooks and major journals

Table 7.1 Useful texts for style (see page xiv for key to levels)

Book	Level	Notes on Content/Style
Crystal 1997a	1	various issues covered and illustrated, but dispersed around book, so use the index
Fairclough 1989	3–4	focus on language and power; discourse-oriented
Fasold 1990	3–4	includes ethnography of communication and conversational implicature
Fasold 1984	3–4	social psychology and sociology of language, including multilingualism, language maintenance and attitudes; qualitative and quantitative research techniques; statistics
Giglioli 1972	3–4	collection of classic papers by Hymes, Searle, Bernstein, Labov and Brown & Gilman, etc.
Hudson 1996	2–3	narrower focus than Wardhaugh 1992; good coverage of modern dialectology

Book	Level	Notes on Content/Style
Montgomery 1995	2	broad coverage; unusual selection of focal topics, e.g. ethnic identity, subcultures, language and representation, etc. Section on language and situation: register provides a useful data analysis framework
O'Donnell and Todd 1991	1–2	focuses on variety, so covers both sociolinguistics and stylistics
Preston 1989	3–4	sociolinguistics of 2LA
Romaine 1984	2–3	sociolinguistics of child language
Saville-Troike 1989	3	focus on ethnography of communication, including children's acquisition of communicative competence
Trudgill 1995	1–2	wide-ranging; chapter titles and sub-headings make it hard to dip in, but the index offsets this
Wardhaugh 1992	3	comprehensive coverage of macro- to microsociolinguistics; easy to use

Apart from the journals noted in Fig. 7.1, reports of studies taking a sociolinguistic perspective on child language, second-language acquisition, conversation, accents and dialects and so on can be found in the journals relating to those areas, as given in other chapters in this book.

English World-Wide	*Language and Communication*
International Journal of the Sociology of Language	*Language and Society*
	Language in Society
Journal of Sociolinguistics	*Language Variation and Change*
Journal of Social Psychology	*Linguistics*
Language	

Fig 7.1 Major journals for research in sociolinguistics

Central themes and project ideas

Because sociolinguistics is concerned with variety in language it can be approached from a number of angles, including what the variation consists of, which groups display it, in which situations it occurs and what approaches can be taken to its analysis. This dimension will be considered first, and then projects will be suggested according to three major approaches to data collection and analysis: **qualitative, quantitative**, and, as a bridge between them, **social networks**.

Types and causes of variation

Language features that vary in precise form from speaker to speaker, such as the dropping of the /h/ from the start of words like *hammer* in some British English accents, and the dialect form *we be* where standard English would have *we are* (Upton and Widdowson 1996: 64), are known as **linguistic variables**. The detailing and analysing of linguistic variables requires tools such as orthographic and phonetic transcription, and draws on the research techniques of conversation analysis, phonetic, phonological and structural analysis, discourse analysis and so on. For ideas on what can be achieved, read the chapters in this book relevant to your interests. The *causes* of variation are known as **extralinguistic variables,** and where there is a relationship between linguistic and extralinguistic variables, this is sometimes referred to as co-variation.

We can identify three main types of extralinguistic variable: speaker, group and situation. The sorts of speaker characteristic that are a backdrop to variation include age, gender, ethnic origin, social background, regional origin, level of education, occupation and religious persuasion. If variation exists between the language varieties of two or more groups, the sociolinguist needs to identify a pre-existing group membership. He or she might decide there are grounds for saying that these people belong to this group and as a result speak differently. Alternatively, there may be evidence that people belong to a group only by virtue of the fact that they speak differently.

Group variation can shed light on **language change**. Labov tried to demonstrate that, contrary to earlier beliefs, it is possible to see language change in progress, if you know where to look. The variability in language use found within a community of speakers, and uncertainty about what constitutes 'correct' or acceptable usage, often give clues to what aspects of language may change in the future. For example, Labov found that the usage of post-vocalic *r* (see Chapter 17) was in the process of change in New York City. After a lengthy period during which it was almost lost, it had suddenly started to increase in frequency during the 1950s. He found that it signalled social 'prestige', which was why speakers were more likely to use it in their more careful speech. Labov's work revealed that the 'prestige' pronunciation was spreading as middle-aged, lower-middle-class women adopted it as a way of elevating their perceived social status. In the process, they displayed **hypercorrection**, and ended up using the form more than speakers in the social groups above them whom they were trying to imitate. The **Labovian paradigm** is the name given to Labov's framework and classification which identifies such concepts as linguistic and extralinguistic variables, co-variation, the observer's paradox (see Chapter 1) and language change in progress, and provides a methodology for sampling speech styles. For a useful introductory summary of Labov's work from the perspective of language change, see Aitchison (1991, chs. 3 and 4).

Situational variables are observable where the same person speaks differently in different environments. Studying language from this angle often means thinking about the role or function which language is playing in a situation. This in turn means that you can gauge the status and mutual familiarity of speakers, and their reasons for needing to communicate, from the style or **register** which they use. Consider, for example, how a politician might speak to his parliamentary colleagues and to prospective voters. The linguistic variation might be seen in the manner of address, including the use of colloquialisms, jargon and regionalisms, in the selection of topic and examples and in the level of detail. Some authors refer to the classification of language according to its use in social situations as **diatypic variation** (see, for example, Gregory and Carroll 1978).

Quantitative approaches

One of the key features of linguistic variables is that they can often be counted or **quantified**. For example, a group of speakers' pronunciations of /t/ in words like *better* and *bottle* can be scored according to whether or not they use the RP [t], the non-standard glottal stop [?] or something in between. Scores for different sexes, social backgrounds or age groups can then be compared to see whether there are consistent patterns of usage by different groups. Features in the speech of the same person in different situations can also be counted and compared. Labov devised a means of eliciting five different **speech styles** in interview situations. He elicited a careful or formal style by asking subjects to read 'minimal pairs' (pairs of words which differ by just one key sound – see Chapter 17), and gained increasingly less formal styles from, respectively, read lists of words, read passages, careful and casual conversation.

The Labovian paradigm (see above) is heavily associated with the quantitative study of accent features, and much of it, devised largely in the 1960s, was developed as part of Labov's dialectological work in the United States, especially in Martha's Vineyard and New York City (Labov 1972). Trudgill's (1972, 1974) work on Norwich speech, built on the same paradigm, was also quantitative in nature. Trudgill gathered subjects' responses to recordings of particular words, pronounced with accents ranging from RP to broad local ones, and compared these to the tally of features in their own spontaneous language. He was able to demonstrate that women often 'over-reported', claiming that they used pronunciations that were nearer to RP more frequently than they actually did, whereas men often 'under-reported'. Trudgill concluded that the men and women had different notions of 'prestige language'.

PROJECTS

137. Study one or two features of the pronunciation or grammar of a chosen variety, to find out who uses them and when. Whether or not the variety is one that you know well, check in the published literature for information on the most characteristic features of that accent or dialect. For example, Trudgill (1974) looked at *-ing* in Norwich speech (see above) and Cheshire (1978) looked at forms of *do* (amongst other things) used by Reading teenagers. A good source for pronunciation features in various accents of British English is Hughes and Trudgill (1996), and for non-British English, Trudgill and Hannah (1985). Audio tapes of the data are available for both books. Vowel pronunciations (**continuous** variables) are more 'fluid' and can therefore be very difficult to distinguish and score for. Consonants, especially where you are simply listening for their presence or absence (as in /h/ dropping on words likes *hammer*), are often easier to handle and score, e.g. the presence of /h/ can score 1 each time it occurs in a subject's speech, while its absence scores 0. Reduce extralinguistic variation by using subjects who are as similar as possible in all respects except for the one you are interested in.

138. Undertake a study of the pronunciation and/or dialect features of a group of speakers, eliciting samples of language from them using methodology similar to that of the Labovian paradigm (see above). This should yield information on how the speakers actually use language. Then, by replicating an aspect of Trudgill's work (see above), investigate their attitudes to the accent, to ascertain whether these are in any way linked to current changes in the local accent or dialect.

139. Compare two varieties of international English, taking account of the social and historical forces which have brought about the differences. To what extent has the 'new' variety of English taken on systematic new forms which are causing it to diverge from British English? Are these divergences more marked in younger or older speakers? Are they more marked in men or women? For information on features of international English, see Trudgill and Hannah (1985).

Social networks

One of the criticisms of Labov's work was that he concentrated too heavily on collecting data from rather superficially defined 'social class' groupings. The concepts of 'social groups', 'speech communities' and, moreover, of 'social networks', were borrowed from the social sciences by sociolinguists such as Gumperz (e.g. 1982). His aim was to find ways of showing how membership and allegiance to certain clearly defined social *groups* (such as adolescent peer groups, unusually tight-knit communities, and so on), rather than 'classes', was linked to language use. Speakers often consciously or unconsciously use language to convey their social identity, so members of a group may sound alike in their speech. Sounding alike also helps groups to seem distinctive when compared with others. The concept of social networks is explained very simply in Coates (1993, ch. 5). More detail is given in Wardhaugh (1992, ch. 5), Downes (1984: 93 ff.) and especially Milroy (1987b), whose study of Belfast pronunciation was based on the social network framework.

While large-scale studies, such as Labov's New York City work, lose the profiles of individuals in the group scores, this approach allows a much closer examination of the individual, and is far more ethnographic in nature.

PROJECTS

140. After reading about the work of Labov (1972, also summarized in Hudson 1996, sections 5.4.2 to 5.4.3), Cheshire (1978, 1982) or Milroy and Milroy (1978), Milroy (1987b) to see how language can be used, even at a sub-conscious level, as a 'badge' of belonging to particular groups, look for comparable groups in your own life or in that of someone close to you. Using a mixture of observation and interview, collect data which could enable you to judge whether commitment to the group affects individual members' language. You may be able to judge how central a member someone is by the strength or frequency with which they use the group's speech forms (such as catch phrases, special vocabulary or grammatical structures). Many types of groups may be appropriate for this kind of study, including sports or drama clubs, students' union committees, or a group of friends that meets regularly together. However, groups that share an ideology, or who have a strong motivation for seeming 'different', should be particularly fruitful: examples would be church groups, environmental action groups and political parties.

141. Make a study of a family that is well known to you. Examine specific language features used by different members of the family and compare them. To what extent can differences be attributed to different group membership? Are there any *similarities* that might relate to the family being a group in its own right?

Qualitative approaches

These, by definition, involve description and analysis rather than, for example, the counting of features. They often have much in common with linguistic work on discourse, conversation and/or pragmatics (see Chapters 4 and 9). The emphasis is on exploring the types of strategy – the **qualities** – in the data and ascertaining why particular speakers used them in specific contexts with particular people. For example, how does a hospital consultant or GP (a 'high-status participant'), inform a patient that he or she must take more exercise and stop smoking? Is it achieved by negotiation (e.g. *How about losing some weight? Could you try to take some exercise?*) or with a bald imperative (e.g. *Stop smoking and lose weight now*)?

This kind of research often involves longer-term observation, very detailed and close perusal of the data and relatively small numbers of subjects. Findings can therefore only be said to hold true for that particular group until comparative work can be undertaken with other groups. Some researchers feel that purely qualitative approaches lack the rigour of research which can be supported by figures to show how commonly or frequently certain patterns crop up. They feel that, without such figures, no generalizations about trends in language usage can be made. Others hotly contest the validity of quantitative approaches, however. They feel that to elicit data which is suitable for counting and comparisons, it is necessary to use techniques which prevent truly 'natural' and spontaneous language from being produced (the 'observer's paradox' – see Chapter 1).

It is possible to combine elements of all the approaches. Qualitative work might document a pattern, and a quantitative approach establish how frequently the features occur. Cheshire managed to do this in some of her social network research with teenagers in Reading. In other words, Cheshire not only examined the frequency of certain types of language structure (such as *you was* as opposed to *you were*), but also explored how these forms were used by individuals on particular occasions, for example, one speaker's use of non-standard *what* in *Are you the little bastards what hit my son over the head?* (Coates 1993: 94). Cheshire was able to show a connection between this speaker's use of vernacular forms and his central position in one of the teenage gangs.

PROJECTS

142. Document the key daily routines in the lives of recent immigrants to your country or region. What part does language (in general, or one language in particular) play in these routines? Are special registers (or styles) of language used for particular activities (such as religious worship, speaking to elders)?

143. Focusing on **diglossia** (the use by a whole community of different languages or distinct language varieties in different situations), make a study as described in project 142, but looking at the way in which your subjects switch between languages during their day according to where they are and what they are doing.

144. Investigate the phenomena of **code-switching** (where bilingual speakers switch between their two languages on the basis of topic and/or addressee) and **code-mixing** (where they mix languages within a single conversation or even a single sentence). What appears to determine when they use each language? For further information, see Appel and Muysken (1987) or Romaine (1995).

145. Make a study of a language (such as Welsh or Irish) or a language variety which is under threat from a dominant surrounding language or variety. For example, if you know Welsh, use data from Welsh TV and radio programmes to examine borrowing from English. What kinds of words are borrowed from the dominant language and why do you think this happens? Your study could incorporate both quantitative and qualitative techniques.

OTHER PROJECT IDEAS

146. Focusing your project on language change, collect samples of written and/or spoken English, and look for aspects of usage about which people seem unsure (what might be termed 'inconsistent usage'). Obvious examples are constructions such as *would of, could of* instead of the standard *would have, could have,* and the linking of words in writing, as in the case of *aswell, alot* (see also project 202 in Chapter 9). How frequently do the constructions appear in your sample? Who uses them? Are they more common in written as opposed to spoken language? Why might they be occurring, and is there any reason to believe that they indicate language change? Your study could incorporate both quantitative and qualitative techniques. For more ideas and examples, see Aitchison (1991, ch. 3).

147. Follow the last suggestion, but place the emphasis on *attitudes* to language change. Rather than collecting a sizeable corpus of data, examine people's responses to inconsistent usage (all the better if this could involve some of the people who generated your examples in the first place). Embed some examples in sentences or, even better, in paragraphs. Then present the texts to a range of 'judges' selected carefully with respect to such characteristics as age, gender, background or regional origins. Ask if the language samples are acceptable to them and, if not, where the problems are and how they would resolve them. Have your judges identified the 'inconsistent' constructions as problematic? Decide in advance whether you want your data to be quantitative, qualitative or both, and use the appropriate techniques (see Chapters 14 to 16). For examples of similar types of study, see Freeborn *et al.* (1993, ch. 1).

148. Examine the emerging English of a recent (non-English-speaking) immigrant to an English-speaking area. If possible, observe his or her progress over a period of several months. To what extent does the emerging language resemble a pidgin in terms of structure and the situations where it is used? Does your subject cope with the distinction between colloquial and formal language? Does your study shed any light for you on how pidgins develop and change, or on how pidgins, and the social and linguistic forces associated with them, might contribute to the shaping of major languages over time? For introductory information about pidgins and creoles, see O'Donnell and Todd (1991, ch. 3).

149. Undertake a primarily qualitative study of the language used with elderly people. To what extent does it resemble the 'carer talk' used with children (see Chapter 3) or 'foreigner talk'? Does the selection of this 'register' seem necessary for successful communication in the situations where it is used? You might ascertain this by finding out whether *all* people speaking to an elderly person appear to see the need for features of this register to make themselves understood, and whether elderly people seem to understand less well when the features are not used. What does your study tell you about how elderly people are viewed by society? For fuller discussion of language and the elderly, see Coupland *et al.* (1991).

150. Make a study of language and power by observing the forms of address or politeness strategies used in one of the following situations: a university tutorial setting; transactions at a bar, shop or some other form of agency. What range of linguistic structures or strategies is used? Are there any patterns regarding which types of people are most polite? Determining factors might be: age, apparent social status or occupation, gender, and so on. If you have the means of recording and analysing them, extend your study to include intonational features or paralinguistic features such as gesture or facial expression. Your study could incorporate both quantitative and qualitative techniques. For further ideas see, for example, Brouwer *et al.* (1979).

151. Investigate the attitudes of some carefully selected subjects towards language varieties by surveying their reactions to particular accents. This could involve using the Matched Guise technique (see Chapter 14).

152. We know that many people have a 'telephone voice'. People often adapt their pronunciation to fit particular situations and/or to blend in with other speakers. The latter, in particular, is **convergence** – part of what linguists call **accommodation**. The opposite of this is called **divergence** – when someone changes their accent or dialect (or even their language choice) on a specific occasion in order to distance themselves from the people they are among. Collect samples of a subject's language from several situations in which contrasting varieties of English are used by the other speakers involved. Observe the extent to which your subject converges or diverges from the language of the others present. One way to do this would be to ask someone to tape their telephone conversations for a week, using their home answerphone. (Allow your subject to delete any conversations that they consider too personal or private in nature.) Avoid revealing the true focus of your interest in the data, as knowing what you are looking for may affect they way your subject speaks. Look for things like style-shifting between the subject's initial phone-answering style and his or her subsequent accent and dialect use, as he or she accommodates to the language variety used by the caller. For more information on accommodation, see Fasold (1984: 188–209). Mugglestone (1995) is useful for information on the social uses of accent.

8

Accents and dialects of English

Accents and dialects are a focus of interest for various groups of linguists. The main two are sociolinguists studying how people use their variety's pronunciation, vocabulary and grammar to express and retain social identity, and phoneticians and phonologists, who study the sound systems of accents. Although this chapter focuses on varieties of English, most of the methods would be the same if you were collecting information about another language.

The sorts of questions that you might ask in research into accents and dialects include:

- where are the geographical borders between different pronunciations of the same word?
- where are the geographical borders between different words or expressions for the same entity, action, and so on?
- are such borders consistent across a large set of words or expressions, or must they be differently drawn for each?
- how are past settlements of communities reflected in the pronunciation, vocabulary and grammar of a local variety?
- what differences are there between the pronunciation and vocabulary of men and women using the same regional variety?
- in what ways do TV and film actors exaggerate, under-represent or successfully reproduce a given regional accent?
- how do the grammatical forms of a given dialect differ from standard English, or from another variety, and why?
- how mutually comprehensible are dialects and accents from different places?
- to what extent is, and should, dialect be used in schools?
- what subtle differences in pronunciation and vocabulary mark out subgroups within a single local community?

Research on accent and dialect requires a baseline for comparison. You should expect to use your national 'standard', or else the variety used in the books you are referring to (such as, for accent, British Received Pronunciation). Work on pronunciation will require phonetic script. Phonemic transcription will probably not be sufficient to capture the detail you need, and in any case, it builds in assumptions about the phonological system that may not apply to the variety under investigation. See Chapter 17 for guidance on transcription.

If you are short of actual data to analyse, you could try the old BBC recordings of non-British English accents, *English with an Accent* (Polydor Mono Rec 166) and regional British English accents, the mis-named *English with a Dialect* (Polydor Mono Rec 173), though the accents are not always strong and the speech is often very unnatural-sounding. If you can get to a sound archive, such as the National Sound Archive in London, you can listen to endless good-quality material there. However, check first whether you will be able to make a copy to take away, as this isn't always permissible. Local radio programmes and national radio phone-ins are another good source of data. Television news bulletins where onlookers to an incident are interviewed can provide usable, though short, sound-bites.

Terminology

The terms **accent** and **dialect** are often used rather imprecisely, even interchangeably. Wakelin (1977: 1) provides the following definition of them: '*Dialect* refers to all the linguistic elements in one form of a language – phonological, grammatical and lexical – while *accent* refers only to pronunciations. Accent is thus the phonetic or phonological aspect of dialect.'

Linguists avoid the suggestion that some people have an accent and dialect while others do not: '*all* of us speak with an accent, and *all* of us speak a dialect' (Trudgill 1990: 2). For more information on the various ways in which the term 'dialect' is used, see Malmkjær (1991: 93ff.), where you can also find a very useful outline of the focus of research in dialectology since the nineteenth century.

Textbooks

Table 8.1 Useful texts for accents and dialects (see page xiv for key to levels)

Book	Level	Notes on Content/Style
Aitchison 1991	1–2	some coverage of accent & dialect variation
Brook 1978	3	old-fashioned approach, incl. traditional dialect studies, history of English dialects, representation of dialect in literature
Crystal 1995, chs. 20 and 21	1	brief, well-illustrated account of regional and social variation

Book	Level	Notes on Content/Style
Freeborn *et al.* 1993, chs. 1–4	1–2	attitudes to variation, modern English accents and dialects and their history
Hughes and Trudgill 1996	2	introduction (ch. 1) and accounts of accent and dialect variation with examples; valuable set of analyses of individual varieties; tape of data is available
Trudgill 1978	3	collection of papers on specific British varieties
Trudgill 1990	1–2	description of pronunciation and grammar of major British dialects, with maps; does not use phonetic transcription
Trudgill and Hannah 1985	2	non-British varieties (native and non-native); detailed; tape of data is available
Wakelin 1977	3–4	introduction in ch. 1, then technical accounts of dialect studies, with detailed discussion of individual varieties
Wells 1982	4	detailed study of accents of English, not for the faint-hearted

Other resources

Be aware of specialist publications for specialist jobs. These include dictionaries and books on place-names and surnames, dialect dictionaries, and dictionaries of slang, jargon and euphemism.

For examples of how data can be collected, look at the publications spawned by the major national surveys, including the *Survey of English Dialects* (Orton *et al.* 1962–1971), the *Linguistic Atlas of England* (Orton *et al.* 1978), the *Linguistic Atlas of Scotland* (Mather and Speitel 1975), *A Word Geography of the Eastern United States* (Kurath 1949) and *The Linguistic Atlas of the Gulf States [of the USA]* (Pederson *et al.* 1986). Samples of the data in these is given in Crystal (1995, ch. 20). For other languages, see the rather older surveys of German (Wrede and Mitzka 1926–1956; Mitzka and Schmidt 1953–1978) and French (Gilliéron and Edmont 1902–1910). These are briefly described in Malmkjaer (1991: 268–9). In such sources you can find lists of words and forms that you can use as stimuli; also, much of a practical nature can be gleaned from using Hughes and Trudgill's (1996) book in conjunction with their tape.

For information on particular varieties use local libraries and bookshops, which will often have books or pamphlets not easy to come by outside of that area (for example, the Yorkshire Dialect Society publications). Bear in mind, however, that not all of these will be taking a strictly 'linguistic' approach. There is a short list of publications focused on the varieties of particular places in Wakelin (1977: 174–5) – it would be well worth checking whether the place you are interested in is covered by one of these. Classic accounts of specific varieties include the work by Labov on New York and Martha's Vineyard (Labov 1972) and Black Vernacular English (Labov 1969), Trudgill (1972, 1974) on male–female differences in Norwich, Cheshire (1978, 1982) on Reading, and Milroy (1987b) on East and West Belfast. Much of this work is reviewed in Aitchison (1991, chs. 3 to 5) and in Chapter 7 in this book.

Major journals

Educational Review	*Journal of Phonetics*
English and Germanic Studies	*Journal of the Lakeland Dialect Society*
English Studies	*Journal of the Lancashire Dialect*
English World-Wide	*Society*
Folklore	*Language and Speech*
International Journal of the Sociology of	*Orbis*
Language	*Speech Monographs*
Journal of the International Phonetic	*Transactions of the Yorkshire Dialect*
Association	*Society*
Journal of Linguistics	*Word*

Fig 8.1 Major journals for research in accents and dialects

Which accent/dialect to choose

An important question to consider is whether you are going to study a variety that you use yourself. The advantage of studying your own variety is that you are yourself a source of data. This means that if a form or a pronunciation is missing, you know what it is and can confidently add it to the list. Working with a variety that is not your own can make it difficult to identify the pattern underlying a set of features, because it is hard to judge what another example would do. This problem can be eased by using published work on the same or a similar variety to get some ideas. Other advantages are that you can plan with more confidence how to elicit the forms you need, and that when interviewing informants you are not putting them off by using a different pronunciation or vocabulary.

However, there are some serious disadvantages too. You may not have an identical variety to that of your informant, and you may unwittingly remove some of the more subtle layers of data by influencing the informant into your way of speech. Studying a variety requires some perspective, and it is very hard to get this when it is very familiar to you. It may be difficult for you to tell which words are part of standard English (or a 'national slang') and which are only part of your own variety. We can tend to be quite blind to aspects of our own speech, so you may miss some detail. You can reduce the risk of this by getting a friend who does not use that variety to listen to your data and check your assumptions.

A variety you know very well, but which is not your only variety, may provide a compromise, offering the advantages of both scenarios above.

Broadly speaking, there are three types of accent/dialect. **Native regional** varieties are those of speakers whose first language is English but who do not speak the standard. In Britain, examples might be the English of Yorkshire, Cornwall or Glasgow. **Native national** varieties are found in speakers whose first language is English but who are not from the same country as you, such as Australia, America, Canada, Ireland or the UK. **Non-native** varieties are those of speakers whose first language is not English. We can identify three types of these. First, there are speakers from places where English is one of the official languages, so there is a recognized national variety taught by local teachers, as with India, parts of Africa and parts of Malaysia. Second, there are speakers from places where English is a foreign language, such as France, Spain and Poland. And third, there are speakers whose native language is not English but who live in an English-speaking environment, like Punjabis in Britain, Greeks in Canada, Hispanics in the US and so on. In this case you may get some interesting mixes of non-native and regional features, such as where an Italian informant has been brought up in Lancashire.

What to look for in an accent

If you are interested in pronunciation, structure your study by listening out for specific sounds and transcribing them in some detail. A list of English phonemes, based on British Received Pronunciation (RP), is provided in Chapter 17. Use this to write down your own examples phonetically next to the appropriate phoneme. Try to find several examples of each phoneme, in case it is pronounced in different ways in different environments in that variety. As your chosen variety may have a different set of phonemes to those of RP, do not be surprised if some categories collapse together and others divide: that is something that you can write about in your study. Kreidler's (1989) representation of English variety types, as determined by their phonemic inventories (pp. 49–56), may help you. Hughes and Trudgill (1996: p. iv, or p. 42 in the 1987 edition) also provide a wordlist suitable for eliciting all the phonemes of RP.

What to look for in a dialect

In order to analyse a dialect you need an understanding of basic grammatical categories, both so that you can accurately describe what you find and so that you know what sorts of phenomena to look for. You may find it helpful to write a 'translation' of your material in standard English alongside the original, so that the differences become clear. You must categorize your data according to word classes, and really get to grips with morphology (word forms and endings) and grammar as well as vocabulary. The relationship between grammar and vocabulary on the one hand, and pronunciation on the other, is not always clear-cut. Some words which seem to just be 'lazy' pronunciations of the standard form are actually very different, with a separate history. For example, 'em' in *sort 'em out* appears to be a shortened form of *them*, but it is not (Brook 1978: 105). If you have enough data you should be able to construct tables of pronoun and verb forms. Use the lists of standard forms below to help draw up a corresponding set of dialect forms.

Pronouns and possessives

Subject:	*I, you, he, she, it, we, they, who, which*
Object:	*me, you, him, her, it, us, them, who(m), which*
Possessive:	*my, your, his, her, its, our, their, whose*
	mine, yours, his, hers, its, ours, theirs, whose

Some languages, and indeed some varieties of English, may have additional forms which you need to check for, including: a difference between singular and plural *you* forms, a difference in politeness and/or intimacy in *you* forms, a difference between plural forms referring to two and to more than two, a difference between *we* forms which include and exclude the addressee, and separate *they* forms for male and female.

For further details on pronouns, see Trudgill (1990: 81–94). Remember to note carefully the pronunciation of all pronoun forms, along with the context in which they have occurred.

Verbs

Besides variations in the meaning or inventory of verbs from place to place (such as *starving with cold* in the north of England or *abba* in South African English, meaning to carry a child on one's back), the key things to look for are the different tense forms (present, past, past participle), especially those of the common irregular verbs such as *to be* and *to go*. If you find an unusual form of a verb, check the rest of its forms. Dialect forms are likely to differ from the standard by having a different strong past tense form, or else a weak (*-ed*) form instead of a strong one, or vice versa. Different varieties can also sometimes use the verb tenses differently. For example, a British southerner would say: *The burglar broke into the house and he ransacked the place*, while some northerners might say: *The burglar* *has broken into the house and he's ransacked the place*, using the perfect rather than the simple past. There may also be contrasts in the use of conditionals and subjunctives: where a British English speaker says *If I had seen him I would have chased him*, an American might say *If I would have seen him I would have chased him*. If you do not use the variety yourself you may need to go back to your informant with specific questions, or look up descriptions of that variety in published sources.

Nouns

You should find the richest pickings of regional vocabulary here, particularly, of course, where a word is needed locally for something that does not exist elsewhere. (For illustrations of regional variation in nouns, see Crystal 1995, ch. 20.) Some terms require local or topical knowledge to explain: according to the *Dictionary of South African English* (1996), Township vernacular contains the words *Mary Dekker* (a fast police vehicle) and *Zola Budd* (a slow one), named after an American and a South African who were rival athletes in the 1980s. In addition, look out for non-standard plural forms of familiar words.

Negative forms

Languages have many ways of forming negatives, but even within English grammar there is regional variation. Some people say *don't you?* and others say *Do you not?* Some varieties use the **double negatives**, e.g. *I ain't seen nothing*. Trudgill (1990) is a very useful source of insight into this.

Tags

Tag questions are a hallmark of English. Compare: *It's raining, is it?, It's raining, isn't it?* and *It's not raining, is it?* Different varieties use tags in different ways. In South Wales you might hear: *So you've moved into your flat, is it?* Other varieties replace the standard tag forms with a general *yes (yeah)* and *no*: *So it's raining, yeah?*

Adverbs

Differences between varieties in their use of adverbs can be quite striking when heard for the first time. The following example illustrates how an analysis might progress. In Yorkshire it is common to hear *He was well happy* and *They were well tired* for *He was very happy* and *They were very tired*. What is the underlying pattern? One might hypothesize that Yorkshire English simply uses *well* wherever Standard English would use *very*, but this is refuted by the fact that Yorkshire English does not say *You're the well person I was looking for*. To understand how Yorkshire English works, it is necessary to examine the way that Standard English itself distributes *very* and *well* (e.g. *She had been well taught;* **She had been very taught; The tyres were well worn; The tyres were very worn*) (the asterisk indicates that the sentence is ungrammatical). If it is the case that *very* is used with adjectives and *well* with verb-forms, then where does *He was well pleased* fit in? It turns out that there is a subtle relationship between adjectives and past participle forms in Standard English and, returning to the Yorkshire variety, this leads to the following question: does the difference between the two varieties lie in the meanings of *very* and *well* themselves, or in the underlying categories of the words they are modifying?

Possible angles and project ideas

You can, of course, just focus your work directly on the variety. However, it is often useful to get an 'angle'. This gives you something to aim at and provides a motivation for exploring some aspects more than others. Most importantly, it can help you avoid simply ending up with a list of forms you have found, without anything very much to say about them.

Comparing the speech of three generations

This is a study of how a variety is changing at the moment. Providing you can get access to compatible recordings of three related individuals a generation apart, you can potentially uncover interesting differences that may characterize change within their variety across time. However, remember that other variables may explain the differences which you are attributing to age. For example, it has been suggested that males tend to display more pronounced regional characteristics than females (see Trudgill 1972 and the discussion in Aitchison 1991: 65–7). Avoid this variable by studying only one gender. Alternatively, perhaps the informants have had different amounts and types of contact with outsiders (such as travel, war experiences or employment). Perhaps they watch different quantities of TV or different programmes, and/or are differently influenced by them. Remember here that it is clearly not reasonable to say that the youth are exposed to youth culture through TV and yet to deny that older generations are also exposed to external cultures. You need to take a sensible sociolinguistic approach to the whole question of identity (see Chapter 7).

PROJECTS

153. If you have family members who have lived for several generations in the same area, compare the language of a grandparent, parent and sibling or cousin. Bear in mind the following advantages and disadvantages to this sort of a study. There is a good chance of getting good quality data without very much effort, and the research is fairly well controlled, provided the only major difference between the informants is age (not place of birth or residence, social class, extent of travel, gender, level of education and so on). However, while you bring an insight and intuition to a description of your own family's variety, it can also be quite difficult to detach yourself from it and see it for what it is (see above). Furthermore, the chances are there that there is little, if any, published material about the variety used in your town or village. This is not disastrous, but it can leave you out on a limb, particularly with those observations that you find hard to interpret. For guidance on sociolinguistic factors that may be relevant to this, see project 141 in Chapter 7.

154. Rather than studying your own or a friend's family, find recordings of the royal family and compare their accents.

155. Or, using videos of classic films and TV programmes, study the accents of members from three generations of one of the great acting families such as the Redgraves.

Explaining why a variety has come about

This is a study of the accent or dialect of a place, incorporating its history. Clearly, you are going to have to rely on reading for a considerable chunk of your work. This is fine, providing that the language of the place you choose has been fairly extensively studied before. Do check first that that is so. Unless you're looking at a variety with a high profile like Geordie (Newcastle) or Scouse (Liverpool) you may have considerable difficulty in finding more than the odd page in a few books about the history of the place, let alone its language. Writing about the history of settlement in a place is not the same as writing a linguistic history, and if you are not careful you will end up with a political or social history of the area that you cannot easily relate to the modern variety of English except to say that the dialect 'probably reflects the history of settlement in the area'. Unless you know a bit about Norse, Anglo-Saxon and/or Celtic languages, any 'analysis' is likely to be far too superficial to say anything much.

PROJECTS

156. Focus a study on one of the historical centres of immigration, such as inner London or Liverpool, on one of the industrial cities that drew rural

populations to them in the nineteenth century, or one of the new towns
created in the twentieth century. The later the settlement, the better documented it is likely to be. There may be useful local records about the
origins of settlers in the US, Canada and Australia, if your study is
focused there. To identify linguistic signs of the settlement in an urban
accent, compare it with the less-influenced surrounding variety. Can you
spot specific features that relate to the variety (or foreign language) spoken by the immigrant population?

157. Find a locality that has a specific story of recent unusual settlement. For
     example, Corby in Northamptonshire (in the southern Midlands of
     England) received a sizeable settlement of Scots workers when a steel
     plant was relocated there. Collect data from the original settlers (if any
     survive), their descendants, and individuals (or their descendants) who
     were part of the receiving community. Compare the varieties used for
     signs of a retained social identity and/or linguistic integration.

The political dimension of a variety

This approach takes a sociolinguistic or historical perspective, focusing on
the status of a variety within a community. Read Chapter 7 in this book for
background on the social aspects of accent and dialect use. For ideas on the
specific social impact of certain dialects, look at Burke and Porter (1991),
where the papers include a study of the significance of dialect at the beginnings of the trade union movement, Quaker language, an account of the
research done by a seventeenth-century dialectologist and how language is
affected by political conquest.

PROJECTS

158. Gather data on attitudes to non-standard English in the education sys-
     tem. This is a large and lively issue, so use newspaper archives to
     assemble recent views and reactions to official Reports like the Bullock
     Report (DES 1975) and *English in the National Curriculum* (DFE 1995).
     You could make recordings in a school in an area where the variety is
     particularly strong, to see how 'standard' the English is in different con-
     texts, such as assembly, formal teaching, discussion and group work,
     sports or gym, recreational time, staff meetings and in the staff room at
     breaks. Malmkjaer (1991: 254–5) provides some further information on
     the political issues.

159. Write a carefully considered account of the differences there might be in
     the accents and dialects of a country if some political event or policy or
     the status quo had been different: for example, if York had been the capi-
     tal of England in the Middle Ages, if Edinburgh, rather than London, had
     developed as the centre of British culture or if Australia had been settled
     largely by Scots rather than English emigrants. In every case you will

need to assess the long-term effects of the political domination of a variety. Some study of the way that standard English came about will help to give you insight (for general references, see Chapter 10).

Accent and dialect in literature

This is a study of an accent or dialect as depicted by a certain author, and it offers an interesting slant on accent and dialect work because authors are not dialectologists, and their purpose is not linguistic. When examining accents in literature, take a linguist's eye to what is, in effect, a literary device. You may well find that the author permits him/herself certain liberties in 'spelling' words 'phonetically' (for example, keeping silent letters in a word to help indicate the meaning, as in *y knaa* for 'you know', where the 'k' is actually silent). Use phonemic script to clarify your understanding of what is depicted in 'spelled' forms.

PROJECTS

160. Do an analysis of, say, the London accent of one or more of Dickens's characters, the West Country accent or dialect in Hardy's novels, or the speech of the yokels in Shakespeare. Evaluate its accuracy against published descriptions. Assess the extent to which the differences are simply a function of the time-lapse between the literary description and the more recent linguistic account. Alternatively, draw on a linguistic description that is contemporaneous with the work of literature, to remove this variable.

161. Compare an author's depiction of an accent or dialect (as above) with your own data from the same area.

162. Compare an actor's rendering of a local accent with the real thing (try to use an actor who is not from that area). A notorious example is Dick van Dyke's attempt at a Cockney accent in the film *Mary Poppins*. At the other extreme, Meryl Streep is one actor who has tackled many accents with success. What tends to make an actor's rendition more or less convincing? Does a bad attempt tend to exaggerate, under-represent, misplace or incorrectly define features?

Update study

This is a comparison of a published description of a variety with data of your own, and it has the makings of an excellent study. Instead of simply making observations which, while valid in their own right, may not fit easily into a wider pre-established context, you can anchor everything that *you* find into something that has been found, or not found, before. It is best if you can replicate as many aspects of the original work as possible – ask the same questions in a similar way, use a similar questionnaire, record in a similar environment with people of the same age, sex and background as the original, etc. Beware of becoming too simplistic and narrow when you have a good single source for comparing your data. Read other descriptions of the variety and see in what ways your chosen study differs from others of the time: if there wasn't full agreement at the time about what this variety was like in its finest detail, it will not be surprising if your findings are different too!

PROJECTS

163. Find a study from, say, 40 years ago. The Survey of English Dialects, carried out between 1948 and 1961 is one place to look; use Crystal (1995: 318 ff.) to get general information about this and to orientate yourself. Replicate the procedures of the original study as closely as you can. Concentrate your discussion on whether any differences in your findings are a function of the 40-year gap or not. You should, in this case, consider some of the other factors that might make a difference, such as the procedures used, how comparable the informants were, the precise geographical area they came from, and how the population of an area may have altered in nature.

164. Using the maps in the *Linguistic Atlas of England* (Orton *et al.* 1978) or a similar publication (see earlier in this chapter), identify, for your geographical area of interest, a boundary between two pronunciations, dialect words, morphological forms or structures. For example, the *Linguistic Atlas* map for the words for a headache indicates two areas in East Anglia in which the term *skullache* is used, while *headache* is used in the areas surrounding and between them (Crystal 1995: 321). Conduct your own survey to see whether the boundaries are still in the same place as they were when the Survey of English Dialects was carried out.

Comparison of two varieties

In one sense any study of a single variety entails this anyway, because there will be implicit or explicit comparisons with standard English. However, there is no intrinsic reason why standard English (British or otherwise) should represent the point of comparison. If you choose to compare two non-standard varieties, the rationale for your choice should be made obvious: a historical or geographical link, or else one relating to cultural or educational influence.

PROJECTS

165. Compare a Scots variety with Geordie, or with Northern Irish (in both cases there are historical links that make them sensible to compare).

166. Find out the national and regional origins of settlers in a particular area of a former colony of Britain (for example, Canada, Australia, New Zealand or the

USA) and compare the varieties used today in the two places. For example, are there similarities between London Cockney and the variety used in an Australian settlement originally founded for or by London (ex)convicts?

167. Compare the varieties used in two adjacent towns or villages.

168. Compare the English of, say, two French informants, one of whom loves British culture and one of whom identifies with American culture.

Things to think about

- To explain why a variety is as it is, and put it into context, read up on the history of English. Features of regional varieties often shed light on the historical development of the standard language and/or retain features that used to exist in standard English. In their turn, historical developments can often help explain regional differences.

- On the whole, you will get stronger accent and dialect features if: (a) you can understand your informants when they use their variety – if you have to keep asking them what they meant, then they are likely to modify towards the standard to accommodate you; (b) the informant speaks about particular subjects such as family or home life. Children talking about such things as playground games, and elderly people talking about their childhood are also fruitful subjects.

- Beware of a tendency for informants to make value-judgements about the language variety that they speak, and perhaps to understate what they know and/or use.

- Be aware that an informant may tell you that they use a form which they don't actually use but think they ought to: it may be the one their grandparents used, and they may genuinely think they do use it, even though they don't. This is clearly problematic if you are trying to get an accurate picture of the variety as it is today, especially if you are comparing different ages of speaker. But it can be turned to your advantage in a couple of ways. If you focus on identifying the features of the variety *in general*, it may not matter that your informant's perception of it is rather old-fashioned. Simply mention this somewhere in your study, as a feature of the way people can sometimes identify with defunct forms. Alternatively, if you have enough data, you could compare *what* your informants say with *how* they say it, looking for examples in their speech of the things they have described. Thus you can take the interesting angle, for all or part of your study, of how speakers may have limited ability to recognize the form of their own language.

|9|

Structure and meaning

In this chapter we look at some of the research that might fall under the headings of **grammar, syntax, morphology, semantics** and **pragmatics**. Each of these areas extends considerably beyond what we cover here, however, and if you want information about the full range of topics covered in any of these, you should go to a specialist textbook on the subject. The sorts of questions that you might want to ask in a project on structure and meaning include:

- how does a speaker convey messages indirectly, i.e. ones that are not explicitly carried in the words themselves?
- how does a speaker express subtle differences in meaning by shifting elements of the sentence around, or by choosing one word rather than another?
- how do we express politeness through structure?
- what makes jokes funny?
- why are some sentences ambiguous?
- what restrictions are there regarding which words can go with which others?
- what does a word mean, and who decides?
- how do intonation and punctuation contribute to meaning?
- what is 'correct' grammar?
- how are words constructed?
- what role does the hearer play in making sure the speaker's utterance is correctly understood?
- how do languages vary in the way they express meaning through words and through strings of words?

Textbooks and major journals

Table 9.1 Useful texts for structure and meaning (see page xiv for key to levels)

Book	Level	Notes on Content/Style
Aitchison 1992, chs. 6, 8, 9, 14–16	1–2	ch. 6: introduction to morphology; ch. 8: brief account of semantics; ch. 9: pragmatics; ch. 14–16: clear, simple explanation of syntactic theory, incl. the principles of Government and Binding; invaluable for orientation
Baker 1995	3	general but detailed account of how syntax works; examples; useful appendix of the tree diagrams for basic English structures
Bloor and Bloor 1995	2–3	introduction to Systemic Functional Grammar; easier than Halliday 1985
Bornstein 1976	3–4	valuable collection of early key papers in syntax
Borsley 1991	3	coursebook for syntax; needs methodical study
Burton-Roberts 1986	2–3	introduction to syntax, covering tree diagrams and constituent structure; more detailed than Thomas 1993 or Kuiper and Allan 1996 and takes more concentration
Carter 1987	2–3	morphology and lexical semantics; theory is applied to stylistic analysis, lexicography and vocabulary learning/teaching
Chierchia and McConnell-Ginet 1990	4	formal semantic theory; technical, not recommended without lecture backup or a friendly tutor
Cook and Newson 1996	3	clear overview of Chomsky's Universal Grammar
Crystal 1988b	1	introduction to what grammar is and why it's worth studying; basic sentence analysis
Crystal 1995, chs. 13–16	1	comprehensive introduction to the grammatical structure of English
Crystal 1997a, ch. 16	1	brief account of how levels of language combine to express meaning; useful table of grammatical categories (p. 93)
Eggins 1994	2–3	introduction to Systemic Functional Grammar; useful overview in ch. 1
Fromkin and Rodman 1993, chs. 2, 4	1–2	ch. 2: introduction to morphology; ch. 4: brief outline of semantic theory including pragmatics

Table 9.1 (*continued*)

Book	Level	Notes on Content/Style
Green and Morgan 1996	2–3	trouble-shooting book for those already conversant with syntactic concepts; clarifies terminology, demonstrates how to present an analysis, ideas for projects
Greenbaum 1991	2	basic grammatical concepts; glossary of terms; how grammar is manipulated in literature; appendix on English spelling
Halliday 1985	3–4	key text for Systemic Functional Grammar
Hurford 1994	2	alphabetical guide to concepts with examples
Hurford and Heasley 1983	2–3	introduction to semantics
Jackson 1988	2	focus on words and how they convey meaning; includes a study of dictionaries
Jackson 1990	2	starts from meaning and shows how grammar encodes it; not compatible with standard syntactic approaches but offers insights they cannot
Kess 1992, ch. 5	2–3	drawing on psycholinguistics, puts syntactic theory in a wider context, so it's easier to see why it's worth studying
Kuiper and Allan 1996, chs. 5–8	1–2	chs. 5–6: form and function of words; glossary of terms; chs. 7–8: introduction to syntax, covering tree diagrams and constituent structure; user-friendly
Leech 1992	1–2	alphabetical guide to concepts with examples
Leech *et al.* 1982	2	principles of grammatical analysis and how they apply to sample texts
Levinson 1983	3	pragmatic theory in some depth
Malmkjaer 1991, pp. 314–24, 354–8, 389–98	3	brief overview of background and scope of morphological study (314–24), pragmatics (354–8) and semantic theory (389–98)
McCloskey 1988	3	step by step guide to syntactic analysis; needs a methodical approach
Oxford Guide to the English Language 1984	1–2	general reference book including information on 'correct' forms
Palmer 1981	2–3	introduction to semantics
Pinker 1994, pp. 106–12	2	basic description of recent syntactic theory including X-bar and principles and parameters; useful for orientation

Book	Level	Notes on Content/Style
Quirk and Greenbaum 1973, Quirk *et al.* 1972, 1985	2	comprehensive guides (Quirk *et al.* 1985 has 1779 pages) to English grammar including the relationship between form and meaning
Thomas 1993	1	introduction to syntax, covering tree diagrams and constituent structure; recommended for the terrified
Webelhuth 1995	4	dedicated chapters on specific syntactic theories and approaches
Young 1984	1	practical workbook with exercises

Analysis	*Linguistic Inquiry*
Journal of Applied Linguistics	*Linguistics and Philosophy*
Journal of Linguistic Research	*Philosophica*
Journal of Linguistics	*Philosophical Review*
Language	*The Linguistic Review*
Language Research	

Fig 9.1 Major journals for research in structure and meaning

Central themes and project ideas

Pragmatics

Much of our verbal communication is expressed in rather indirect ways, creating a potential obstacle course for the hearer. For example, arriving at someone's house on a muddy day, we might be expected to interpret *I'll see if I can find my spare slippers* as an invitation to take our shoes off at the door. However, such indirect communication is risky for the speaker: we might genuinely not pick up the hidden message, or we might wilfully ignore it. In our day-to-day interaction, there is more than an exchange of words: there is a social dance, and we, as the listener, may choose to keep in step or to clumsily upset the rhythm of the communication by not listening to the music. Pragmatics deals with the hidden messages.

In **Speech Act Theory** (Austin 1961, 1962; Searle 1965, 1975, 1979) the way in which apparently straightforward utterances perform complex interactional tasks is revealed. For example, **performatives,** easily identified by the possibility of inserting the word *hereby*, have a permanent effect upon the state of the world (e.g. *I name this ship HMS Endurance; I bet you £5 he loses the match; I promise to return the book*). A clear description of the theory is given in Malmkjaer (1991: 416–24), and an overview, including a review of its critics' objections, can be found in Sadock (1988).

For one important application of Speech Act Theory see Shuy (1993), who explores the forensic role of the linguist in ascertaining whether or not an individual has committed a crime that hinges on a performative speech act. The subtlety of such research lies in the fact that it is rare for an illegal offer such as a bribe to be made explicitly, and in the absence of a recording that contains the words 'I'm offering you a bribe', it is obviously difficult to be sure that the speech act (verbal agreement) was actually carried out.

Grice's (1975) theory of **Conversational Implicature** takes account of the need for the speaker and hearer to enter into a pact regarding how things will be said and interpreted if communication is to be successful and efficient. Grice's four classes of **maxims** characterize this co-operation: the hearer will assume that the speaker is only saying things that are relevant to the current state of the conversation, giving neither too little nor too much information, speaking truthfully and avoiding ambiguity and obscurity. The speaker may deliberately flout a maxim in order to deceive the hearer (for example, by telling a lie), something that is made easier by the hearer's expectation of co-operation (i.e. assuming the truth will be told). Hearers or readers will work very hard to find relevance in an utterance, as can be seen from our ability to interpret an exchange such as: *A: Is there any more butter? B: I didn't leave work till seven.* Besides Grice's own (1975) paper, you can read about conversational implicature in Malmkjaer (1991: 355 ff.), Horn (1988: 117–33) and Levinson (1983: 97–166).

In 1986 Sperber and Wilson first published their influential book on **Relevance Theory** (Sperber and Wilson 1995). It is based on the belief that 'human attention and thought . . . automatically turn toward information which seems relevant' (Sperber and Wilson 1987: 697/460). Their account solves the problem inherent in assuming that communication is only successful if the speaker and hearer are each aware of how much information about the situation the other has (**mutual knowledge**). Rather, they invoke the notion of **mutual manifestness**, whereby certain assumptions about the situation are *available* to you (you could work them out, or even simply perceive them, if you paid attention to them), even though you are not necessarily taking them into account. As a speaker, you can make guesses about what is manifest to your hearer: that is, what the hearer may not know but will be able to work out once you draw attention to it either directly or indirectly. Relevance Theory is not easy to get to grips with. Rather than reading the whole book, try Sperber and Wilson's (1987) précis of it, or Blakemore (1992, ch. 2).

PROJECTS

169. Examine the text of a play for evidence of implicit messages, and consider what the playwright is deliberately conveying about the attitudes and personality of the characters.

170. Write two scripts for the same sequence of events, one that is totally explicit, and one that expresses the same information by implication, shared assumptions and so on. Get three people to judge each one for naturalness or plausibility, and to describe their reaction to the characters.

171. Examine one or more comedy TV sketches that rely on pragmatic manipulation for their humour (*The Two Ronnies* are particularly good for this).

172. What we say when we want to get something done provides interesting paradigms, in which a decreasing scale of directness may reflect increasing levels of politeness. For example, all of the following could be used as a request for a book: *Give me that; Could I have that please? Would you mind passing me that book? I haven't seen that book; That book looks interesting.*

    Examine data from, say, episodes of a soap opera, to evaluate how the level of directness reflects the relationships between the characters, as independently demonstrated by their behaviour and the content of their utterances (for example, Do two people who dislike each other use more direct framings? Do two people of unequal status contrast in their politeness markers when talking to each other?).

173. Analyse different types of joke (puns, shaggy dog stories and so forth) for ways in which they flout Grice's maxims (for example, consider what the person hearing a joke is expecting).

Metaphor

Whilst we are accustomed to seeing metaphor as a feature of literary language, it is clear that we also use it in everyday life. We talk about the *journey through life*, about *battling something out* and about *sailing serenely through an exam*. Research on metaphor obviously needs to do more than just list examples, so you need to find out about the major theoretical approaches to understanding it. Amongst these is the **constructivist** approach, which you can read about first hand in Lakoff and Johnson (1980). They propose that, rather than being an abstraction away from a more fundamental, literal way of seeing things, metaphor is the very basis of the way in which we make sense of the world, and, in effect, is what our 'reality' is based upon. A useful overview of this and other theories can be found in Malmkjaer (1991: 308–12). For concise definitions of **metaphor** and other devices, see Crystal (1995: 421; 1997a: 70).

PROJECTS

174. Identify the metaphors in a passage from a novel, and systematically replace them with a more literal expression. Show the new passage to informants and ask them to rate it for readability, interest and style. Then show them the original and ask them to rate that. Is it possible to say that the use of metaphor always produces better prose?

175. If you are familiar with Old or Middle English, compare the metaphors used then with ones used in a similar (that is, literary) context today. Crystal (1995: 23) gives some examples of metaphors in Old English, including *hronrād* (*whale-road*) for *sea*, and *bānhūs* (*bone-house*) for *human body*. One way to test how similar our 'feel' for metaphors is to that of years ago is to see whether modern informants can make sense of a modernized version of the old ones. If the choice of metaphors then and now is essentially similar, what does that tell us? If old and modern metaphors seem quite different in kind, why might that be?

176. Consider the claim that 'most lexical items [are] dead metaphors' (Sadock 1979: 48), by conducting an etymological study of English vocabulary. For example, Partridge (1966) gives the origin of *lord* as Old English *hlāfweard* (*loaf-guardian*) and that of *lady* as *hlāfdīge* (*loaf-kneader*). To keep a focus, pick one sub-area of vocabulary for the study, such as words for people, tools and so forth. Remember to link your findings back into a theoretical discussion of the nature and function of metaphor.

Sentence structure

The precise way in which words are strung together can subtly affect the meaning. For example, at surface level, word order can change the topic (focus). Compare: *There's a tiger on the church roof; It's a tiger that's on the church roof* and *It's the church roof that a tiger's on*. Omitting information can also have a marked effect on the slant of the message. Compare: *The soldier fired his gun at the protester at point blank range; The gun was fired at the protester at point blank range; The gun fired at the protester at point blank range* and *The protester was shot at point blank range*. To understand this kind of variation it helps to identify the **roles** of the different participants in the events. Here, the soldier is always the person firing the gun (**actor**), even when he is not mentioned and some other noun phrase is the subject of the sentence. The gun is always the **instrument**, irrespective of whether the phrase *the gun* is subject, object, object of a preposition, or not mentioned at all. The protester is always the **patient**, i.e. the one who is shot. A useful introduction to semantic roles is Jackson (1990). There are also some examples, with discussion, in Pinker (1994: 114). For some insight into the subtleties of our linguistic understanding compared to that of a logical machine, see Pinker (1994: 78–81).

Not all differences in meaning are explicit on the surface, however. Syntactic theory examines the structures that underpin sentences and attempts to account for a range of phenomena, such as unexpectedly ungrammatical sequences and ones that are apparently similar but where structural differences exist, like: *The pupils are usually easy to help* and *The pupils are usually eager to help*. Here, it seems as if there has been a straightforward replacement of one adjective with another, but this is not so, as we can see if we ask *who does the helping?* You can gain insights into major issues in syntactic theory by reading Pinker's (1994: 219 ff.) description.

Syntax also addresses issues of ambiguity, as in *Biting insects can be unpleasant.* You can learn a lot about the nature of English by trying to make up further examples of this. One particular type of ambiguity is the garden-path sentence, where there is, in fact, only one grammatical reading, but we are fooled by the sequence of words into looking for a different one (e.g. *The soup boiled vigorously spilt over; The ball bounced past the goal-post burst*). These are grammatical only if you read them as a (legitimately) shortened version of sentences with *that was* after the subject noun phrase. Again, trying to make up your own examples of garden-path sentences will soon indicate to you how they work. You can read about them in Pinker (1994: 212–17) and in Kess (1992: 129 ff.), where you will also find accounts of psycholinguistic experiments using them. They are also briefly mentioned in Chapter 2 of this book. For general references on syntax, see Table 9.1 above.

PROJECTS

177. Compare newspaper accounts of an event (something with strong political implications is best, such as a scandal at the heart of a political party), using publications which are likely to take sides. Look for different ways in which the same story can be told so that a different emphasis (e.g. about blame) is achieved. For guidelines on how to do this, see Freeborn *et al.* (1993, ch. 9).

178. Examine the writing of a 9, 11 and 13-year-old for evidence of a developing ability to manipulate the structure of English for the purposes of subtle expression.

179. For one or more other languages that you know, work out whether garden-path sentences can be made in the same way, and if so, why. If not, why not? If they can, do native speakers have more or less trouble seeing the meaning than native speakers of English do with English ones? If they don't, expand your study to look for other types of structural ambiguity.

180. Collect grammatical slips of the tongue such as *She doesn't do anything once she gets there, except be's there*, and *That's a whole nother issue*, and account for them structurally, using tree diagrams (Burton-Roberts 1986, Thomas 1993 or Baker 1995 will help you here). Begin by considering what was intended and how else it might have been said, and try swapping other words in (e.g. *stay(s)* in the first example and *new* in the second).

Lexicon and collocation

Although one might think that a language would only have one word for each idea, and that words would fit together quite simply to express relationships, this is actually not true. Words often have quite restricted usages, dictated by words with which they **collocate** (co-occur). For example, we say that humans eat *food*, while animals eat *feed*; you *melt* cheese and metal, but you *smelt* ore; you *pinpoint* a distant building but you *sight* a distant animal. Collocations can create some odd anomalies: why can we say *Merry Christmas*, *Happy Christmas* and *Happy New Year* but not *Merry New Year*? You can find out about many of the curiosities of collocation by looking at works derived from the Cobuild project, such as Sinclair (1991) and Collins Cobuild (1991, 1996).

In specialist areas, vocabulary can be remarkably specific, as the terminology in Table 9.2, taken from Farb (1973: 177), shows.

Table 9.2 Terms for animals

	Cattle	Horses	Sheep	Swine
Female	cow	mare	ewe	sow
Intact male	bull	stallion	ram	boar
Castrated male	steer	gelding	wether	barrow
Immature	heifer	colt/filly	lamb	shoat/gilt
Newborn	calf	foal	yeanling	piglet

Source: Farb (1973: 177)

Some specific subject areas have a vocabulary, even a grammar, that is incomprehensible to the uninitiated. Heraldry is a particularly striking case, as this extract from Tim Lewis's satirical novel *Pisspote's Progress* shows.

> The shield was per bend sinister, or a witch's hat gules, sable a cat embowed sable on an increscent moon argent, and chief sable a crucible and crossed mortars or. Above it was the crest, a king's head sanguine in a cauldron sable above a royal crown on a gold helm with seven bars, a torse or and azure, mantelling azure turned or, with crossbone supporters argent above a compartment of magrobs or in a chest sable. (Lewis 1991: 331)

Another focus of interest is what a word 'means'. Does 'gay' *still* mean 'happy'? Does it *only* mean 'happy'? and so on. In *Alice Through the Looking Glass* Humpty Dumpty tells Alice, 'When I use a word, it means just what I choose it to mean – neither more nor less' (Carroll 1865/1971: 114). Much has been written about this idea of meaning residing only in usage. In his play *Dogg's Our Pet* (1971), Tom Stoppard experiments with Wittgenstein's ideas by giving certain words new meanings. Although this is initially confusing, the audience soon adjust to this new language.

PROJECTS

181. Table 9.3 shows this writer's grid of acceptability for intensifications (*good, strong, high*) of four words that are very close in meaning (*likelihood, probability, possibility, chance*). Do you agree with the judgments? Bolinger (1981: 55) does not. Try the grid out on some informants. Is there a pattern? (You might look for similarities in use within a family, or differences according to age or gender, or place of origin, and so on.) What is the significance of disagreements for our perception of the English language as an entity? You might also address the difficulty that informants often have in deciding what is acceptable and what isn't. If they are not always sure, what does that tell us about language?

Table 9.3 Collocations of adjectives and nouns

	good	strong	high
likelihood	✓	✓	x
probability	x	✓	✓
possibility	✓	✓	x
chance	✓	✓	✓

182. Pawley and Syder (1983) suggest that one of the ways in which even highly proficient non-native speakers can give themselves away is by their use of grammatical sequences of the language that are not idiomatic. Using the techniques of **error analysis** (see Chapter 5 in this book for references), assess the extent to which the spoken or written language of one or more fluent non-native speakers does indeed mark itself out in this way. Consider *who decides* what is idiomatic, and under what circumstances non-native usage might come to be adopted more widely.

183. Choose an area that interests you (such as cookery or equestrianism) and identify specialist words and the words they collocate with. For example, in cooking, what can be *browned, griddled, poached or sautéed*? (See Cook 1997: 98–9 for a brief exploration of cookery terminology.) If English had to reduce its vocabulary by one third, which words from this field could be discarded, and which others could expand to cover the gap they left? Is specialist vocabulary necessary, or just the product of history? What effect would such simplification have on communication?

184. On p. 1 of Collins Cobuild (1996) there is a list of **meaning groups** for verbs, including the words they collocate with. Take these meaning groups and try to account for how or why the English language divides things up this way (does it reflect the language itself? human perception? history? culture?). Is there a conscious aspect to these sets, or do native speakers have no idea about them? Show some native speakers the lists and ask for their reactions.

185. Remove the terms from the grid in Table 9 2 above, and see how many of Farb's terms native speakers can fill in. Are there patterns regarding what people know and don't know? Why might some terms be more central to our common vocabulary than others? Use a word frequency list (see Chapter 1) to check whether it is the least-used words that are least well-known. If it is, consider whether infrequency causes unfamiliarity or the reverse.

186. Construct a list of common collective nouns (e.g. *flock of sheep, pride of lions, shoal of fish*). How have they come about, and how long have they been in use? (Use the full *Oxford English Dictionary* or a good etymological dictionary – references are given in Chapter 10). Why do we need such terms (if at all)? Under what circumstances might newly coined ones end up coming into common usage?

187. Compared with some other languages, English has very few kinship terms. What is the sociocultural significance of a lack of different words, for example, for *mother's sister* and *father's sister* in English? Make a comparison with other languages that you know.

188. Investigate the meaning that informants give to words such as *barely* in a sentence like *He barely has ten books on his shelf*. How many has he? More than ten, fewer or exactly ten? Another interesting word is *orphan*. Precisely who counts as one? Can you cease to be one? If you were brought up by foster parents while your own parents were still alive, who would have to die for you to become an orphan? Use examples like this to explore the agreement, or lack of it, between native speakers about precise definitions, and to discuss whether or not it matters.

189. Explore the meaning of the word *edition*, carefully identifying its range of uses (including *special edition* chocolate bars and cars). Ask informants what the word means (a) in isolation, (b) in its different contexts. How easy is it to pin down a central core to its meaning, and how does that relate to the history of the word's use? Find other words used in an extended way, probably also in advertising or marketing, and investigate them similarly (e.g. *'fresh' orange juice/cream; light/lite; bio*).

Morphology and etymology

The morpheme is the smallest unit of meaning. Some morphemes (**free morphemes**) stand alone, such as *dog, smile, black, from, also*. Others are **bound,** needing to combine with other morphemes, e.g. *-s* (plural), *un-,-ish, pseudo-*. You can find examples of the prefixes and suffixes of English in Crystal (1995, ch. 14). English is a particularly fascinating language to study, because its history of borrowing from other languages has left it with an enormous collection of morphemes, not all of which still have meanings that are recognizable without recourse to a dictionary. Because of this history, for English the studies of morphology (how we make up words today) and etymology (how words have come to have the form they do) are closely allied. For more information and suggestions for projects on etymology, see Chapter 10. For a simple introduction to morphology, see Aitchison (1992: 53–8), Fromkin and Rodman (1993: ch. 2) or Kuiper and Allan (1996: ch. 5). For more detail, use Atkinson, Kilby and Roca (1988: ch. 5) or Malmkjaer (1991: 314–24) and for a technical overview of the field see Anderson (1988) or Coates (1987).

PROJECTS

190. Look through teenage magazines for words that are new to the language, or interview some children about the current playground vocabulary, what it means and how they use it. Investigate the way in which these words have been constructed and/or where they have been borrowed from. If they are borrowed, have they had their meaning changed? When and how have they first appeared? Do they express an idea for which there was previously no word? If not, what was wrong with the old word? Is there any way of telling which of the words will last, becoming fully established in mainstream English, and which will soon fall into disuse again?

191. Look through magazines from the 1950s or 1960s, and try to identify words that were new then. Divide them into two categories – those which have survived and those which have not – and look for reasons why each word may have undergone its fate.

192. Find out about the construction of vocabulary in a sign language used by deaf people. What happens when a new sign is needed? Who introduces it and under what circumstances? How does the sign language express things like past tense, plural or the conditional? Interview signers who also speak English about the way in which the two languages are the same and different.

193. Take a passage from a novel or a document, and attempt to rewrite it using only monomorphemic words (i.e. words that cannot be broken down any further into meaning components). What problems arise with: availability of vocabulary, deciding whether a word is monomorphemic or not, style, and so on?

194. Anderson (1988: 185 ff.) explores the restrictions on English vocabulary formation, which outlaw *He sang *goodly; She stared in *amazion; The bruise began to blacken and *bluen; Delia Smith is a good *cooker* (the asterisk indicates that the word does not exist). Use this as a basis for an analysis of idiosyncratic vocabulary in the work of a poet such as Gerard Manley Hopkins or e. e. cummings. What determines whether words of this kind are seen as humorous on the one hand, or beautiful and creative coinages on the other?

195. Make a list of words that, if split, have a different meaning, such as *altogether/all together; into/in to; however/how ever; everyone/every one; layby/lay by.* Ask informants to pin down the differences in meaning. Research the history of the words, to find out whether the opposition has always existed. Pay attention to the syntactic classes of the words and the structures in which they appear. For further examples, see Greenbaum (1991: 200).

Punctuation

Punctuation plays various roles in clarifying meaning. Putting a word in inverted commas, for example, can indicate that the writer considers it unfamiliar, inappropriate, and so on. Commas are used to indicate the structure of the sentence, sometimes clarifying potential ambiguity, and without punctuation a string of words may be complete nonsense. One well-known example is *Jones, where Smith had had 'had', had had 'had had'. 'Had had' had had the teacher's approval* (about a school translation exercise).

PROJECTS

196. Remove the punctuation from some texts, and get informants to put it back. To what extent do they agree? Categorize the conventions into those which genuinely make the meaning clear, and those which could be dispensed with. Do your informants have most difficulty with those aspects of punctuation that play the least role in clarifying the meaning? Survey their attitudes to and problems with 'correct' punctuation.

197. Research the history of punctuation in English, both in books about the history of the language and by looking at original texts from Old, Middle and Modern English. Was there ever no punctuation at all? Which usages have existed longest? Has their scope of application changed?

198. The poet e.e. cummings makes very limited use of punctuation. Show some of his poems to informants and compare their reactions and their understanding of the meaning. Does the poet's approach permit subtle expressions of meaning that would be destroyed by using punctuation more conventionally, or is it just a gimmick?

'Correct' grammar

In order to understand the issue of *correctness* in grammar, it is necessary to differentiate between **linguistic** and **social** judgements. A descriptive linguistic approach recognizes that many of the features that are considered 'incorrect' in English are in fact simply *non-standard,* and within their own variety they are entirely grammatical and consistent. However, the existence of a 'standard' English indicates that there is a variety of the language that is socially and culturally more acceptable than the others. Forms that do not adhere to it are often seen as 'incorrect'. See Freeborn

(1995) for a review of the arguments regarding what constitutes 'good' and 'correct' English, and for examples of how actual text does not always conform to the 'rules'. Freeborn *et al.* (1993, ch. 1) and Crystal (1995: 366–7) also discuss the question of correctness, and Wray (1996) explores the conflicts between prescriptivism and descriptivism that arise when academic linguists have to correct the work of their students. Cameron (1995) gives a spirited account of the debate in her chapter 'Dr Syntax and Mrs Grundy: the great grammar crusade'. On the other hand, Marenbon (1994) suggests that descriptivism and prescriptivism are mutually supportive: 'by describing how a certain language is spoken or written, the grammarian prescribes usage for those who wish to speak or write that language' (p. 20).

PROJECTS

199. Compare the grammar of two strong dialects of English (such as Scots, Geordie, Black English Vernacular, Indian English), or compare one of them with standard English. What things can be expressed by one and not the other? For some ideas on this, see Pinker's (1994: 29 ff.) commentary on Labov's Black English Vernacular data. Consider the implications for the expressive potential of an individual of accepting or rejecting his or her variety as a legitimate form of English in its own right.

200. Research the history of a prescriptive feature of English grammar, such as not splitting infinitives, or not ending sentences with a preposition. Use textbooks on the history of English (see Chapter 10) and original sources where possible. Does a rule have more, or less, credibility if it reflects (a) a long-standing convention, (b) a recent imposition?

201. Do school pupils, teachers, school governors and employers in business and in the public services have the same opinions about what is good English? Show the same stimuli to pupils and one of the other groups above, and compare the responses. For example stimuli, see Freeborn *et al.* (1993: 11–12).

202. Find examples of *alot*, *aswell* and other non-standard spellings of this kind. Collect data by borrowing essays from a local school or your fellow students. Which word strings are now being perceived as single items and which remain consistently separate? Use basic phrase-structure analysis (such as Burton-Roberts 1986, Thomas 1993) to establish whether there are structural reasons for this. For some background and example data, see Wray (1996).

203. Explore the role of dictionaries as prescribers or describers. By comparing their forewords, their format and what information they include, find out who they are targeted at and what their aims are. Interview native and non-native speakers of English about how and why they use dictionaries, whether they always believe what they find there, and what they do if they can't find the word or meaning they are looking for.

OTHER PROJECT IDEAS

204. Investigate the form and usage of idiomatic and 'rule-breaking' expressions such as *He was sleeping like the proverbial* or *I've just had himself on the phone*. Explore the nature of their form and usage, taking account of the syntax (including any restrictions they violate) and the pragmatics (shared information, about whom or in what circumstances they would be used, the effect of using them rather than an alternative and so on).

205. Take a selection of jokes from a joke book and catalogue them for humour based on pragmatics, ambiguity (phonological, lexical and structural) and non-linguistic factors such as situation. Give the jokes (intermixed) to groups of subjects and get them to rate them for funniness. Do 10-year-olds give consistently different ratings from adults for the different types? What about men and women? Nash (1985) and Chiaro (1992) will give you a good introduction to the pragmatics of humour and ideas to follow up for projects. For further insight into the structure of jokes, try the *Usborne Book of Silly Jokes* (pp. 30–1), which demonstrates how certain types can be made up by formula.

206. Take Monty Python's *Parrot Sketch*, or a sketch of similar anarchic complexity, and categorize the lexical, structural and pragmatic sources of its humour.

You can find lots of information that will inspire ideas for projects by reading chapters 8 to 12 of Crystal (1995).

10

Historical linguistics

However big you may conceive historical linguistics to be as a field, it is bigger still. There are innumerable questions to be asked about a language at every point of its history, about every aspect of its form and function, and about the relationship between the language forms at different times. And whatever may be asked about one language can be asked about every other, though languages vary considerably in the amount of research already done on them and, indeed, in the amount of primary documentation that is available for researching them.

For convenience, most of the ideas put forward below will make reference to English. This is undoubtedly one of the best-documented and most-researched languages, as well as being one that is unusually rich in its mixture of vocabulary. It also has a striking **diachronic** ('across time') profile, largely because of its political and economic history. In many cases the suggestions made for English can be transferred to the study of other languages, but it will be important to establish that the information you need, be it historical documents or commentaries upon them, is available.

There are two basic ways of finding out what a language used to be like. Where possible, evidence comes directly from written records. However, writing is not only a recent phenomenon in man's cultural development: it is also highly selective, and much of the information that would most interest the linguist is therefore simply not available that way. Where there are no written records it is possible, to some extent, to reconstruct features of a language using either other linguistic information from that time, or information that we have about one or more languages, from a subsequent period, that have descended from it. In this way it has been possible for scholars to reconstruct aspects of the vocabulary and grammar of the prehistoric language Proto-Indo-European, using information from its many descendants today. The same method could be used, however, to reconstruct the dialect of the 'criminal' class in London in the eighteenth and nineteenth centuries, by using the modern London dialects and the variety of Australian English that developed in the penal colonies.

Because we cannot time-travel, care must be taken, when working on the history of a language, to ask only questions that it is possible to answer from where we are today. This immediately excludes, for example, questions such as how much aspiration Shakespeare's wife used on a word-initial /t/, or whether the English nobility at the time of the Norman Conquest spoke French as fluently as they wrote it. Unless these specific things happen to have been written about at the time, there is obviously no way of finding them out.

It may seem, then, that the only questions we can ask are the ones that are, by definition, already answered. But this is far from being the case. Nor is it true that we cannot know anything about the spoken, as opposed to the written, language. The body of linguistic information that was documented at the time, combined with the many superb surveys and investigations done since, can provide you with both the materials and the theoretical background for exploring a wide range of questions.

Textbooks, reference sources and major journals

Table 10.1 Useful texts for historical linguistics (see page xiv for key to levels)

Book	Level	Notes on Content/Style
Aitchison 1991	1–2	language change, both historical and contemporary; simple but reliable account
Barber 1993 (revision of *The Story of Language*, 1972)	2	history of English; comprehensive introductory coverage; includes prehistory of languages, language change
Barber 1997	2–3	Early Modern English
Baugh and Cable 1993	2	history of English, full of example texts and contemporary quotes; includes prehistory, attitudes towards English, spelling
Blake 1996	2–3	history of development of standard English, including sociolinguistic aspects
Boas 1911/1966	3–4	American Indian languages and their inter-relationship
Cambridge History of the English Language (e.g. Hogg 1992, Blake 1992, Burchfield 1994)	3–4	history of English: separate volumes for different periods and themes, giving overviews of current thinking in the field; not suitable as an introduction
Cavalli-Sforza 1991	1	movement, settlement and languages of early man
Crystal 1995, part I and ch. 10, etc.	1	considerable coverage of history of English with excellent illustrations

Book	Level	Notes on Content/Style
Crystal 1997a, chs. 50–4	1–2	how languages are related (chs. 50–3); general account of language change (ch. 54); further reading list, p. 447 (IX)
Fisher and Bornstein 1974	2	text-based analysis of the history of English; tape available with historical pronunciation
Freeborn 1992	1	history of English, illustrated with analyses of contemporary texts; tape available with historical pronunciation
Gamkredlidze and Ivanov 1990	1	Nostratic, ancestor of Indo-European
Görlach 1991	3	Early Modern English; many example texts
Graddol *et al.* 1996	2	history of English; themed chapters that may inspire project ideas
Greenberg 1970	4	African languages and their inter-relationship
Keller 1994	2–3	language change: whimsical account, giving interesting personal view; not representative of introductory books
Lockwood 1969	3	prehistory; comparisons of related languages
McCrum *et al.* 1992	1	history of English, including modern variation; derived from a TV series; patchy and superficial but engrossing; find videos of the TV version and invite your friends over
McMahon 1994	3	detailed account of language change with comprehensive reviews of recent research and current issues; may be worth reading Aitchison 1991 first, for orientation
Malmkjaer 1991, pp. 196–213	3	explanations with examples of language change (phonology, morphology, syntax); social and psychological aspects of change (196–209); prehistory and Indo-European (209–13)
Myers and Hoffman 1979	3	history of English, including prehistory; later chapters are thematic, including a partial history of linguistics
Onions 1966	2–3	reference book for English etymology
Oxford English Dictionary	3	not to be confused with anything less than 12 volumes and supplements; gives meanings and first recorded uses of more words than you can dream of; also available in electronic form

continued overleaf

Table 10.1 (*continued*)

Book	Level	Notes on Content/Style
Partridge 1966	2	reference book for English etymology; particularly inviting style
Potter 1975, ch. 7	2	the prehistory of English
Pyles and Algeo 1993	2–3	history of English, including prehistory, history of writing and spelling, word formation and borrowing
Renfrew 1987	2–3	in-depth account of the Indo-Europeans and their language, using archeological theory
Renfrew 1989, 1994	1	movement, settlement and languages of early man
Room 1982, 1991, 1992	2–3	reference books for origin of commercial names (1982), changes in word meaning (1991), origin of proper names (1992)
Ross 1991	1	Nostratic, ancestor of Indo-European
Samuels 1972	4	language change: one theory put into practice; not for the beginner
Smith 1996	3	processes of dynamic change
Strang 1970	3–4	history of English in reverse chronological order; dense but detailed and careful; includes relationship between synchronic and diachronic change (ch. 1)
Wadler 1948	2–3	old and quirky, arguing for a single original language, but full of examples that could be used for other things
Wakelin 1988	2–3	history of English with full recognition of dialects; includes chapter on prehistory
Williams 1975	2	history of English; many unusual features, including chronologies of political and linguistic events (there is a shorter but similar list in Crystal 1988a)

Much of the research on historical linguistics is highly technical, and takes for granted a firm understanding of linguistic theory. It is still worth looking through the journals, though, as given in Fig. 10.1, for ideas on what people consider interesting to study and how they go about it.

Diachronica	*Lingua*
English Studies	*Linguistics*
Folia Linguistica Historica	*Scottish Language*
Foundations of Language	*Shakespeare Studies*
Glossa	*Studia Linguistica Diachronica et*
Journal of Linguistics	*Synchronica*
Language	*Studies in Philology*
Language and Communication	*Transactions of the Philological Society*

Fig 10.1 Major journals for research in historical linguistics

Central themes and project ideas

Researching words

Many people find the history of English words very interesting, but a project on words must be very carefully managed, not least because it is excessively tedious to look up word after word in dictionaries, particularly as you really need to check each one in more than one place. For the sake of your sanity and that of your assessor, you must find something more engaging than a straight list of histories and/or definitions: such a list is boring, two-dimensional and, because it involves no engagement or real thought, it won't get you good marks.

SURNAMES

Much less is genuinely known about the history of surnames than you will be led to believe by any given book on the subject. Look a name up in one book and you may feel confident of knowing its origin. But look the same name up again elsewhere, and it will probably seem less certain that any of them have got it right! So, be very sceptical about what you read. Look for interesting questions to ask. For example, whilst it is true that many surnames derive from placenames or geographical features, occupations, physical characteristics or personal names, some apparently straightforward cases are more obscure. At first glance, 'Pope', 'Monk' and 'King' might seem to have derived from occupations, with the surname passed from father to son in the normal way, but a moment's thought indicates that this is fairly unlikely!

PROJECTS

207. Choose a small number of surnames, look them up in every book you can find, and make a critical comparison of what the different sources say. Then try to account for the variation and discuss the significance of it.

208. Choose two very different areas of the country and, using the telephone directory, find out what the most popular local surnames are. Use this as a way of discussing possible differences in the communities today and in the past. For example, London has been a target for waves of immigrants: French Huguenots, Eastern European Jews, Indians and so on, whereas a rural area may have had a very settled local community for many generations.

209. Draw up a list of specific queries to investigate, such as: why *are* there so many people with the surnames 'Pope', 'Monk' and 'King'? Why is the name 'Smith' spelled in so many different ways? What surnames *don't* exist that could, and why (e.g. Mrs Computer-programmer; Mr Obese; Ms Tea-drinker; Mrs Pylon and so on)?

210. Take a wider, more comparative, approach, asking why surnames arose in the first place, and how different communities (local and worldwide) have dealt differently with the same problem that surnames were intended to solve. Ask whether they are appropriate and/or sufficient in our modern world and if they are not, how naming practices could be reformed.

PLACENAMES

Placenames can be easier to research than surnames, because while people move from place to place, taking their name with them, places tend to stay put, so you can trace at least the spellings of a placename as far back as there are maps or local records. Again, different books may give different meanings to the same name. The best single source for placename meanings is the 69 volumes of the English Placename Society, such as *The Placenames of Dorset* (vol. 1, 1977; vol. 2, 1980) and *The Placenames of Rutland* (1994). To avoid just ending up with a list, find a way of *using* placename research to address a slightly different question than 'what is the origin of these placenames?'

PROJECTS

211. Focusing on a local area of interest to you, find out how the placenames have changed their spelling (and pronunciation, if you can manage it) over the years and why. Who would have determined how the name was spelled, and what would the status of any given spelling have been?

212. Are there patterns to the placenames in an area which indicate the history of settlements of different peoples? Yorkshire is particularly good for this. Look for indications of who lived on the hills and who lived in the valleys. You don't need to live in the area to do this sort of work: get a good map and read up about it. You may find Cameron (1965) a useful model. He looks at how placenames in the five boroughs of Derby, Nottingham, Lincoln, Leicester and Stamford reflect Viking settlement patterns.

213. What do street names tell us about the history of an area? Consider how the basic vocabulary for thoroughfares must have changed its meaning over the years: what was the difference between a *road*, a *street* and a *lane* 300 years ago? What do they mean today? Focus on a suburb and use modern and old maps to trace its development as a residential area. Extend your study to look at new towns and/or street names in new estates. Find out who decides what to call them, and look for patterns in the choices from place to place.

214. Look at a particular recurrent word or syllable in placenames. What pattern is there to its occurrence within an area and across a region or beyond? Among the useful sources are Zachrisson (1909) on Anglo-Norman influences, Ekwall (1923, 1925, 1928) on placenames with *-ing* and on river names, and Sandred (1963) on *-stead*.

215. Make a critical analysis of pub names. Rather than simply recounting the history of a few interesting ones, interview publicans and brewers to find out their preferences and policy on keeping or replacing long-standing names and choosing new names (do they tend to make a new pub *sound* traditional, or might they call one *The Website* or *The Heliport*?). Do they feel that the name of a pub has an influence on its image, so that different names would be used for different clientele? By examining the names that pubs have been given in past centuries, attempt to ascertain whether the influences then (such as market forces) were the same as they are now.

ETYMOLOGY

The ordinary vocabulary of English is particularly rich, and derives from a great many different sources. However, it isn't always very obvious what to do with a set of word definitions – just putting them down in a list, even organized under *words from French, words from Arabic* and so on, will not convince your assessor that you have done much thinking! It is therefore important to provide yourself with a solid theme that allows you to *interpret* your data.

PROJECT

216. Choose a theme and look up the words that relate to it. This could be equestrianism, things you eat for breakfast, words for modern machinery and gadgets (many of which are much older than the things they describe), plant names, names for zoo animals or words relating to warfare (see Partridge 1948). Then *use* what you find out to account for the ways in which words come about in languages, and how technological advances, or changes in a culture or society, will require new words. Read up on language change so that you can back up your claims. Useful reading, especially for ideas and serendipity, includes Groom (1934), Ayers (1965) and Barfield (1953). A wide-ranging source well worth using is Serjeantson (1935). To look up specific words use Onions (1966) and Partridge (1966). The latter usefully indicates the links between rather

unlikely words, such as *turban* and *tulip, asterisk* and *disaster, shrub* and *sorbet, wench* and *lapwing,* and so on.

Pronunciation and spelling

English has a fascinating history as far as pronunciation is concerned, and our modern spelling system bears witness to much of it. Almost all the introductory books will give you an overview both of the sound changes and the spelling system, and there are specialized works by Bradley (1916), Brook (1957), Gimson (1962), Barber (1997), Burchfield (1985), Kökeritz (1953), Zachrisson (1913), Vallins (1954) and many more. For spelling, Baugh and Cable (1993) is useful and includes, on pages 414–20, examples of contemporary writings to illustrate the spelling changes that English has undergone. For a recent study of the nature of English spelling see Mitton (1996).

PROJECTS

217. For many native speakers of English, all of the following words have the vowel /u: /: *flew, approve, fool, wound* (noun), *rule, blue, fruit, neurotic, new.* Find out how 'characteristic' different spellings are of their pronunciation, by reading out made-up words to subjects. Tell them that they will have to read the words back to you with the correct pronunciation and that they should write them down in a way that helps them do that. (Do *not* use linguistics students for this, as they will probably use phonetic script!) Do the subjects all tend to spell a sound in the same way when being impressionistic? (For example, is /u:/ always written *oo*, or are *ue* and *ough* also used?) Are the preferred spellings of each sound today the most long-standing ones (for example, has *oo* represented the sound /u:/ for longer than the other spellings?). Vallins (1954: 46–9) gives lists of the different spellings for each sound.

218. Take a piece of verse (by Shakespeare, for example) and identify which rhymes still work and which don't. What about puns? What pronunciation changes are reflected by them? Argue in a balanced way for and against performing works of literature in their original pronunciation. What wider implications are there for the arts?

219. What have been the motivations of the spelling reformers in England (and France, perhaps) during the last few centuries? For some ideas to get you started, look up the *inkhorns,* the *Academie* and *George Bernard Shaw.*

220. What would we lose by modernizing our spelling system to match modern pronunciation? Why has no such reform been achieved before now? When did spelling start diverging from pronunciation, why, and what was people's reaction?

221. Go to one of the books issued in facsimile by the Scolar Press, for a contemporary view of the issues. For example, read the introductory note to

Mulcaster's *The First Part of the Elementary* (1582) for an idea of his attitudes towards spelling, before embarking on the description of the alphabet that he presents. Alternatively, use John Hart's *An Orthographie* (1569), one of the most linguistically informed and accurate descriptions of English pronunciation of its time, and incorporating his own phonetic spelling system.

222. Write a critical evaluation of a nineteenth- or early-twentieth-century essay on the 'decay' of language, such as Bridges (1913). Use the modern descriptive linguistic approach to put the other side of the arguments.

223. Interview actors and musicians about the validity of performing works from the sixteenth century and earlier in original pronunciation. For insight into the issues, see Wray (1992b and c, 1995).

History of English dialects

Be careful what you choose here, because some dialects are better documented than others. Read Skeat (1911) to gain a clear idea of how the four major dialects of Old English fit together, and work forwards from there. Try to avoid giving just a straightforward chronicle of developments.

PROJECTS

224. Investigate why it was that the variety of English spoken in the East Midlands became the standard English. By careful reading about Northumbrian and about the nature of standardization, speculate about what English would be like now if Northumbrian had continued to be the high-prestige variety that it was in Bede's day.

225. Draw on a range of reading to ask to what extent a topography of the British Isles can account for the development of standard English.

The profile of a feature of English across time

Aspects of English grammar, meaning and style have all changed across time, and there are plenty of documents that provide evidence of this. Use what you know of syntactic, semantic or discourse theory to inform your analysis.

PROJECT

226. Focus on a feature such as the passive, the subjunctive, the negative or how speech is quoted, and compare its occurrence in a couple of sample texts for each of, say, three periods between Chaucer and the late eighteenth century or even up to modern times. You can keep the variability down by

choosing a text that has been rewritten many times, such as a Bible passage. Examples of such passages can be found in many textbooks, including Fisher and Bornstein (1974), Burnley (1992) and Freeborn (1992).

Socio-political trends and influences on English

One much-described aspect of the history of our language is the way in which the Norman Conquest affected, among other things, the vocabulary of English. There has also been some interesting work done on the later 'social' history of English, including the way in which dialects were used to support the trade union movement (Joyce 1991). See Burke and Porter (1987, 1991) for ideas, and Leith (1983) for a more general but socially oriented view of the history of English.

PROJECTS

227. Using the chronologies in Williams (1975), write an account of what linguistic life would have been like in Norman England for, say, three or four individuals from different social classes. What language would they have used when, and with whom? How does this relate to the changes in the vocabulary of English between 1066 and 1400?

228. Draw up a list of the proverbs mentioned in Obelkevich (1987). Interview a small group of elderly people and ask them which ones they know, what they mean and in what circumstances (for example, in conversation with whom) they might use them. Do the same with a group of young adults or children. Comment on the following possibilities: the use of proverbs is dying out; proverbs vary from generation to generation; you only really learn (or learn to use) proverbs later on in your life.

229. Make a study of euphemisms and when they are used. Read the introductory pages of dictionaries of euphemisms for an impression of their range. Make a list of euphemisms for the same thing (for example, words for having sex, for excrement, or for parts of the body) and interview a group of informants about when they would use each one. Which do they consider shocking, which 'cute' and which old-fashioned? What words do they consider to be non-euphemistic (i.e. the direct term) for each concept? Look these words up to establish whether they too used to be euphemisms. Consider the 'shelf-life' of euphemisms, and when they need replacing. For an outline of the scope of taboo words, including their use as swear-words, see Crystal (1995: 172–4).

English as a world language

Read Crystal (1995, ch. 7 or 1997b) to gain a clear impression of the current status of English as a world language. There are many interesting questions that we can ask, including how English came to be such a widespread and influential language, what mark it has left on other languages, and what mark they have left on it.

PROJECTS

230. Assuming an unaltered basic political history for Europe and America, how would foreign policy and/or social structures have had to be different for the English language *not* to have become so important? You can get ideas by looking at other nations which have had plenty of political, but less linguistic, influence. This sort of project is based on speculation, and to be successful as a piece of research you *must* draw upon a range of established theories to support the points you make. You will need to research the processes by which English became so important, and draw on sociolinguistic research to demonstrate how social and political influences filter through to the individuals in a speech community, leading them to decisions about their own needs and priorities.

231. Make a comparison between English today and Arabic in the Middle East or Latin during the Roman occupation of Europe.

The influence of literacy on language

By researching the history of basic literacy education in Britain over the last thousand years, and linking that in to who had influence over whom as far as language was concerned, one can develop a picture of the effect that being able to read and write has on the development of a language. Remember to consider the people at both edges of literacy: those who maybe had to write letters from time to time, but who had almost no schooling, and those who were highly educated in not only English but also French, Greek and Latin. There is plenty of information about the latter in introductory books like Baugh and Cable (1993) and Crystal (1995).

PROJECT

232. Find out who was teaching the basic literacy skills to the less-privileged in a period of history of your choosing. How good were *their* skills? Link this debate into literacy practice in the modern world, both locally and internationally, but remember to consider to what extent the demands of our society today require different levels of literacy and education from those of the past.

Things to think about

- It is possible to download from the Internet lengthy texts that may not be easily available any other way, by doing a Search on a name such as

Paston (a family whose letters through the fifteenth century have been much studied), or the name of an event or monarch.

- Studies of pronunciation require a working knowledge of phonetic script; phonemic script will not be sufficient for anything other than the most general kinds of observations. For the difference between these two transcription systems, see Chapter 17.
- The more research you do into the history of a language, the more you will realize how much of what is presented as *fact* is actually an *interpretation* of often rather ambiguous and confusing original data. Don't be content with reading just one account; expect another one to be different, and take note of where the disagreements occur. The art of writing a good project is to use the disagreement as a pivot for developing your own views (see Chapter 22).

|11|

Language and gender

The study of language and gender is concerned with how gender affects the ways in which we use language and others use language with us. Gender is one of the key determiners of linguistic variation, yet until recently the study of variation in language in general, let alone gender differences in language use, was relatively neglected. Even when language variation was systematically studied, in fieldwork projects such as the *Survey of English Dialects* (see, for example, Orton 1962), women subjects were virtually excluded, since men were thought to use the vernacular more often, more consistently and more 'genuinely' than women (Chambers and Trudgill 1980: 35). The earliest systematic studies were in the late 1950s and early 1960s (for example, Fischer 1958, summarized in Romaine 1984, ch. 4, and Labov's work in Martha's Vineyard (1963) and New York (1996) summarized in Aitchison 1991, Wardhaugh 1992 and Hudson 1996). Since the early 1970s, partly due to the rise of the women's movement in the USA, language and gender has developed and diversified rapidly as a field.

Among the questions addressed by research into language and gender are:

- in what ways do males and females use language differently (for example, grammar, pronunciation, vocabulary choice, amount of talk, topics selected for talk, strategies selected in conversation, use of taboo words, politeness, accuracy in written language)?
- are the patterns equally observable in all societies?
- do males and females speak differently in single-sex groups and mixed groups?
- what are people's attitudes towards male and female language, how do they relate to the genuine observable differences found through research, and are they changing?
- how are males and females portrayed as communicators in literature, commercials, comedy, and so on?

- what happens to individuals whose language does not fit the popular stereotype of how a man or a woman should behave?
- what is the role of gender differences in linguistic change?
- what is linguistic sexism, where does it exist and why?
- can political correctness change people's attitudes and behaviour regarding language and sexism?
- how do children learn to speak and write appropriately for their gender?

Terminology

In the context of language and gender research, gender is not just a synonym for sex: '*Sex* refers to a biological distinction, while *gender* is the term to describe socially constructed categories based on sex' (Coates 1993: 4). By this Coates means that our identity as men and women is shaped to a considerable degree by our surroundings: parents, siblings, friends, other role models in our society, cultural taboos, ways in which we show our sexual orientation, and so on.

Useful skills and knowledge

As for most linguistics projects, a good piece of work in this area will almost certainly require you to use one or more of the following skills, even if only at a basic level: grammatical analysis, phonetic or phonemic transcription and analysis, orthographic transcription and conversation analysis. You may need to know about questionnaire design and processing, and the quantitative (counting features/statistics) and qualitative handling of data. There is guidance on how to approach data collection and analysis elsewhere in this book.

Textbooks

Most introductory books are written from a linguistic perspective, but you will find that some textbooks intended for students of sociology, politics, history, education and women's studies also contain useful information. Booksellers and librarians sometimes shelve books in rather inappropriate places, since they are not always aware that a particular author is a noted linguist as opposed to a sociologist, and it is not clear from the title which section the book belongs to. This can be confusing, and important too, if the book you obtain turns out to be written from an inappropriate standpoint (usually this means too little specific linguistic comment). If in doubt, stick to the linguistics section of your bookshop and library and look for the names of key writers in the field, such as Jennifer Coates, Deborah Cameron, Deborah Tannen, Janet Holmes, Dale Spender and Joan Swann.

Table 11.1 Useful texts (see page xiv for key to levels)

Book	Level	Notes on Content/Style
Bergvall *et al.* 1996	3–4	challenges the simplistic male–female dichotomy; includes language of a rape trial, radio talk shows, etc.
Coates 1993	2–3	broad-ranging and systematic; all main areas, including children's acquisition of gender-specific language; clear headings
Coates 1996	2–3	women's conversation
Coates and Cameron 1989	3–4	collection including language of black British women, gossip, classroom talk, Gujarati wedding songs; requires prior knowledge of the field
Crystal 1995, pp. 368–9; 1997a, pp. 21, 46–7	1	brief account of some issues; tends not to name the researchers, so hard to derive further references from; useful examples
Fasold 1990, ch. 4	3	covers main areas and gives references to others; summary of issues at the end
Freeborn *et al.* 1993, section 12.3	1	brief and limited account of issues in language and sexism, politically correct language; useful for examples and ideas
Fromkin and Rodman 1993, pp. 306–12	1–2	brief account of language and sexism
Graddol and Swann 1989	3	education perspective; broad coverage; focus on theory; headings can be cryptic
Holmes 1995	2–3	gender differences in politeness behaviour
Johnson and Meinhof 1996	3	men's language, including gossip and turn-taking
Mills 1995	3	top researchers on current issues in the field; requires knowledge of the field
Smith 1985	3–4	more about the role than form of male–female language; examines speaker's and hearer's perspective; little on accent and dialect; headings not always transparent
Spender 1985	3	focuses on 'male control of language'; radical and idiosyncratic; significant work
Swann 1992	2–3	broad coverage; focus on gender differences in children's language; clearly structured, but reading up on adult differences first may help
Tannen 1991	1–2	bestseller, not academic in style; hard to find information and can lack detail needed for research; a good read, useful for ideas

continued overleaf

Table 11.1 (*continued*)

Book	Level	Notes on Content/Style
Trudgill 1995, ch. 4	1–2	focus on male–female differences in dialect form and use; barely mentions conversation or style differences
Wardhaugh 1992, ch. 13	2–3	covers main areas, in less detail than Fasold 1990. Discussion questions may inspire projects; some mention of gender issues in chapters other than 13

Major journals

Because of the broad scope of the area, there are many journals where papers on language and gender issues might appear. These include those given in Fig. 11.1.

```
Applied Linguistics                        Language and Speech
Discourse Processes                        Language and Society
Discourse and Society                      Language in Society
Educational Review                         Language Teaching
English World-Wide                         Language Variation and Change
International Journal of the Sociology of   Linguistics
   Language                                Merril-Palmer Quarterly
Journal of Language and Social             Psychology of Women Quarterly
   Psychology                              Small Group Behaviour
Journal of Pragmatics                      Social Problems
Language                                   Studia Linguistica
Language and Communication                 Women's Studies International
Language and Education                        Quarterly
```

Fig 11.1 Major journals for research in language and gender

Central themes and project ideas

Due to the popularity of projects in language and gender, it can sometimes feel as though topics have been 'done to death'. Consider whether you can select a focus which adds something new, no matter how small, to the field. Discussion with a tutor should help with this.

The history and development of language and gender as a branch of linguistics

In spite of their training, many linguists in the past were not curious about gender differences in language, sometimes because they allowed themselves to be influenced in a very unscientific manner by popular opinions on female language (see *Attitudes*, below). Coates (1993) gives a good overview of some of the main themes, particularly in chapters 2 and 3. Chambers and Trudgill (1980) give coverage on the methods of traditional and urban dialectology.

PROJECTS

233. Look in detail at some of the material from a major linguistic survey, such as the *Survey of English Dialects,* and examine the extent to which the questionnaires reflected issues of interest or relevance to women. Many good university libraries have copies of the full survey and related publications.

234. Contact researchers who have worked on published surveys which have taken gender as a variable. Try to establish where their motivation for studying gender comes from and how they view early work in the field.

235. Survey recent books and journal articles to find out what the most popular issues in language and gender research currently are. You could combine this with a survey of the questions and approaches followed in these studies.

Attitudes towards male and female language

Study in this area involves looking not at real language use, but at societies' perceptions, attitudes and stereotypes of it. These are sometimes termed 'folk-linguistic beliefs'. If attitudes and stereotypes are not based on truth, how and why have they arisen? Do they exert any influence on how males and females acquire or use language?

Use Coates (1993, chs. 2 and 3) as a starting-point for information on attitudes in Western society. Studies which have sought opinions on features of male and female language include Kramer (1977). Other examples can be found in Smith (1985).

PROJECTS

236. Using Coates (1993, chs. 2 and 3) as a reference resource, survey key writings of prominent authors, commentators and early linguists, to investigate the kinds of opinions which were held concerning male and female language. Supplement this with general reading from books about language written in the nineteenth and early twentieth centuries.

237. If you have contacts with native speakers of other languages, especially if they are from markedly contrasting cultures, probe their perceptions of male and female language, at the same time asking about wider beliefs in their culture. This may involve using some kind of structured interview technique or questionnaire (see Smith 1985, Kramer 1977 and Chapters 14 and 15 in this book).

238. What do children think of adult male and female speech, and at what age are their perceptions strongest? Again, Coates (1993) can provide some orientation. Source studies include Edelsky (1976).

239. How is male and female speech portrayed in novels, cartoons or TV and radio drama? Investigating these issues can be an oblique way of asking questions about society's attitudes. One source reference for cartoons is Kramer (1974). Smith (1985) has summary coverage of relevant issues.

240. Replicate or adapt Trudgill's (1972) study of male and female speech. He found that women tended to think they used standard forms more than their real language data showed they did, whereas men did the opposite. The roles of males and females in society have changed since then – will that lead to different results? For similar ideas, but with a different slant, see projects 138 and 242.

Male–female differences in accent and dialect

Studies in this area involve looking at aspects of accent (pronunciation, intonation) or dialect (word order/syntax, morphology and lexis/semantics). Often grouped under the heading of (modern/urban) dialectology, they have not always been set up with gender as a key focus, but this is often studied as one possible source of variation and change, alongside social background, age, and so on.

Several key studies, such as Labov (1966) and Trudgill (1974), have identified certain groups of women as the driving force behind pronunciation change within their communities, and have provided insights into the different models of prestige which males and females adopt, as well as helping to shape a picture of how and why accents change. For a summary, see Wardhaugh (1992: 152, 164–6 and 199–200).

Coates (1993, chs. 4 and 5) gives a good overview of key studies, and also describes recent moves in methodology towards a more 'group-centred', social-network approach rather than a society-wide, more anonymous one (see also Chapter 7 in this book, Wardhaugh 1992, chs. 2, 6 and 7, and Fasold 1990, ch. 4).

Formal studies are now less popular than studies focusing on interaction between speakers of one or both genders. Formal studies placed emphasis on quantitative techniques, relatively small units of language (sounds, words), large groups of subjects about whom comparatively little is known, and relatively small samples of speech collected from a fairly restricted range of situations, using structured questions in an interview format. The more recent methodological approaches are described later on in this chapter.

Jenny Cheshire (1978; see Coates 1993, ch. 5 for a summary) studied non-standard verb forms used by three adolescent peer groups (two male, one female) in Reading, 'hanging out' with the groups and becoming accepted by them. Cheshire also saw how language use reflected an individual's position in and allegiance to the group, and how the girls and boys became socialized into their adult roles and linguistic patterns. This type of approach, because it takes the emphasis away from gender differences and places it on gender 'behaviour', legitimizes studies that look at only one of the sexes, such as Reid (1978).

PROJECTS

241. Conduct a study of your local dialect, paying attention to the gender dimension. Replicate or adapt the methodology of one of the key studies, and write about the particular problems encountered in making the adaptation and/or in collecting representative data from both sexes.

242. Much of what we know about male and female dialect patterns stems from work done more than 20 years ago. Social conditions have changed markedly since then. Conduct your own survey of male and female language and compare your findings with those of an older study in the same locality. You will need to gather information on any changes in lifestyle, employment, population (immigration and emigration, for example) that might have led to changes in the roles of males and females with a corresponding change in their language.

Differences in conversation and style of language use

Studies following this theme tend to focus on differences in **communicative competence**, that is, broad features of language use including the issue of *appropriate* language use (Coates 1993: 106 ff.). One central question is that of whether males and females have different models of communicative competence, such that there are identifiably male and female 'styles'.

One of the pioneer studies in this area was Lakoff (1975, reviewed in Coates 1993). She proposed a set of so-called **women's language** features. Although Lakoff's list was based largely on her intuitions and informal observations of friends rather than on systematically gathered evidence, it was for many years a starting-point for other studies which set out to find empirical evidence for or against the existence of these features. One informative 'spin-off' study is published as chapter 7 in Coates and Cameron (1989). Other key sources include Kramarae (1981), Maltz and Borker (1982) and Thorne and Henley (1975).

Lakoff's work has encouraged and inspired research in several areas.

One is **gender patterns in conversational styles and strategies,** including turn-taking, topic selection and control, minimal responses/backchannel behaviour/sympathetic circularity, interruption and overlapping speech, and the initiation and ending of conversation. Studies have tended to find that women are far less domineering in conversation and tend to favour cooperative or supportive participation. Coates (1993) provides an excellent starting-point on these issues, and Coates (1996) gives a more detailed account. Johnson and Meinhof (1996) explore the issues from the hitherto neglected male perspective. **Politeness** also reveals gender patterns. Although 'politeness' clearly involves more than saying 'please', 'may I' and so on, writers differ in what they put under this heading. Holmes (1995) considers 'hedges' and 'tag questions', apologies and compliments as politeness features, whereas Coates (1993), for example, sometimes classifies them differently. Findings on these features have usually suggested that women use more politeness strategies than men. As regards **talkativeness,** Western society often stereotypes women as the more talkative gender. However, research has frequently indicated that this is not the case. Summaries of key studies on these issues can be found in Coates (1993, ch. 6) and Spender (1985). Coates and Cameron (1989, ch. 8) and Johnson and Meinhof (1996) cover 'gossip' from female and male perspectives respectively. **Swearing and taboo language** is another of Lakoff's themes where folk-linguistic beliefs seem to be undermined by research findings, though there are relatively few key studies so far on this topic. Both genders seem to swear more in single-sex company than in mixed, but there is only limited evidence to support the view that men swear more than females overall (see Coates 1993, ch. 6).

PROJECTS

243. One interesting issue is whether there are gender differences in forms of address. Brouwer *et al.* (1979) investigated politeness and forms of address used by males and females at the ticket office of Amsterdam Central Station. Both ticket sellers and customers were studied. Find an environment where you could collect data from a large number of transactional exchanges (do you know anyone who owns a shop or works in a bar and can give you permission to observe or record exchanges?). You might find yourself looking at a relatively small range of speech features and variations, but your work would have a clear focus and the features would be easy to count. Remember to consider the ethics of recording in specific environments (are you likely to capture material which you shouldn't record without the speaker's consent?) and problems with background noise if you are using a tape recorder.

244. As noted above, there are still relatively few studies on swearing and taboo language. Observe a mixed group of friends, and examine the frequency of swearing, the 'strength' of the terms used (this could be evaluated by a questionnaire to the subjects after recording) and the parts of speech which swear words typically occupy (such as noun, verb or adjective). Are there male–female differences in any of these criteria?

245. To examine single- and mixed-sex conversational strategies, try the following procedure. Ask a small group of mutual friends, half of them male and the other female, to your house for a meal. Ask the females to arrive earlier than the males (or vice versa) and record their conversation. When the other gender group arrives, record some mixed-sex conversation and, at some point, arrange for the first group to leave the room. You can then record the second group talking. This methodology has the advantage of using the same informants for each gender in both the single- and mixed-sex interactions, and gives you data-sets from the same time and context.

Explanations of difference

There have been various explanations of gender differences in language, starting with those claiming the mental or cognitive inferiority of women. Subsequent explanations were less judgemental, but suggested that biologically programmed tendencies or properties account for the differences (see Coates 1993, ch. 3). Explanations of gender differences in language *acquisition* commonly fall into this category too (see below). Accounts in the 1960s and 1970s focused on women's status in society. Trudgill (1972) suggested that women's greater tendency to use prestige forms was the result of the profile of their lives: they were less likely to be able to signal their status via their occupation, so they did so by the way they spoke. Lakoff (1975) suggested that women's social inequality made them unassertive, and her work has become associated with so-called 'dominance' explanations. Some women reacted to this viewpoint by trying to eliminate the 'female' characteristics from their language style, and by striving to be more assertive, which often meant copying male speech strategies. O'Barr and Atkins (1980) used data from courtrooms to suggest that Lakoff's features related not to gender but status, and proposed that they be renamed **powerless language**. However, subsequent research has challenged this (see Coates 1993, ch. 6).

In the 1980s there was some re-evaluation of the features of **women's language**. Coates, for example, has stressed the co-operative (rather than weak or unassertive) nature of female style (see Coates 1993, ch. 6; Coates 1996; Coates and Cameron 1989; Cameron 1995). This links with accounts of how children are pushed towards different interactional styles by socialization in predominantly single-sex groups (see Maltz and Borker 1982). In making sense of all these explanations, one very useful framework to be aware of is Tajfel's theory of inter-group relations and social change, which is described in Coates (1993, ch. 1).

PROJECT

246. Investigate the language of an informant who has an untypical male lifestyle (for example, acting as prime child-carer). Does he display any of the characteristics of the typical female cooperative style? If so, is the style 'female' at all, or just the product of a social role (Coates 1993: 4), and is he displaying female language because of his role; or does he find the role more comfortable than most men because of his 'female side'?

Language and sexism

Sexist language can be sought in adverts, film dialogue, posters, comedy, many types of written document and conversation. Some sexism is inherent in language, such as the generic *he* in English. Graddol and Swann (1989) point out that English 'has no direct feminine equivalent of *virility*' to reflect female sexual potency (p. 110). Some research investigates how derogatory or potentially patronizing terms are applied to women. One antidote to sexism in language has been political correctness. Is political correctness a good thing? What do people understand it to be in relation to gender? Does it change attitudes? You can read about these issues in Lakoff (1975, especially Part I, section 3), Spender (1985), Graddol and Swann (1989, ch. 5), Smith (1985, ch. 3) and (in less detail) Freeborn *et al.* (1993).

PROJECTS

247. Investigate the forms of address used with men and women of equivalent positions and ages. If there are differences, could they be linked to sexism?

248. Investigate the assumptions made about gender for people in certain jobs. Examples would be a nurse, cleaner, mechanic, hairdresser, brain surgeon, judge and so on. Does the vocabulary of English offer the possibility of non-sexist job-descriptions?

249. Ask two groups of different ages to provide specific types of terms for men and women (for example, relating to sexual promiscuity or untidy personal appearance). Does your data bear out the claim that there are more derogatory terms for women, and that they are considered 'stronger'? If there are differences between the two age groups, what is the significance of these?

250. If you have a working knowledge of another language, focus on one of the above issues from the perspective of speakers of that language, and compare the results with patterns identified in English which you have found in textbooks.

Gender-differentiated language in first-language acquisition

Much of the research into the **acquisition of structures** has focused on the rate of development of grammar, phonology or lexis. Early work either assumed or suggested that girls acquire language faster and better than boys, perhaps because of earlier maturation. However, later research has questioned whether girls' acquisition patterns are markedly superior at all. For a summary of views see Coates (1993, ch. 7) and Wells (1986b). Research on **communicative competence** concerns how girls and boys learn what it means to speak and write appropriately for their gender in a given society. Edelsky (1976) investigated how children perceived stereotypes of male and female language and how these perceptions might influence them (see Coates 1993, Swann 1992). There is some evidence that girls become aware far earlier than boys of the need to 'style shift' towards standard pronunciation in formal contexts (Romaine 1984, ch. 4).

Other studies have focused on how parents speak to children of each gender and the way they encourage girls and boys to speak to others. One question has been whether parents provide a good model of the language they require from their children (for example, does the father constantly tell his son not to interrupt his sister and then interrupt her himself?). Wells's (1986b: 124) study on when and with which gender parents will initiate conversations found a focus on 'helping/non-play' activities with girls and on 'playing with an adult' contexts with boys. Recent studies on **socialization** have suggested that girls and boys are socialized in single-sex peer groups, and that this is a key means by which they learn how to talk like boys and girls. Coates (1993, ch. 7) reviews studies suggesting that adult female 'cooperative discourse' can already be seen in the ways in which girls' peer groups are structured and in the activities they engage in.

PROJECTS

251. Conduct a case study of a pair of mixed-sex twins. By studying brother and sister you eliminate extra-linguistic variables, like differences in social background and family structure. If, in spite of both subjects belonging to the same family, there are differences in their stages of language development (see Chapter 3), accent and dialect or conversational style, is it reasonable to attribute these to the gender differences? What else might have caused them (for example, parental models, friends, other models from TV)? You may have to be satisfied with tentative suggestions, rather than a proven answer.

252. Compare male and female children of the same age, background and educational level describing a picture or retelling a story they have previously watched on video. Do the girls exhibit the sorts of style features found in adult female language? Is the boys' language different in specific ways and, if so, how would you evaluate the differences?

Language, gender and education

Are gender differences in children's oral and written language the result of boys and girls being treated differently by teachers? Conversely, do teachers treat boys and girls differently because the children use language differently in the first place? Both of these questions make the assumptions that teachers might or do treat girls and boys differently, and that there are indeed gender differences in the children's output, so the major part of any study on this must be to establish if this is so. Related issues are: whether teachers exercise as much equality as they intend to or believe they do; strategies that boys use to get more conversational turns than girls in classroom settings; and the implications, for their educational achievement, of girls' tendency to be more quiet and passive than boys in the classroom (see Coates 1993 and Swann 1992).

White (1986) explores the ways in which some girls' literacy skills, combined with more modest career expectations, lead them into low-status secretarial jobs rather than other professions, and the extent to which girls' literacy skills lead them away from science-based topics at school, college or university (see Swann 1992). Changes in educational curricula, such as in the National Curriculum in Britain, which upgrade the value of 'female' oracy skills like cooperative discourse features (see Swann 1992), may lead to some interesting developments.

PROJECTS

253. Study the types of reading material (such as fiction or non-fiction, and sub-genres within these) used by a mixed group of children. How far can you identify patterns of preference, according to gender, for particular types of material? Can these be linked in any way to styles of language (such as descriptive, imaginative or factual)? What might the implications of your findings be?

254. Investigate how a group of girls and boys feel about the writing tasks they are asked to do at school. Which tasks do they enjoy most, and why? Collect samples of their writing and analyse the styles, or the presentation, punctuation, spelling, use of non-standard grammar and so on. Do any trends emerge?

TECHNIQUES FOR COLLECTING DATA

|12|

Tape-recording data

Audio and video recording is a support to many types of work, where it may save the researcher from having to make frantic notes at the time and risk missing important information. But in linguistics, where the speech itself is the subject of analysis, it is especially important to have a good quality recording. Recorded data is suitable for a range of projects, including those in:

- first-language acquisition
- second-language acquisition
- sociolinguistics
- accent and dialect studies
- conversation analysis.

A major issue, clearly, is the extent to which your recording provides you with naturalistic material. In actual fact, the inhibitions associated with informants knowing that they are being recorded are usually fairly short-lived. Therefore, although you may want to consider concealing your microphone or camera, do not assume that this is the only way of getting the data you need. Most people will soon forget about the recording as they become involved in the activities.

Places to get data

Provided you take note of possible problems due to such things as background noise (see below), the following sources may furnish interesting data: your family home, a pub, a train, a café, the radio, old recordings, a school, schools' programmes on TV, an old people's home, the house of an old person, a student room, a club or meeting, a consultation, and so on.

Audio or video?

In most circumstances audio data is sufficient, but it is certainly worth considering using video equipment. On the whole, you will get better quality sound from audio recordings, but if you have several informants, especially children, it may be difficult to tell their voices apart if there is no visual corroboration.

Ethics and legality

There are important ethical considerations when it comes to recording people. Either ask their permission first or, if you feel that your data will be less 'genuine' if they know you are recording, ask them afterwards. You should be prepared to let them hear what you have recorded and you must give them the option of asking for part, or all, of it to be erased.

Recording from the radio or television does not entail such ethical problems, as broadcasts are in the public domain. However, broadcast material is copyright, and if you intend to use it in a publication or other public presentation you should ask the permission of the relevant broadcasting company.

Quality

Golden rule number one in collecting recorded data is to remember that you will have to listen to it *over and over again*, till you're sick of it. You will need to listen for detail, so it must be well-recorded, otherwise background noise will increasingly become a problem. When you are deciding where to record, think about the noise implications. Pubs, trains, cafes, schools and old people's homes can offer wonderful opportunities for natural conversation or interviews, but they can also be excessively noisy, so do a trial recording before you commit yourself to collecting the data there.

Practicalities

- Use a good machine, and make sure you know how it operates. If it runs on batteries, carry sufficient spares to change the entire set at once.
- Use new, good-quality tapes, and ensure you have plenty. If you will use several, label them in advance and use them in order. In any case, make sure all your data tapes are labelled by the end of the day, or you will forget which is which.
- Consider using two machines, with the second one set up ready to

record. When the tape in the first machine is nearly finished, the second is turned on, so there is a short overlap which helps with continuity later. This avoids the panic of changing over a tape quickly, and the loss of material while the leader tape runs through. It also reduces the problem of interviewees being abruptly reminded that they are being recorded. Another obvious advantage is that you can still continue with the collection even if one machine breaks down.

- Avoid recording on dictaphone, as the quality is poor even before the data is transferred onto normal-sized cassettes. If you are recording digitally, check that your assessors have the means to play it back!
- If possible, use an external microphone. In particular, try to avoid using a machine with a built-in condensor mike that is right next to the motor, as the background hum will be a problem.
- If using video, consider whether you want to hand-hold the camera (more flexible but quite intrusive) or put it on a tripod (leaving you free, but risking the action falling outside the frame).
- If you decide to conceal a camera or tape recorder, plan carefully how you will achieve this. If there is any danger of it being discovered midway through the recording, or if you will have trouble secretly retrieving it afterwards, you might be better off making it visible in the first place.
- Where possible, get informants to identify themselves on the tape, so that you have a reference to link their voice and their name later. When a new speaker contributes, make a note of their name and the tape counter number.
- You may want to plan to collect data from more subjects than you need, in case anything goes wrong with the recording.
- Make a copy onto another tape of just those parts of the data that you are focusing on; this avoids getting lost in endless fast-forwarding and reversing.

Things to think about

- How well do you know your informants? It can save a lot of time if you already know them, and many friends and family members will be pleased to help you with your research. On the other hand, a small child who knows you well may mess around, whereas one who knows you less well might be more co-operative.
- If recording in a public place, remember that not everyone will necessarily take kindly to being on your recording!
- Particularly if there is a high risk of extraneous noise, find, or ask for, a quiet room if possible.
- Plan carefully who you will record, how long for, and what the agenda will be.

- TV and radio programmes provide good-quality sound. Remember that the sound from a TV doesn't come out of the screen where the mouths are, but from a speaker, often round the side or back!
- Scripted speech may not be appropriate to your study, so if you are recording from the radio or TV, look through the schedules to find the most appropriate times to record.
- If you want accent features from TV or radio, target 'passer-by' interviews on news broadcasts, schools programmes which use interviews with children, and 'fly-on-the-wall' documentaries, because these will provide good-quality, naturalistic data from ordinary members of the public.
- Just as you can choose the *source* of your data, so you can also choose what *type* of data you collect. Here are some possibilities: natural conversation (with or without your presence or participation); structured interview (plan what questions you are going to ask); unstructured interview; scripted material, and so on.

How much data do you need?

How long is a piece of string? Be practical. Know what sorts of features you are looking for, and listen to your data as it is collected, in order to gauge how many examples of those features you have accumulated. However much data you collect, expect to analyse no more than 3 to 5 minutes' worth unless you are specifically analysing features that are intrinsic to longer stretches, such as (some) features of conversation.

- If you are simply collecting conversation data, bear in mind that although every conversation is valid in its own right, and therefore it ought to be possible simply to record the first 5 minutes of any conversation, you can help yourself by going for interesting features such as story-telling or argument.
- If you are studying accent you only need a small quantity of recording, because a large proportion of it is likely to be relevant to your needs. However, remember that some of the sounds you will want to find examples of in order to fill in the phoneme chart (Chapter 17) may be quite rare, and it will be frustrating if you find you have too little data to provide everything you need.
- For dialect studies you may need a longer recording, because certain forms and structures may not appear in a 5-minute stretch. Seriously consider doing a structured interview to elicit specific forms. This can be done entirely directly, by saying 'how do you say that'? or by steering the conversation towards certain topics (see Chapter 15).
- If you plan to record on more than one occasion, transcribe or do a preliminary analysis of the data you already have before you get the next lot, as this may help you to see what you still need.

Eliciting data from informants

Interviewing informants is a sensible way to be up-front about the recording aspect. For guidelines on interviewing techniques, see Chapter 15.

|13|

Experiments

Conducting experiments can be very rewarding, but it can be a nightmare if the procedures are not carefully planned and executed at every stage. Do not embark on experimental research unless you have a good supervisor who is, him- or herself, experienced in it. It is vital to design your experiment with your focus firmly on what you will do with the results, as this will determine how you run it. The point of running experiments is to cut to a minimum the natural variation between people and/or situations. You control as many variables as possible and carefully manipulate one (or more) in order to ascertain precisely what effect that variable has on the overall result. The trickiest variable in any behavioural science is the individual person. No single individual can be guaranteed to produce behaviour that is representative of the population as a whole, but if you pool the results from quite a lot of subjects it is likely that they will average out into something that *is* representative.

The skill in running experiments lies in making sure that, except for the factor being investigated, the subjects are compatible and are treated the same way, so that any differences that are noted between two groups under comparison are not attributable to any unintentional variation. For example, if you wanted to compare women with men on some language-based task, it would be important to ensure that there was no major difference in the average age of the two groups or in their educational background, experience or other attributes. If the women performed better than the men and then it turned out that the women were all university graduates in their twenties, whilst the men were all in their sixties and had left school at 14, it would not be possible to determine which of those variables (gender, age or education) accounted for the difference in performance.

Experiments are appropriate for studies in:

- psycholinguistics
- first-language acquisition

- second-language acquisition
- semantics
- some areas of sociolinguistics, including language and gender.

What does experimentation involve?

Subjects

Normally, you will use ordinary people, representative of the general population or some subset of it. Even if you are investigating behaviour that should be the same for everyone, gathering a sample of practical size that genuinely represents the whole population is virtually impossible, so if it is easiest to only use, say, female undergraduates, do so. Just acknowledge the limitations of your subject pool in your write-up, stating that you recognize that it represents only one sub-group of society.

You need a statistically viable number of subjects: what this is depends on the statistical tests you intend to use, so you must decide that first. If the statistics require numbers that are too large to manage, you may be allowed to compromise (check with your supervisor) by using smaller numbers and clearly stating the limitations which they impose on your calculations.

Procedure

You must have a clear-cut, well-planned experiment from the outset. Make it simple and don't be tempted to complicate it while you're running it. It will become complicated of its own accord once you take some basic procedures into account! You should be able to explain in one sentence what you intend to find out and in another one, how you intend to do it.

The task should be carefully chosen to be appropriate to the abilities of the subjects. Plan meticulously and run through the steps in a rehearsal and/or pilot study (see Chapter 1). Locate a suitable environment: this must be available when you need it and be within your control. If you use a language lab, make sure you can operate the machinery; if you use a quiet room, make sure the porter/caretaker/secretary will not come and turn you out midway; if you use your own room, negotiate with your flatmates and unplug the phone. If you are testing subjects in sequence, think ahead about the problems of an appointment system – what if someone is late or doesn't show up? If they're early, will they interrupt proceedings and/or overhear something they shouldn't? Decide if you need an assistant, and if you do, brief him or her thoroughly. An assistant might keep subjects out of the room till the appropriate time, present stimuli or take notes.

Equipment

You may need equipment for the presentation of stimuli (a tape player, a computer screen, flash-cards, toys, and so on) and/or the collection of data (such as a timer, a video camera, a tape recorder). Some procedures used in the published research rely on complex equipment. For example, dichotic listening tests (dlts) entail the subject hearing different stimuli in each ear simultaneously and giving a timed response. Setting this up is a specialized job. Computers can display words or pictures for timed periods and can record reactions to them, accurate to one-tenth of a second. Fairly simple programs can achieve this. More complex programs are needed for presenting stimuli to one visual field only. Be practical about what you can achieve and if necessary, use the old, pre-technology methods of, say, flash-cards and (if it will give sufficient accuracy) a stop-watch. As always, take advice on what is expected of you and how best to achieve your objectives.

Advantages of experimental research

- The history of science in the western world clearly demonstrates how important experimental investigation is seen to be. Indeed, there are many who find it hard to conceive of valid research that is *not* experimental.
- A well-planned experiment gives you results that can be processed in a pre-selected way and provides clear evidence for or against a pre-specified hypothesis.
- There are (in theory) no loose ends or awkward corners, and results are easy to relate to each other and to other experiments done in the same way.
- A clearly described experiment can be improved upon in future work or replicated by others.
- Experimental data is much more focused than, say, a recording of spontaneous speech or informal interview/activity data, so it is easier to make sense of, to process and evaluate.

Disadvantages of experimental research

- Experiments pare the situation down to its bare minimum. Some situations can be treated in this way, but others can't; there is a danger that in the process of controlling the experimental design you lose the very essence of what you are trying to examine.
- It is easy to measure the behaviour of people operating in experimental conditions, but how could you compare it to their behaviour in *non*-experimental conditions? (You couldn't do it by experiment, so what would be your basis for comparison?)

- Experiments usually end up being harder than they look, and it is easy to bite off more than you can chew.
- The more subjects you have, the less likely you are to know a lot about them; there may be hidden variables contributing to your pattern of results. Experiments on people are always subject to much more 'unexplained' variation than those on white rats or vials of potassium permanganate, and they are liable to give ambiguous results. There is a good chance that when you have made your calculations there will be no statistically significant differences at all. However, this *does not* mean that your experiment has been a failure. You can write it up with every bit as much confidence as you would if you had made a major new discovery.
- Some people (children, for example) do not make good experimental subjects; they may have too short an attention span, feel uneasy about being tested, or be inhibited with a researcher.
- It can be difficult to be sure, before you analyse the results, that a subject has really understood what he or she is supposed to do.
- Avoiding design faults, such as potential ambiguities in the stimuli or instructions, can be difficult.

Designing an experiment

If possible, base your experimental design on one that has been run before. You can try to match it exactly (**replication**) or alter one dimension. Published experimental reports vary as to how much information they give you regarding exactly what was done and what stimuli were used, so you may only be able to approximate to previous work. Try to identify in it, however, what they felt was central to the experimental design. Experimental comparisons can be made in different ways, and may require different statistical treatments (see Chapter 23). The major comparisons are:

Two identical groups . . .

The assumption is that the two groups would perform the same way given the same conditions and input, so that if you *vary* the conditions or input, that is why their performance varies. Assigning people to groups can be done randomly if the numbers are large enough. Alternatively, share the genders and ages equally between the groups. Do the same for any other factor that you feel could be relevant (such as ethnic origin, past experience, educational background or handedness). Don't go mad, though: hair colour and favourite ice-cream flavour are unlikely to have a bearing on most experiments!

. . . Doing different things

Here, the experiment is based on the assumption that Group A would perform like Group B if it was given Group B's task and vice versa. The reason for not giving both groups both tasks (which is certainly permissible in the right circumstances) is that doing one task spoils you for doing the other. Example: memorizing household items on a tray, compared with memorizing the names of those objects on a list (see project 2 in Chapter 2).

. . . Doing the same thing in different conditions

There are several variations on this, including the following:

- Both groups perform the same task, but Group A is prepared one way, Group B another: do different things happen? (Look at project 27.)
- Group A undergoes a process (such as training), Group B doesn't: do different things happen? Here, B is acting as 'control' group, against which the effect of a process can be measured: in medical trials one group receives the new drug and another receives a dummy (placebo) drug, to see whether any recovery is due to the drug itself or due to the patient's reaction to being treated (as in project 3).
- Both groups complete the same task, but the conditions under which they complete it are different (see project 1).

Two groups that are different in some specific way, doing the same thing

Here, you want to keep the stimuli, training and procedures the same and just compare the effect of being a Group A person as opposed to a Group B person. You need to be able to explain *why* you think the two groups might perform differently: are you assuming that their brains are wired up differently? that different lifetime experiences will influence their behaviour? that one group will have more confidence than the other? Examples: a comparison of children of different ages; a comparison of males with females; a comparison of native speakers with non-native speakers.

One group doing two different tasks, or one task in two different conditions

This is appropriate where doing the first task (or in the first condition) will not invalidate the results of the second. It is best to take precautions, however, against possible order and practice effects (see below). For example: subjects recite familar nursery rhymes (or days of the week) and a poem they've only just memorized while bouncing a table-tennis ball on a bat: is their physical accuracy different when they have to think more about what to say next?

Using published results as your control

If you are replicating a published experiment, you can compare your results with those in the original, instead of building a comparison into your own experiment. However, this really does require you to have matched your stimuli, subjects and conditions very closely with those of the work you are replicating.

More than two groups?

You can compare more than two groups or conditions, but this complicates the results because each group and condition needs comparing with each other one.

Things to think about

- Will you tell your subjects what you're looking for before they do the experiment? What effect would it have? If you *don't* tell them, are they likely to try and guess (thereby adjusting their behaviour in uncontrollable ways)?
- Will your subjects be intimidated by the experimental setup? How can you alleviate this without compromising the rigour of the experiment?
- Are your stimuli unambiguous? For example, young children may have difficulty interpreting line drawings. Do the stimuli reflect any cultural and social stereotypes that may be inappropriate for some of your subjects?
- What exactly are you testing? How will you know if you have found an effect? Does your experiment really measure what you intended? How will you score or assess the data?
- Where are you going to get enough subjects and will they be homogeneous enough?
- How will subjects, parents, teachers and so on feel about the 'testing' dimension? Can you explain clearly your plans and how the data will be used?
- Where can you run it? Do you intend to bring the subjects to one unfamiliar place, so that none of them have the advantage of feeling at home? Can you avoid external interruptions?
- Will you have to run the experiment lots of times (on individuals or small groups)? If so, how will you ensure that all the conditions are identical each time?

- Do you need special skills or techniques for presenting the stimuli (with child subjects, in operating puppets convincingly, for example)?
- Look after your data: summarize your data into clear tables and remember to label them fully. Refer to the content of the tables explicitly, pointing out the important information. Do calculations carefully and check them. Make sure that totals tally.

Order effects

If one group is doing more than one task, or in more than one condition, or with a series of stimuli, how are you to be sure that any differences you find are not simply to do with the order in which the tasks or stimuli were presented? The most straightforward way to cancel out order effects is to split the group in two and present the tasks or conditions in one order to one group and the other order to the other. Then add the results together. If subjects always scored better on, say, the first task or condition, then the differences will cancel out, because half the subjects will have done one task or condition first and half the other.

Floor and ceiling effects

If you make a task too difficult, then everyone will score zero and you'll have nothing to compare! This is called the 'floor' effect. If it is too easy, everyone will score the maximum and the same problem will occur. This is called the 'ceiling' effect. Your task should be pitched so that everyone performs well within the range of possible performances (so that, say, if the score potential is 0–20 then the lowest score is about 3 and the highest about 17). Don't expect to know intuitively how to achieve this: that's what a pilot study is for (see Chapter 1).

Practice and fatigue effects

If you were to draw a graph of an individual's performance in a task, you wouldn't be surprised to find that they performed better as they got more accustomed to the task (the 'practice' effect) and worse as they got tired and/or bored (the 'fatigue' effect). Provided that everyone's scores went up and down symmetrically for practice and fatigue and that everyone practised and fatigued at the same rate up to and from the same point in the procedures, you could find a way of making allowances for this. But people aren't like that! However, there are ways of reducing the potential of these two effects to skew the results:

- Give everyone some practice sessions, so that they don't use the experiment itself to build up to speed.

- Design the experiment so that the activities don't go on too long. Obviously, you can't pre-empt at what stage people will become tired, but you can use a pilot study to ensure that you don't seriously over-step the mark.
- If some important types of stimuli are positioned at the beginning of the test, and there is a general tendency for the scores to be lower than on later ones, you will not be able to tell whether this is due to the nature of the stimuli or the practice effect. Counter this by dividing the different types of stimuli randomly across the test and having different random orders for two randomly split groups. The idea is that a practice or fatigue effect will show on the first or last stimuli irrespective of what those stimuli are, while a genuine stimulus-specific effect should show up on those specific stimuli irrespective of when they are presented. Do not aim to run statistical comparisons on the two groups who get the stimuli in different orders. The results should be pooled, to minimize the effect of those orders.

Emergencies

It can be very distressing if, after all your hard work, your experiment 'goes wrong', whether that simply means that you can't support your hypothesis or that the procedure is actually unworkable, though the latter can be avoided in most cases by running a pilot study. Unforeseen circumstances such as a fire in the building or a breakdown of the equipment are just bad luck. However, many apparent 'disasters' are salvageable:

- If the results are inconclusive, that is a result in itself – maybe the phenomenon is not as you foresaw or is not measurable in the way you thought. Try to find some possible reasons why you got what you did, especially identifying whether there was any problem with the experimental design. This is how real research actually works: you use each experiment as a way of understanding the bigger picture and working out what to do next time.
- If the procedure has gone completely awry, you may have time (or be able to negotiate time) to re-run the experiment, in which case you can treat the original as a(nother) pilot; alternatively, you may be able to salvage some of the results.
- If there really is nothing to show for it, obviously you need to negotiate with your tutor, but do so in the confidence that anyone who has run experiments has experienced bad luck or bad judgement and so you should get a sympathetic hearing. Offer to write up the experimental design critically and discuss what the various possible results *would have meant*. Add a section on ways in which problems of the kind you experienced could be avoided in the future.

- Occasionally, an experiment turns out to have been a poor way of finding out the thing it was designed for, but incidentally to have ended up measuring something else. So consider whether it is possible to find other patterns in it: you may find that you have another experiment embedded within the one you actually ran. Obviously, however, be careful with this strategy and take advice, because it is not difficult to end up with something that is too far from the real world to be acceptable.

|14|

Questionnaires

In this chapter we look at the general design of questionnaires and issues relating to administering written and spoken questionnaires.

What is a questionnaire?

A questionnaire is 'a set of questions on a topic or group of topics designed to be answered by a respondent' (Richards *et al.* 1992: 303). At their most tightly controlled, questionnaires can allow data to be collected in the same, replicable way from a large number of informants. This makes comparison of the results easier and conclusions clearer.

Students sometimes seem to view questionnaires as an easy way to avoid having to transcribe lengthy tapes of 'messy' conversation data and/or engage in 'technical' (grammatical, phonetic or other) analysis. However, questionnaires are neither as restricted nor as straightforward as this view implies. Furthermore, many linguists feel that questionnaires are best used in association with other types of data elicitation (see, for example, Milroy 1987a:10; Saville-Troike 1989:129), because a fuller picture of the data can be accessed if it is approached from more than one angle. Because of this, questionnaires often do not operate as a substitute for transcription and analysis, but rather complement them.

Using questionnaires should not be embarked upon lightly, for they are difficult to handle well. 'Designing questionnaires which are valid, reliable and unambiguous is a very important issue' (Richards *et al.* 1992: 303).

What research areas can a questionnaire be used for?

- Traditional dialectology, to help produce linguistic maps and atlases.
- Urban dialectology, to elicit information on how speakers' accents and

dialects may change between informal and formal situations, vary according to sex, age and social background, and change over time.

- Sociolinguistic work on attitudes towards language, including such matters as non-standard accents and dialects (see Hughes and Trudgill 1996: 9; Fasold 1984, ch. 6; Giles *et al.* 1975), slang, new vocabulary or pronunciations, female *vs.* male speech features (see Coates 1993; Edelsky 1976), dying or minority languages (see Romaine 1995: 302–19) and multilingualism.
- Second- or foreign-language teaching and learning, including the importance of motivation for the successful learning of a language (see Fasold 1984; Lambert *et al.* 1968), and needs analysis and assessment (see Richards *et al.* 1992: 242–3).
- Language surveys, investigating, for example, which languages are spoken in a specific area, when these languages are used, and proficiency levels in the different generations of speakers (see Richards *et al.* 1992: 205).
- Ethnographic ('whole culture') research (see Chapter 7), where they are used to gather a wide range of information about aspects of specific cultures and societies, including linguistic data.

Subjects

Any subjects can be used, providing they are able to understand the questions and can provide responses (usually this means they are able to write and/or speak intelligibly in at least one language or dialect shared with the researcher). See Saville-Troike (1989: 123–9) for details of considerations and problems entailed in selecting subjects, including child respondents.

Although questionnaires can be used with any number of subjects, their true usefulness is with large numbers. A large sample will be more representative and can lend greater weight to your claims. The way you design and implement the questionnaire may depend on the number and type of subjects it is intended for.

As in most fieldwork, the subjects have to be selected carefully to ensure that as reliable and representative a sample as possible has been obtained. You may work either with a 'random' sample, where 'everyone in the population to be sampled has an equal chance of being selected' (Wardhaugh 1992: 153), or with a 'judgement' sample, where you select your participants according to your preferred criteria, or a range of representative criteria such as social class, age, gender or education. Wardhaugh (1992) points out that 'a judgement sample is obviously less adequate than a random sample' (p. 153).

If you use a judgement sample, you need to consider two major things: **compatibility** and **representativeness**. To ensure **compatibility**, you need, where feasible, to obtain at least minimal reliable background information on your subjects/respondents. To compare responses from a group there need to be some base-line features in common, so that it is clear why a comparison is valid. For example, if you were comparing attitudes to mother-tongue teaching in a Polish and an Indian community, it would make sense to ensure that all your interviewees had children, all used the mother-tongue to a similar extent at home, and perhaps, even, that all of them were of the same sex, as any of these variables could otherwise confound your results.

As you will normally be intending to make inferences, on the basis of your sample, about some larger group, your subjects must be representative of it. This is not always easy to achieve. Saville-Troike (1989) comments that 'often the people who make themselves most readily available to an outsider are those who are marginal to the community, and may thus convey inaccurate or incomplete information' (p. 127). She also notes that such 'marginal' group members may 'interfere with the acceptance of the researcher by other members of the group'.

Handling personal information

In seeking personal information, a balance needs to be found between getting what you need and being intrusive or costing people time and extra work. With child subjects, be aware that they may not even know their own name and address, and that school records may not be up to date.

If you promise anonymity or confidentiality to subjects, you must ensure that this is achieved in full. Anonymity means you will not request the respondents' names; but it also precludes you from using any sort of code number that can lead even you back to an identity for each respondent. If you feel you will need to know, for example, who has and who has not returned their questionnaire, or if you may need to do follow-up interviews, then do not offer anonymity, but rather confidentiality. This means that you can know who is who, but you will make it impossible for anyone else to do so. You might favour the anonymous completion of questionnaires when, for example, you are investigating delicate issues, such as names for intimate parts of the body. It is often assumed that respondents will be more candid when anonymous. However, they can also be less responsible, and you may be left unsure about the validity of their answers.

Presenting a questionnaire

Questionnaires can be constructed and administered in various forms. One basic division is between those presented and completed orally and those that are in written form. However, it is also possible to have a mixture of the above by, for example, administering the questions in writing and having the respondents record their spoken responses on audio or video cassette, or administering the questions orally and having the respondent write the responses down.

A further distinction is between those questionnaires administered by the researcher and those completed in his or her absence. If the researcher is to be present, then a large time commitment is entailed. This could be an important consideration if a large number of subjects is involved. One possible way around the time problem is to administer the questionnaire simultaneously to a group rather than to individuals. This is not procedurally difficult where the answers are written down, and the questions can be presented to the subjects either orally or on paper.

There are a number of advantages to being present when the data is collected. With a 'captive' audience you are guaranteed a relatively high completion rate, and if anyone finds a question unclear you can explain what you meant and what type of answer is required. On the other hand, if the respondents have too many queries you may compromise the whole data-collection exercise, especially if, by trying to clarify a question, you unconsciously lead the respondents towards particular answers. Certainly, any discussion of this kind should be monitored carefully across different sessions of data collection, so that all respondents are given the same information.

If the researcher is *not* to be present the questionnaire can be administered by a proxy, sent out and returned by post, or handed to the respondents for completion in their own time. The advantages of this include the possibility of reaching individuals from a much larger geographical area than it would be possible to bring together in one place or visit in person. However, there are several disadvantages too.

First, you will probably have a low response rate (perhaps only 20 to 30 per cent), simply because the questions have left your hands. Second, the return rate may be further jeopardized if even a single question is judged at all confusing or intrusive. Because of this, any questionnaire completed in the repondent's own time must be carefully presented, with the questions clear and easy to answer, and the task appearing worthwhile. Third, where the response rate is low, this may skew the sample. Those who take the trouble to reply may, in doing so, be demonstrating a personality trait which will be reflected in the answers they give to the questions. Those who do not respond might have given different answers. Fourth, it may be impossible to ascertain whether the right person has filled the questionnaire out, whether the questions have been answered in the right order – this could be important, especially if **cross-referencing** questions (see below) have been included to monitor the informant's consistency – whether all the respondents have taken roughly the same amount of time to complete the form, whether all of them have done it in one sitting, and whether all of them have completed it in comparable circumstances: one might have done it in a rush over breakfast, while another took a relaxed approach one evening. Finally, leaving the administration of a questionnaire to someone else is a risk. No-one will understand the aims as clearly, or be as committed to obtaining good data, as you are. If you send out questionnaires to, say, teachers, for distribution to 'suitable subjects', you lose control of the balance and distribution of the subjects, and you may end up, unwittingly perhaps, with data that is biased (see Milroy 1987a: 11).

Try to be aware of how your respondents view questionnaires. They are relatively unfamiliar in some communities, and respondents may not be sure how to deal with them. Children may never have filled one in before. Some people may be suspicious of what looks like an official form. People with low levels of literacy, or whose native language is not that in which the questionnaire is written, may find the whole exercise intimidating. And people can suffer from 'questionnaire fatigue', if they have been confronted with too many other questionnaires before yours. This may make them less willing to take part or they may tend to give irresponsible answers.

Designing a questionnaire

You can learn a great deal about the design of questionnaires by considering your own response to the ones that you have had to complete in the past, whether on paper or in a street interview. For example, have you ever: not felt that any of the answers on offer actually reflected your view? not really understood what the question was getting at? not wanted to answer a particular question because it was too personal, painful or difficult? not really cared whether you gave accurate or truthful answers, because the whole thing seemed rather silly, or ill-thought-out? been reluctant to give certain details because the questioner wanted your name and address and you were worried about where the information would end up? These common reactions, and many others, can seriously compromise the success of a questionnaire survey. Do a careful pilot study (see Chapter 1) to ensure that you have not made it in any way difficult for your respondents to provide accurate and honest information.

Framing questions

- Questions must be simple and unambiguous. Be careful not to embed one question within another, so that it is possible for each part to require a different answer – you won't know which part has been answered. Also, avoid loaded questions, where one proposition has to be taken as true for the question to be answerable, such as *Why do people think that the Birmingham accent is unpleasant?*
- Wording can subtly influence the answer obtained if the respondent consciously or subconsciously detects an expectation or bias on your part. Questions like: *Do you think women swear less than men? Do you think that women are more polite than men? Do you think that women*

talk more than men? could build up a bias in the respondent's mind. In a question like: *If someone has a strong regional accent and dialect, don't you expect them to be from a lower social class?* the use of *don't* might lead an undecided informant to the answer *yes*, because it somehow appeared to be the 'right' answer.

- Do not try to fool your respondents – if they see through it they will feel compromised. There are certainly circumstances in which an 'agenda' is built into what appears to be an innocuous questionnaire, such as in charity advertising. A current Oxfam 'questionnaire' contains the following:

  – Oxfam believes that the only effective long-term answer to Third World poverty is to help poor people develop their own solution to their problems. Do you agree? Agree/Disagree
  – It can cost Oxfam as little as £2 a month, over a year, to help villages build wells to provide a clean, safe water supply for 12 people. Do you think this is expensive/about what you'd expect/good value for money?
  – Oxfam relies on public support to continue its fight against poverty throughout the world. Would you personally be willing to help Oxfam by giving just £2 a month? Yes/No.

These sorts of questions are very difficult to answer without painting yourself into a corner; unless you depict yourself as totally inhumane, you cannot avoid the implication that you should donate money. What is important to realize, however, is that the most common response by far to such a 'questionnaire' is to throw it in the bin. In writing your questionnaire, every measure must be taken to reduce the likelihood of this happening, so there must be no lingering agenda to make the respondent feel uneasy.

- If you provide a choice of answers, make sure that it covers all the possibilities. Try to imagine a range of different people trying to find an answer to match their precise circumstances.
- Begin the questionnaire with some easy questions, so that the respondents feel they are getting on well. If there are several harder or more time-consuming ones, space them out, or, alternatively, preface them with a statement such as: *The following three questions require slightly more detailed answers.* This indicates to the respondent the nature of the new task and how much of it there is.
- Include one or two **cross-referencing** questions, in which you ask, in different words, for the same information as in a previous question. This gives you a check on the reliability of the responses. It is often possible to 'turn the question round' so that a positive response in one version corresponds to a negative one in the other. Be particularly careful, however, that in doing this you do not alter the emphasis. For the answers to be comparable, you must have asked for exactly the same information.
- It is easy to end up with too few or too many questions for your needs. You need a clear idea of what information is necessary for a successful analysis, and all relevant questions must be included. Any questions that

are superfluous to your aim should be removed, as it is a waste of the respondents' time to answer them and of yours to process them. Use your pilot study (see Chapter 1) to fine-tune the coverage of the questionnaire in this regard.

Types of data

It is important to think carefully about the best way to get the information you need, and this includes deciding how explicit and/or truthful you will be about what you say you are looking for.

Direct (explicit) approach

There are certainly advantages to being straight and truthful about your study, as it reduces the risk that you are misunderstood. However, there can be disadvantages too. Saville-Troike (1989: 128) notes that respondents sometimes answer to please the fieldworker (**courtesy bias**) or deliberately try to mislead the researcher (**sucker bias**). In addition, if they associate the topic of the questionnaire with stigmatized issues or ones they strongly dislike, such as, say, political correctness, then they may feel negatively about participating. Even if you are unsure about stating why you are doing your study, you could still use direct questioning. You might simply ask your subjects directly about their opinions (for example what they think about one language or dialect as compared with another) without telling them why you are interested in knowing.

Indirect (inexplicit) approach

This means keeping your subjects from knowing what aspect of language is being focused on, or maybe even that language is the focus at all. A good example of this, involving the extent to which Muslim speakers of Hebrew and Arabic viewed Hebrew as a more effective language for scientific arguments, is cited in Fasold (1984: 149). The advantage of this approach is that the informants' responses are reliable in the sense that there is less motivation to hide or distort anything. On the other hand, it is more difficult to ensure that all your data is relevant, as the informants will certainly develop some sort of opinion about what you are looking for, and perhaps, in trying to be helpful, may go off at an irrelevant tangent.

Open and closed questions

A question is **open** if it does not require a one word or curtailed answer. An example would be *Describe your reactions to this speaker*, after a tape of the speaker's voice had been played. Advantages include the fact that the respondent has 'maximum freedom to present her views' (Fasold, 1984: 192), and that the researcher–respondent interaction can be quite like spontaneous conversation. This can reduce the risk of an **observer effect**, where the presence of the researcher makes a difference to what data is obtained. Disadvantages include the danger of digression, so that little of relevance is collected in the time available.

If the linguistic features under investigation (such as certain sounds, grammatical structures and so on), are likely to crop up frequently in spontaneous speech, then open questions are a good way to elicit **general** data (see Chapter 15). However, if your open questions are specifically about language, as opposed to simply being a means of stimulating the production of speech for later analysis, then you may find that the information they contain is too varied in form to be easily summarized or scored for.

A **closed** question can only be answered in a limited way, for example: *What do you call a baby sheep? What was the name of the woman in the story?* Traditional dialect studies developed two types of closed question. The **naming** type elicited either a single word or a slightly longer response, such as *What can you make from milk?* (butter, cheese); *What's the barn for and where is it?* (Chambers and Trudgill, 1980: 25–6). The **completing** type required the respondent to fill in a gap in a sentence structure to provide a desired lexical item, such as *You sweeten your tea with* _____ (Chambers and Trudgill, 1980: 25–6).

One drawback with all closed questions is that they can often be so directive as to be patronizing. Informants do not want to feel that they are being treated like an idiot; and you run the risk of receiving flippant, unhelpful answers. On the other hand, such questions obviously enable you to steer the interview with precision in whichever direction you choose. This is an advantage if you are primarily interested in the answers that you are given; but if you are just trying to stimulate general speech, then closed questions will give very little return. Another disadvantage of closed questions is that they prejudge the issues and possible responses. Open questions might reveal things you did not know were even there to ask about.

The reason why closed questions nevertheless remain a popular and valued means of gathering data is because they provide answers that are easier to process and score for. Closed questions make possible a range of formats for tallying and comparing responses. The following closed-question designs illustrate this.

SEMANTIC DIFFERENTIAL

This gauges respondents' subjective reactions to words, speakers' voices on tape, and so on. Respondents indicate their opinions or attitudes by locating their response on rating scales. The scale typically contains a pair of adjectives with opposite meanings, and the respondent indicates the approximate position on the continuum between the two in which their judgement falls (Fig. 14.1). For further information see Fasold (1984: 150–1, 177) and Richards *et al.* (1992: 328).

WORD (e.g. *democracy*)					
good	—	—	—	—	bad
weak	—	—	—	—	strong
rough	—	—	—	—	smooth
active	—	—	—	—	passive

Fig 14.1 Semantic differential
Source: Richards *et al.* (1992: 328)

In Fig. 14.2, where the ratings could indicate respondents' reactions to a voice heard on tape, the numbers indicate how scoring information can be added by the researcher *after* the questionnaire has been completed. This avoids influencing the informants, for example, into believing that a high number is a desirable number. Numbers make it easier to process the data. For fuller information on how information from semantic differentials can be analysed, what problems can arise and so on, see Fasold (1984: 150–2). For examples in second language research, see Larsen-Freeman and Long (1991: 35–6).

intelligent	–	–	–	–	–	–	–	unintelligent
	7	6	5	4	3	2	1	

Fig 14.2 Typical seven-point semantic differential scale
Source: Fasold (1984: 151)

LIKERT SCALE (ATTITUDE SCALE)

Like semantic differentials, this method elicits informants' subjective responses. A statement embodying an attitude is presented, and the respondents indicate how strongly they agree or disagree (Fig. 14.3). This kind of

Foreign languages are important for all educated adults.						
1	2	3	4	5	6	7
strongly disagree			agree			strongly agree

Fig 14.3 Likert scale
Source: Richards *et al.* (1992: 25)

question is commonly used in research into foreign-language learners' motivation (see, for example, Larsen-Freeman and Long 1991: 35–6).

NOTES ON USING SCALES

- Look carefully at the orientation of your Likert scale or semantic differential. Is the positive adjective (semantic differential) always on the same side of the scale? Does *strongly agree* always appear on the right (Likert scale)? It can seem like a good test of the respondents' attention to change the scale around (to ensure that they don't just go through the form without the reading the questions). However, in reality, if you do reverse the scale, you can sometimes see from optional comments that the respondents have not noticed the switch. Where this has occurred, their answers will not be valid, but it can be difficult to be entirely sure that they really have made a mistake and that they do not hold the view they have expressed, so you cannot really adjust their answer with confidence.
- You may be forcing people to choose from a range of responses none of which really fits their ideas. You will find that respondents sometimes complicate your subsequent processing of the data by altering your categories by hand, or by refusing to indicate a response on the scale.

RANKING SCHEMES

This approach will be familiar to you if you have ever entered a product promotion competition where you had to put a set of desirable features into their order of importance. In the linguistic domain, Dorian (1981) asked English/Gaelic speakers to order a set of 13 reasons for being a Gaelic speaker into their order of importance (see Dorian 1981: 166 and Romaine 1995: 313–14). For general information see Fasold (1984: 152).

MULTIPLE CHOICE

This is probably the most commonly used approach where unequivocal responses that can be automatically counted are required. The respondent is presented with a question or incomplete statement (**stem**) and must select the appropriate answer from a list of several possible alternatives (Fig. 14.4). The wrong answers are termed **distractors** (Richards *et al.* 1992:

I have known her_____three years now.

(a) whilst   (b) for   (c) since   (d) besides   (e) at

Fig 14.4 Multiple choice

239). This method yields non-subjective (that is, objective) responses to questions.

There are some pitfalls with this approach. Take a question like this: *Who is most likely to use standard English? (a) a judge (b) a doctor (c) a teacher (d) a docker.* The potential problem here is that the choices are strongly weighted towards stereotypes. Anyone who has these stereotypes will simply fulfil the built-in expectations of the question. Anyone without those stereotypes will be puzzled, and might end up writing *it depends.* Also, the alternatives appear in order of descending social status, with the person most likely to use standard English first.

TRUE/FALSE QUESTIONS

As the name implies, these require a 'true' or 'false' response. They can be used as objective questions, as shown in Fig. 14.5.

English sentences generally follow a Subject plus Verb plus Object order.

(circle the right answer)   True   False

Fig 14.5 True–false

YES/NO QUESTIONS

These are rarely useful in linguistic research, because, on their own, they give so little information. For example:

> *Do you think that women and men talk differently? Yes/ No/ Don't know.*

WHICH TO USE WHEN

The relative merits and problems inherent in open and closed questions mean that the most successful outcome can often be achieved by using open questions in a preliminary study, and then using the results from this to construct a closed questionnaire (Fasold 1984: 152).

Specific techniques

Matched guise technique

This is often used in association with a questionnaire investigation of language attitudes. Though the precise format may vary, the basic technique usually involves respondents being played recordings of voices and then being asked to evaluate them, using semantic differential scales (see above). The technique can reveal respondents' attitudes towards different language or dialect groups, for example. Respondents are commonly asked to evaluate speakers on a range of criteria including intelligence, friendliness, co-operativeness, reliability, honesty, and so on. On the basis of results from this type of test, several large companies have located their telephone sales or services departments in regions where the local accent is one associated with high ratings for intelligence, friendliness and trustworthiness.

The recordings typically involve a person speaking first in one dialect, accent or language and then in another (that is, in two 'guises'), giving the same information. The respondents must not realize that both recordings are made by the same person. See Fasold (1984: 149–58) for more information, variations on the technique and example studies (including ones where informants have not even been aware that they were participating in any sort of linguistic study). Hughes and Trudgill (1996: 9) and Wardhaugh (1992) also provide summary examples.

Self-evaluation tests/subjective reaction tests

These are often used in association with studies of actual language usage (such as regional accent and dialect) to establish whether respondents' evaluations and perceptions of their own language are accurate. For example, Trudgill (1974: 195–201) asked people whether they liked the way people spoke in Norwich. He then asked them to listen to pronunciations of words and state whether they used the pronunciations themselves. Finally, he asked them to give opinions on ten sets of words and to tick the form they thought was correct and underline the form they would use, whether or not it was the same form.

Things to think about

- It is very important to run a pilot study (see Chapter 1).
- As in most fieldwork, respondents will tend to behave in a more relaxed and perhaps more typical manner if they are familiar with the researcher. By getting to know a group of potential respondents, you can target the most suitable ones more easily. A period of familiarization may therefore be useful before you begin the data collection. This is obviously not possible if you send out questionnaires to people you do not know.
- Research over the last 30 years has highlighted the effects of *mismatch* between interviewer and respondent in terms of age, sex, ethnic origin, education level, accent, dialect, native language and so on (see, for

example, Saville-Troike 1989: 124–9 and Labov 1969). This is something to be aware of. For example, the gender of researchers in traditional and later dialectological work has probably biased the selection of informants as well as the choice of language issue and the overall methodology (see Coates 1993, ch. 3).

Relating the questionnaire to the study

Since questionnaires can be used for a variety of purposes, and can take on different forms for each, the best way to find out how to tailor a questionnaire to the specific task is to read about other work in the same area. Work on local dialect forms and local accent forms is reported in Montgomery (1995: 79 ff.) and Trudgill (1994). A large number of questionnaire studies, dealing both with 'real' accent and dialect data, and with attitudes towards language, are reviewed in Fasold (1984). For information on eliciting a range of speech styles see Trudgill (1974: 195–201) or Wardhaugh's (1992: 151–2) description of the same work. The methodology for investigating motivation and attitudes in second- or foreign-language learners is described in Larsen-Freeman and Long (1991: 35–6) and Lambert *et al.* (1968). For examples of work on bilingualism, see Romaine (1995: 301–19).

Written questionnaires

These can be expensive to administer, as you need multiple copies of the questionnaire form, produced on a good-quality photocopier, and a possibly also a supply of pens if it is being completed in your presence, a stamped addressed envelope for each form if it is to be returned by post, and a covering letter or other form of explanation of who you are, what you are doing and why, and why the respondents' help will be so valuable to you. The letter should also make a statement about confidentiality or anonymity (see earlier, 'Handling personal information') if appropriate.

When organizing the layout, use a clear typeface and set the questions out uniformly and logically. Make the pages look attractive, and avoid cramping the questions together, even if this means you use extra sheets. It will help you later if you ensure that the responses will be easy to locate quickly on the page. Give clear, friendly, general instructions at the beginning, and provide specific instructions for each new type of question-and-answer format. Leave sufficient room for the responses, especially if you are asking an open question (see earlier, 'Open and closed questions'). It can be useful in some sorts of study to leave space for and invite comments after each question, as these can provide valuable insight into why a particular response has been given. However, this easily changes relatively

straightforward *quantitative* into *qualitative* data, making it much more difficult to generalize about it or to make direct comparisons between responses.

If the questionnaire is only two sides long, print it on both sides of a single sheet to avoid the danger of the pages getting separated. At the bottom
of each page, give an instruction to turn over. It may seem obvious, but it is
not worth risking even one respondent missing a whole page or more of
questions by not realizing they were there. Unless you are guaranteeing
anonymity, give a clear request *on every page* for the respondent's name, so
that if the pages do become separated you can match them up again.

At the end of the questionnaire, leave a space for and invite final comments, thank the respondents for their trouble, and provide give clear
instructions about who it is to be returned to, how, and by when.

Detailed guidelines for the construction and use of questionnaires are
included in Oppenheim (1966) and Bailey (1981).

Spoken questionnaires

The use of a spoken questionnaire is closely tied up with general interviewing techniques. These are explored in Chapter 15. You will need a carefully
prepared list of questions. If you are interviewing individuals as opposed to
groups, be particularly careful that your questions will really work. If you
modify them during the set of interviews, then you may find that the
answers from the earlier ones and the later ones cannot be pooled or compared.

Spoken questionnaires usually have a set order, and this can be problematic if you use open questions. If the informant digresses, the answers to
some later questions may be given earlier on, or in a way you don't want.
Pressing on with the format for the sake of consistency can feel wrong to
both researcher and respondent. Because they don't fully understand the
'routine' of questionnaires, children are particularly prone to digress and to
think it strange if information which has already been given is asked for
again. As you are asking the questions in person, it is possible to allow the
answer to one question to determine which questions are asked next, creating a series of potential pathways through the questionnaire which leave
aside questions that are irrelevant. This must be carefully prepared for,
however. While it is impossible to anticipate every possible answer, the
more you are ready for, the less likely you are to be disorientated by what a
respondent says.

Be aware of your own personality. How well do you think you will succeed in getting the kind of rapport with your subjects that you need for your
particular study? Doing a pilot study can make this easier to judge, and will
give you practice in approaching the task in a way that works for you.

Remember that 'asking people (in interview or by questionnaire) how
they talk is not always a reliable guide to what they actually do. People

tend to report what they think they ought to do, not necessarily how they actually do speak' (Montgomery 1995: 79). This can include them exaggerating their use of *non*-standard *or* of standard forms. Furthermore, their reporting of the forms themselves may not be accurate, if they are not familiar with them through regular use. If you want to get examples of actual language use (as opposed to opinions on it), spoken questionnaires can be limiting in that you will only elicit one style of speech, usually relatively formal or careful – unless, like Labov and Trudgill, you structure the activities so that a range of speech styles is obtained (see Trudgill 1974: 195–201 and Wardhaugh 1992: 151–2).

For information on how spoken interviews based on a questionnaire format can be incorporated into ethnographic work, see Saville-Troike (1989: 123 ff.).

|15|

Interviews

Interviews are appropriate for projects in many areas of linguistics, including:

- psycholinguistics
- sociolinguistics
- language and gender
- accents and dialects
- first-language acquisition (not suitable for eliciting intuitions)
- second-language acquisition
- semantics
- pragmatics
- syntax (especially eliciting intuitions).

General procedures

Where possible, you should expect to audio- or video-tape interviews. Although this means that you will have to find time to transcribe the key points later, there are a number of advantages. One is that you can concentrate all of your attention on the interviewee(s), rather than continually having to break eye contact by looking away while you write things down. You can also avoid having to make snap judgments about what to note down and what to omit. A third advantage is that you are not a victim of your own handwriting, which may be less than legible during hurried note-taking.

You can interview people individually or in a group. Group interviewing enables you to collect data from a lot of people very quickly, and individuals can spark off ideas in each other. On the other hand you may find that one person influences others, by inhibiting them from saying what they really think, or leading the group into apparent agreement. People may speak at the same time, so it is hard to hear all the different points being made and might possibly be difficult later on to tell who is who on the tape.

Approaches to interviewing

In face-to-face interviewing you have the opportunity to use various approaches to data collection without losing too much control over the situation. These approaches include the direct **elicitation** of language forms, asking for **intuitions**, and general questioning without any direct focus on the language until the analysis stage. Each of these is explored below.

Data elicitation

In elicitation you deliberately set up situations, or ask specific questions, that will give you the data you want. This gives you a considerable level of control. Questions may be concurrent with an activity (for example, *What do you think this is for?*) or may follow it (for example, recounting a story seen on video). They can be direct or indirect, and open or closed (see Chapter 14). One technique for structuring an interview is the spoken questionnaire (see Chapter 14), though this is not suitable for young children.

Questions can be asked either entirely directly (for example, *What is your word for this? Do you like the local accent here?*), or you can elicit forms by tightly controlling the conversation so that they naturally emerge (see Chapter 14). Although direct questioning about language or attitudes towards it is a well-tested technique (as in, for example, the *Survey of English Dialects* – see Chapter 8), it does have its disadvantages. Whilst it is straightforward to ask someone directly about their memories of the War or what their school years were like, asking them questions about language does not always produce useful results, as speakers do not always know much about how their variety works and/or may be self-conscious about it.

Direct questioning takes quite a lot of preparation. Investigating a dialect, you would need to go armed with word lists (or objects/pictures) to elicit pronunciation. To elicit specific vocabulary it is necessary to prepare suitable probing questions. For pronouns, for example, you could have a set of sentences to be 'translated' or a paradigm of 'if it belongs to me, it's mine, if it belongs to you it's yours', etc.

In conversation, the different forms of a verb can be explored by asking questions like: *So, did you do that often?* and *What did you do exactly?* This might provide replies like: *Oh, we were always X-ing* and *We only X-ed when it was a games lesson*. For more guidance on investigating accents and dialects, see Chapter 8.

Asking for intuitions

Seeking intuitions is rather different from general questioning or eliciting linguistic forms, because you are trying to get a 'view round the back' of

the process that has led your informants, or would lead them, to their linguistic responses. As we do not by any means always know what we are
doing when we speak or write, this technique has a limited scope but is
quite useful within that. It requires the subject to have self-knowledge and
the vocabulary to talk about language (**metalanguage**). Unlike other types
of data collection, it is important that you conduct the interviews yourself,
rather than delegating the job to someone else. Questions can be concurrent with a task (such as *Tell me how you're working that out*), retrospec-
tive (such as *Look at the video/listen to the tape and tell me what you were
thinking as you wrote/said that*; *Why do you think you said it* that *way?*) or
even more direct, such as asking a simultaneous interpreter *Do you think
that you plan a whole sentence before you start speaking? Why?*

Subjects' accounts of their own opinions and intuitions, possibly alongside the results of a task they were completing, will appear initially chaotic
and may add up to several hours of taped material. When taping or video-
ing, try out the position of the microphone in advance, as people tend to
speak quietly when they are talking about their thought processes.

There are several advantages to intuition data. There is a real sense in
which you can get inside the mind of the subject. Whereas in experiments
you are trying to interpret the mind of the subject solely from observing his
or her behaviour, here you can actually get the subject to help you. Also,
subjects know that they are being recorded, so there's no need for clandes-
tine activity. The fact of their knowing is unlikely to compromise the
results, unless they are inhibited from being totally honest for some reason
(for example, if you get them doing word-association for sex vocabulary).
Disadvantages, however, include the following.

Data based on people's intuition is scientifically imprecise and will never
give you more than a rather cloudy view of what is 'really' going on. Not
everyone sees intuition studies as valid. It can be argued that intuition is
like an iceberg: nine-tenths hidden, so the little bit you can get at is not
representative of the whole. There is no way of controlling how much
information of a particular type people either have access to or choose to
give, nor whether it is accurate or not (they could even lie). Respondents
who are not used to talking about language may lack the knowledge and
analytic tools to give you anything but brief and vague answers. Finally, the
intuition itself is filtered through the interpretation and expression of both
the informant and the researcher. This is not insignificant: to what extent
are we able to verbalize our intuitions about brain processes at all? And
how compatible are the experiences of two people (interviewer and interviewee), or their vocabulary for talking about internal processes?

As with most types of research, what you get out depends on what you
put in. In this case, what you put in must be designed to access information
that the informant may not even know they had, and also to provide you
with something that you can make sense of.

If you have a long set of comments from different informants, you need to find some way of presenting them thematically, to tell more of a story that you'll get from just listing them.

It's easiest to draw conclusions if you have something firm to compare your results with. Therefore, *before you start*, read around the subject and find out what models are favoured and what predictions they make. Design your work to provide a perspective on it. It doesn't matter if you end up with no earth-shattering conclusions, but you should aim to at least raise some questions for further research.

Gathering general data for later analysis

In this approach you are conducting a general interview simply in order to gather a body of language data. You might do this if you wanted to avoid the subjects knowing what you were looking for (because if they did, they might behave differently). Alternatively, you could simply want to use this 'personal' method to obtain data from particular individuals (such as elderly neighbours), as an alternative to, say, taping speech off the radio.

By definition, you will be letting the conversation go where it will, even if you prompt with questions. Certain types of topic may elicit good accent and dialect material, such as reminiscences; others may increase the likelihood of language that is not influenced by the presence of the interviewer, as in the case, say, of emotive issues, such as recalling a bereavement or an emergency situation. You can usually increase the chances of getting speech that is relaxed and that contains informal features (such as strong dialect or accent) if the speakers talk about things they are familiar and comfortable with, and/or things associated with their childhood. If you want to avoid them knowing you are interested in their language, enlist them to help you draw their family tree, or say that you are studying changing fashions in forenames, the history of games played in the street and playground, childhood pranks and punishments or changes in occupations and work patterns. Alternatively, you could ask about the history of the local area. If possible, have some old photographs, and gen up on the area beforehand.

With children, you may need props in order to elicit the data. Practise in advance with any pictures, toys, games, flash-cards and so on, and have a trial run with subjects like the ones you will use in the data collection. Check with parents or teachers that the activities you have chosen are appropriate for the age of the informants.

Do not use general questioning before you have decided what to study. You could well end up with a lengthy tape of data and *still* not know what to study! In other words, make a *positive* decision to gather data in this way, for reasons related to the specific analysis you have planned.

|16|

Observation and case studies

The terms 'observation study' and 'case study' are not mutually exclusive: you may be doing both. Observation studies involve the collection of data without manipulating it. The researcher simply observes ongoing activities, without making any attempt to control or determine them. In a case study some or all of the data may result from observation, but it is also possible to collect data in other ways. In this chapter we first of all consider observation studies, and then case studies.

Observation studies

Observation is an appropriate technique for studies in:

- psycholinguistics
- first-language acquisition (including carer language)
- second-language acquisition
- literacy (including dyslexia)
- accent and dialect studies
- sociolinguistics
- language and gender
- conversation analysis.

Normally you would study ordinary people or people with some recognized disability, about which generalizations can be made. You can use any number of subjects. Remember, however, that you may need quite a lot of background information on each subject, and that each will produce quite a large quantity of unsorted data, so small numbers are advisable. Data from subjects who are expected to share patterns of behaviour can be pooled. Subjects with contrasting characteristics can be compared. They can be of any age, gender or background, but if you are pooling results, the fewer variables there are of this kind, the more compatible the subjects will be.

You may gather your data in various ways, including secret or open observation, recording from the radio or TV, or reusing data previously collected for some other purpose (but in this case you may not have access to all of the background material that you need).

Observation data is qualitative in the first instance, consisting of recordings, transcriptions and notes relating to your subjects' behaviour and language (spoken and/or written). You may subsequently derive quantitative data from it (such as the number of words in each utterance).

Advantages

While many types of research can only measure *elicited* behaviour, because specific tasks are presented in a controlled environment, observation enables you to examine non-elicited behaviour as and when it occurs (for example, slips of the tongue, paralinguistic behaviour, interactional behaviour and pathological phenomena). This allows a much more 'holistic' view of how language is being used in context. For this reason it is a technique much favoured by ethnographers (see Chapter 7). It is also more flexible than, say, a controlled experiment, where any extraneous or unplanned event could potentially invalidate the results. Another advantage is that observation studies are relatively easy to administer. Indeed, by using pre-recorded or broadcast material, you can avoid many of the practical difficulties of data collection. Observation can be used at the planning stages of other types of project, in order to get ideas or to determine the feasibility of the main procedure, and can supplement information gathered by other methods.

Disadvantages

Secret recordings, if that is what you need, are tricky to do and are considered by some to be an infringement of people's rights. You could end up not getting consent to use your best data – you must ask permission. With child subjects you will almost always need the consent of parents, schools and so on beforehand. Hiding an audio recorder or microphone is not easy – if you are intending to do this, do some trial runs. Remember, you may not need to be secretive, especially if you can afford to discount the first part of the recording (see Chapter 12). Another disadvantage is that some observable phenomena (such as slips of the tongue) are not densely packed in data, so you may need a great deal of material to get even a small set of interesting observations. (However, you do not need to transcribe or analyse anything that is irrelevant to your study.) Also, it can be difficult to predict what sort of material you will get: topics may shift, the things you were looking for may not occur, and observation studies are difficult to replicate on another occasion because there are so many uncontrolled variables. Finally, it may not be easy to produce well-focused conclusions because the data is so unstructured and multi-faceted. It may be hard to decide which parts of the data to submit to the assessor as part of the project, as the points of interest may be spread over a large quantity of material.

Things to think about

- Be very sure of precisely what you are looking for. Whilst you may not be able to envisage what specific *examples* of a phenomenon you will gather, you should know before you start what phenomenon you are investigating. (In other words, don't just switch on a tape recorder and hope that something of interest will materialize!) Try to ensure that you are looking for something that is likely to occur reasonably often.
- Different types of phenomena will come from different sources. For example, if you wanted to look at spontaneous slips of the tongue, there would obviously be no point in recording a play off the radio! Neither would you be likely to find many in an interview between an experienced journalist or presenter and a politician. Slips of the tongue tend to occur when the speaker is tired, nervous, flustered or drunk, so you would need to consider how best to record someone in that state. Asking your subject to read out loud some very complicated, unfamiliar text would be one way to increase the likelihood of observing speech errors.
- Be aware of what role you, as the observer, might be playing in the dynamics of the situation you are observing (see Chapter 1). You might put subjects at their ease by being a full participant in the procedures. You would be counted by them as one of the group and you would join in with what they were doing on an equal basis. However, it is important not to try to direct or manipulate, nor to test or interview, while you are a 'participant observer'.
- Alternatively, you may decide not to be present at all during the recording. In the Bristol Survey of Language Development, begun in 1972, spontaneous speech was recorded by fitting children with radio microphones. Taping was activated at random preset times, so neither subjects nor carers knew when they were being recorded. The researchers then talked through the tapes with the carers to get clarification of any difficult passages and to find out about the concomitant activity. Expensive equipment may well not be available, but you might still consider leaving a tape running while you are out of the room. You can read about the Bristol survey in, for example, Wells (1981, 1985).

If you have several observation sessions, try to ensure that the length of time for each is roughly the same. Make notes on any differences between the circumstances of each observation (such as the time of day, other people present, interruptions or illness). You may decide to scrap some observations if you feel that these differences have affected the observation too much. You may also need to refer back to differences, no matter how insignificant they appeared at the time, to help explain or question results.

To help summarize your results, devise a checklist for features based on other studies and use this as a framework. For each feature, systematically record whether the subject(s) used it or not. At the end of each section you can then produce a table or list, bringing out any patterns. If you have a transcript available, remember to note line numbers for occurrences for features, so that these can be stated in the project.

Consider carefully how to draw conclusions from your results. Focus on finding patterns in the data that relate to your original questions. Are there any differences between individuals for the features you were interested in? If you have not found the differences you expected, explain why this might be. Scrutinize your sampling, data collection and analysis procedures for possible causes. Perhaps previous studies on which your expectations were based were flawed and your results have helped to demonstrate this.

Case studies

A case study is usually most appropriate where a given individual has some behaviour worth observing, but:

- the circumstances are so individual or rare that there would be no benefit in combining the results of observations of that person with those of others (such as specific brain damage or first-language acquisition well after the normal age), or:
- the phenomenon being observed is so complex that a variety of different kinds of data is needed in order to gain a full picture (for example, the process of child language acquisition or foreign-language learning).

Case studies are particularly suitable for longitudinal research (where you observe the individual change over time and the focus is on comparisons of the individual's performance on a sequence of occasions). They are a vehicle for both qualitative and quantitative research, and can be appropriate for projects in:

- first-language acquisition
- second-language acquisition
- language and education (including the acquisition of literacy)
- some areas of psycholinguistics.

Data can be collected using the techniques of observation, interview and/or testing, and will often be supported by additional information, both linguistic and non-linguistic, from parents, carers and official records. Whether you are dealing with language plus a special circumstance, or creating a 'profile' of a normal individual's development or progress in one or more aspects of language, you will also need to accumulate background knowledge of what the range of normal development is, so that you have a baseline against which to interpret the patterns you observe.

You will normally need the consent of the subject and anyone else involved (doctor, speech therapist, teacher, family) and you must be able to demonstrate strict confidentiality. You may have to travel to your subject on several occasions, and fit into their schedule. Remember to take into account the cost in time and money, and to consider how you will transport any equipment you need.

If you are administering tests, you can design your own or ask the therapist, doctor or teacher for access to some of those that are standard as diagnostics.

Advantages

You can study someone you already know, in his or her own home or some other environment familiar to him or her; this increases the likelihood of observing representative behaviour. Often there are good opportunities for observing the language of carers and/or teachers as well. The data is valid in its own right, irrespective of how representative of a population the individual is. If you are conducting a longitudinal study this gives a more genuine picture than can be gained by comparing individuals at each of the different stages (a cross-sectional study). As you become more familiar with the case, you can develop your investigation in new directions.

Disadvantages

Relying totally on data from one person can be risky. The subject's personality, disabilities (or limitations), prejudices and anxieties may be difficult to deal with. If you are collecting data over a period of time, the subject might move away or the circumstances change so that your visits are no longer welcome. Also, if your ideas about the study change as you proceed, your early data may be less useful than you hoped, or you may be stuck with a test design or observation procedure that is not appropriate to what you later want to find out. Working over an extended period it can be difficult to remain objective. Also, a child subject may start to mess around as the level of familarity increases. Other disadvantages of case studies include the time they can consume, not only for you but also for the subject and his or her carers, teachers and so on, the small sample size, which means that few generalizations can be made, and the fact that relevant data can be elusive.

How to set up a case study

Accessing a subject can take time, so it's better to know someone already. If you do not, work through a professional such as a GP, teacher or speech therapist. If you are approaching a patient you don't know, take advice about how to do this, or get yourself introduced by someone they know. Do what you can to make it clear to the patient and his or her family that you are *not* an expert, and that you are there only because they are kindly doing you a favour. If negotiating with a parent about access to their child, explain your intentions in as much detail as possible. Don't insist on the parent being excluded from the room if they would rather stay. Keep the parent on your side by asking for advice and insights.

A foreign- or second-language learner can be contacted through a school or college, or through an agency providing language support. However, you could also set up your own arrangement with a friend who fancies studying a new language; but remember, you will be relying on them to see it through, so make sure they are serious about it and are in a position to continue the study for as long as you need.

Before you begin collecting data, do some initial observation to identify likely areas of interest (you can't look at everything). This will help you to design any tests you need to elicit particular phenomena.

Remember that you are dealing with real people (subject and carers) who may be in a delicate state, and/or sensitive about their language performance or their role in supporting and teaching the subject. So be scrupulous in your preparation, and sensitive and professional in your approach. Ensure that the subject *really* does not mind being observed or tested, and *really* understands what's involved. Think carefully about what you expect the subject to do, and what you will do if they don't, can't or won't. Part of this entails finding out as much as you can about how to do your research *before* you get there: read journals, ask the professionals and be guided by them.

Dealing with the results

Avoid accumulating hours of taped material or other observations without any clear idea of what you will do with it all. Try to transcribe and analyse the data as you go along: it reduces the amount to be done in the final stages, and it gives you a chance to see if any of your data-collection methods need refinement. If you have several types of data to analyse (spoken, written, tests, observed, elicited and so on), keep a careful eye on staying within your project word limit.

It is not sufficient simply to list (even in summarized form) what you have seen; you need to pull out patterns and relate them to models and/or theories. It is fine to home in on one or two interesting aspects and leave the rest aside – don't feel you have to describe everything in equal detail and depth. However, it is important to indicate when you *have* left some things aside, so that your assessor doesn't think you have failed to see them.

PART

III

TOOLS FOR DATA ANALYSIS AND PROJECT WRITING

|17|

Transcribing speech phonetically and phonemically

In most situations, slight differences in the pronunciation of a sound by different people, or by the same person on different occasions or in different linguistic contexts, can be overlooked. It is enough to recognize what the words were, or that a given sound was a kind of 't' or a kind of 's'. But where pronunciation is the focus of your work, you need finer distinctions. The sorts of studies where this may apply include:

- accents
- first-language acquisition
- second-language acquisition
- language impairment
- speech errors
- conversation
- language and gender.

The difference between phonetic and phonemic transcription

If you are focusing on pronunciation, it will soon become clear to you that you need a means of transcribing sounds in some detail. Specifically, you need to be able to demonstrate on paper the often subtle differences between two sounds that do not contribute to any change in the identity of the words, but which are nevertheless salient within the study you are doing. This is done using **phonetic** script, and transcriptions are enclosed in **square brackets**. Yet, in order to write about the *relationships* between two pronunciations, you will also need a transcription system that allows you to consider a sound in general terms, independently of its actual realization on a particular occasion. For this, you need to use **phonemic** script, enclosing transcriptions in **slanted brackets**. This may seem like a mere difference of degree, but it is not.

Phonetic script

Phonetic script can be likened to an infinite palette of paints. It is possible, in theory, to depict in phonetic script differences as subtle as the ear can hear. To achieve this there is a large inventory of symbols, including a set of **diacritics**, which act as pointers to exact articulatory positions or ways of making a sound. Thus, to give just two examples, the diacritic [,] written beneath a symbol indicates *tongue further forward* and [ː] written to the right-hand side of a symbol means *of greater duration*. A full set of symbols, including the diacritics, can be found on the IPA chart on page xvi.

Because the detail that can go into a phonetic transcription is potentially infinite, a phonetician needs to make a decision about what to include and what to leave out. In practice, the relatively untrained ear simply does not hear much of the detail, and so the rule of thumb for most students is *if you can hear it, write it down*. However, as detailed transcription is time-consuming, avoid transcribing material or detail that you know you will not need. A detailed phonetic transcription is termed *narrow*, and a less detailed one *broad*. A broad transcription may use few more symbols than a phonemic transcription, but it is *not* one, for all the reasons outlined in this chapter.

Phonemic script

Phonemic script is like having an infinite palette of colours organized into sets called *green, blue, red* and so on, with any given shade belonging to one of those sets. Each language – indeed, each variety of each language – has a small set of **phonemes** (such as /t/, /m/), and each actual utterance of a sound can be categorized as being an **allophone (phonetic realization)** of one of the phonemes (see below). Most (but not all) allophones have a phonetic identity which is predictable from the surrounding environment. The kind of /p/ that you get at the beginning of a word like *patch* is characteristically an aspirated one [pʰ] and the kind of /d/ that you get at the end of a word like *reward* is normally a devoiced one [d̥]. Linguists have worked out the distributions of the different phonetic realizations of the different phonemes by studying how English works. Each language is different. This implies that you cannot transcribe a language, or language variety, phonemically until you know what phonemic category to put every sound that you hear into. If you do not – and often part of your analysis will be establishing the phonemic categories – you must use phonetic script.

In summary, phonetic script *describes* what you are hearing; phonemic script *interprets* it. Beware of using phonemic script as an easy option: there are hidden implications within it which, if not accounted for, could seriously compromise the validity of your analysis.

A few notes on phonemes

Phonemes are *notional* sounds: they are *categories* of sound. You can't hear a phoneme, only example phonetic realizations of one. Compare the category 'red': it is not a colour in its own right. Rather, to illustrate 'red' you need to find examples of it. In the same way, the label /t/ is just a cover-term for the complete set of its possible phonetic realizations, that is, for what you could actually *hear*. So you will be writing that a speaker's realization of a phoneme /. . ./ is [. . .]. This enables you to compare different speakers (or different speech events in one speaker) whilst being sure that you are comparing like with like.

Two sounds may be superficially rather similar, but belong to different phonemes. We demonstrate these phoneme categories by identifying words which are identical except for the choice of that phoneme. These are called **minimal pairs.** For example, in English, /ɛ/ and /ɪ/ must be phonemes because there are minimal pairs such as *led* and *lid*, in which the difference in the sound of the vowel is the only thing that keeps the words separate. So part of the definition of the phoneme is that if you swap one phoneme with another you can make another word. Contrast this with some sound characteristics that are *not* phonemic for English. Suppose on one occasion a person said *sitting* as [sɪtɪŋ] and on another said it as [sːɪtɪŋ] (that is, with a longer, hissy /s/). This would not stop it being a pronunciation of the word *sitting*, because in English the sounds [s] and [sː] do not contrast in a way that could create a new word. They are therefore not separate phonemes of English, but just different examples (allophones) of the phoneme /s/. However, we can imagine a language in which this contrast *was* phonemic, because there was a minimal pair /sɑrɪt/ (meaning, say, *blossom*) and /sːɑrɪt/ (meaning, say, *big toe*). In this language you would have to be very careful how hissy you made your 's', otherwise you could end up saying that the big toes in the garden smell very beautiful this year. Native speakers of Japanese and Korean sometimes struggle to differentiate the English phonemes /l/ and /r/, because in their languages this phonemic distinction does not exist, and [l] and [ɹ] are just allophones of the same phoneme.

Categorizing the sounds we hear into phonemic classes allows us to retain a view of the phonological structure of a language, even when the pronunciation is rather odd. If we aren't sure what we heard, we use our knowledge of the language at all levels to make sense of the message, so that we can work out which phonemic category the rogue sound must belong to. Thus, if a foreign learner of English said *I sailed on a [ʃiːp]*, we could tell from the context that he meant *ship* and not *sheep*, and conclude that, for him, either [iː] was an allophone of the phoneme /ɪ/, rather than of /iː/ as it would be for native speakers, or else he had not, so far, succeeded in creating two phonemes, /ɪ/ and /iː/, at all (perhaps because his native language did not have that contrast).

You can read more about phonemes in Wells and Colson (1971, ch. 20), Malmkjaer (1991: 339–45), Roach (1991, chs. 5 and 13), Clark and Yallop (1990, ch. 5), or virtually any other introduction to phonetics and phonology.

Hints on writing about pronunciation

When you are writing about a real piece of data (or about how a real piece of data would sound if only you had a recording of it), use square brackets and give as much phonetic detail as you can hear, or as much as you need to make your point. When you want to say that the sound in square brackets is an example of, say, a 't' or an 's', use slanted brackets for the latter (/t/, /s/), because you are referring to the categories, that is, the phonemes.

When you explore the pronunciation of an individual speaker, use a phoneme checklist such as the one given below, or the one in Hughes and Trudgill (1996, p. iv, or p. 42 in the 1987 edition) to guide you into finding examples of each phoneme. Next to the phoneme symbols on the list, transcribe your examples with square brackets (because they are real sounds that you have heard), and put in as much information as you can. You are then in a position to compare the pronunciation you have heard with other possible pronunciations of that phoneme.

Despite what most of the books imply, there is *not* simply one inventory of phonemes for English. In other words, it is not simply the case that different varieties of English have different pronunciations for a given phoneme. In some varieties the actual set of phonemes is slightly different. So look out for examples of a phoneme on the checklist dividing in two parts, or of two phonemes on the checklist collapsing together. The best example of collapse for British English is the phonemes /ʌ/ and /ʊ/. Both phonemes exist in most parts of the south of Britain, giving minimal pairs such as *could* /kʊd/ and *cud* /kʌd/, and *put* /pʊt/ and *putt* /pʌt/. But in many parts of the north of Britain these words all contain the same vowel: /kʊd/, /kʊd/, /pʊt/ and /pʊt/. A second example derives from the fact that some varieties of English are **rhotic** (i.e. pronounce the *r* in *car* and *card*) whilst others are non-rhotic. Non-rhotic varieties may differentiate between words like *law* and *lore*, *spa* and *spar*, which, provided the vowels do not differ, will form minimal pairs in a rhotic variety. Kreidler (1989: 50–63) provides a useful set of phoneme inventories for English, into one of which most, if not all, national and international varieties should fall.

You can see some examples of the phoneme inventories for different varieties of British English in Hughes and Trudgill (1996). A good impression of the way in which phonemic and phonetic transcriptions will differ for the same data can be found in Brown (1977, ch. 4).

Checklist of Phonemes

SYMBOL	EXAMPLE BASED ON BRITISH RP	NOTES
/iː/	beat	
/ɪ/	bit	
/ɛ/	bet	
/a/	bat	also often written /æ/; /a/ is arguably the better choice because the phonetic realization in modern RP is closer to [a] than [æ] which tends to sound old-fashioned
/ɑː/	bard*	
/ɒ/	body	
/ɔː/	bored, board*	
/ʊ/	wood	these two phonemes collapse into one in some parts of Britain. That is, *wood* and *bud* rhyme, whether they both have [ʊ], [u], [ə] or (even) [ʌ]
/ʌ/	mud	
/ɜː/	word*	
/ə/	winner*	
/eɪ/	bait	also to be seen as /ɛɪ/, /ei/ and /ɛi/
/əʊ/	boat	
/aɪ/	bite	also to be seen as /ɑɪ/, /ai/ and /ɑi/
/aʊ/	brown	also to be seen as /ɑʊ/, /au/ and /ɑu/
/ɔɪ/	boy	also to be seen as /ɒɪ/, /ɔi/ and /ɒi/
/ɪə/	beer*	one increasingly common phonetic realization of this in RP is [ɪː]
/ɛə/	bare*	one increasingly common phonetic realization of this in RP is [ɛː]
(/ʊə/	poor*)	this is a prime example of how the phonemic inventory has got out of date. In RP today (except among older and particularly 'posh' speakers) there is no separate phoneme /ʊə/ because it has collapsed with /ɔː/. Wells and Colson (1971) have resorted to using a German place-name to illustrate this pronunciation. When examining data, it is useful to check the pronunciation of the following: *poor, pore, pour, paw* and *pause*. Many regional varieties retain two or more distinct pronunciations for these, though modern RP has only one vowel for them all, approximately [ɔː]

continued overleaf

Checklist of Phonemes (*continued*)

SYMBOL	EXAMPLE BASED ON BRITISH RP	NOTES
(/aə/	fire*)	also written as /aɪə/, and pronounced in a variety of ways, including, by some British southerners, [aː]
/p/	ro*p*e	
/b/	ro*b*e	
/t/	wro*t*e	
/d/	ro*d*e	
/k/	spo*k*e	
/g/	ro*g*ue	
/tʃ/	broo*ch*	
/dʒ/	hu*g*e	
/f/	loa*f*	
/v/	dro*v*e	
/θ/	brea*th*	
/ð/	brea*the*	
/s/	gro*ss*	
/z/	grow*s*	
/ʃ/	fa*sh*ion	
/ʒ/	vi*s*ion	
/h/	*h*eart	
/m/	roa*m*	
/n/	loa*n*	
/ŋ/	wro*ng*	watch out for varieties in which the 'ng' in spelling is pronounced [ŋg]. In these cases there is no phoneme /ŋ/ at all, because [ŋ] only ever occurs before /g/ and /k/ and never on its own; so there are no minimal pairs like the RP ones *win* /wɪn/ and *wing* /wɪŋ/.
/l/	ro*ll*	
/r/	*r*oll	
/j/	*y*ear	
/w/	*w*ear	

* In **non-rhotic** varieties like RP, the *r* after a vowel and before a consonant or word-end is not pronounced and should not appear in the transcription. It is important not to be influenced by *r* in the spelling of words, and to *listen* in order to decide whether there is an /r/ present or not. In **rhotic** varieties you will be able to hear the *r* and should transcribe it.

|18|

Transcribing speech orthographically

For an analysis to be valid, the transcription of the data must be accurate. This is a time-consuming and tiring activity, as you may have to listen to the same stretch of tape many times, especially where several people are speaking at the same time. Two things can help here. Firstly, don't be over-ambitious about the quantity of data you transcribe. Only transcribe what you need, and do not put in detail that is not relevant, such as phonetic details of the speaker's accent, unless you have a reason for doing so. Secondly, enquire about what transcribing aids are available for loan from your department. For example, an audio-typist's foot-pedal control, or a dedicated transcribing machine, also operated by foot-pedal, can keep your hands free for transcribing, and save wear and tear on the forward and reverse controls of an ordinary tape-player. A transcribing machine also offers the facility to slow the speech down, so that the duration of the pauses can be measured more accurately.

The following information is organized in a question-and-answer format, and aims to address the procedures of orthographic transcription from the inexperienced user's point of view. The conventions are based on those of Gail Jefferson, as described in Psathas (1995: 70–8) and Jefferson (1989: 193–6).

Basics

Can I assume that my assessors will know the conventions I'm using?

They will, but you should still provide a key to your symbols. This is partly because not everyone uses the same conventions, partly because there are choices regarding how to transcribe some features, and partly because the assessor wants to be reassured that you know what you're doing.

In my analysis, how can I refer easily to material in the transcription?

Number every line. This makes it possible for the reader to find your examples easily and check the wider context if required. Try to ensure that the numbers are not so far into the left margin that they are obscured by the binding or file grip. There is also a transcription convention for highlighting a particular line in the transcription. This is described later in this chapter.

How do I indicate who is speaking?

As in a play script, name the speaker in the left-hand margin. Use a short form, such as an initial, to save space, giving a key at the beginning or end (each speaker should have a different initial or short form). If you wish to protect the identity of the speakers, use letters such as A, B and C. A line of transcription should have one, and only one, letter or name in the margin. If the same speaker has several lines of speech, it is sufficient to label only the first. If several people speak at once, each should have a separate line (see 'Dealing with complexity' below). The only exception to this would be if two or more people deliberately coordinated an utterance in unison (like singing 'Happy Birthday'); in this case it is acceptable (but not obligatory) to list them on one line:

(1) J: C-come on then
     R: Yeah (.) ri-
     J: (sung) Happy birth =
     J,R,K,S: (sung) =day to you: happy birthday to you . . .

Dealing with silence

How do I indicate a pause?

A pause too short to measure is indicated by a dot in brackets: (.). Pauses of measurable length are indicated in seconds and tenths of seconds. There are several conventions available, and you need to indicate clearly in your key what you have used. Try not to mix conventions unnecessarily. The options are:

- give the duration numerically in brackets, e.g. eight-tenths of a second (0.8); one-and-two-tenths seconds: (1.2). This is the most commonly used convention.
- in brackets, use dashes for tenths of seconds with a plus for the one that

makes up a full second, e.g. eight-tenths of a second: (– – – – – – – –);
one-and-two-tenths seconds: (– – – – – – – – + – –)

- in brackets, use plus signs for tenths of seconds, with a gap between each
  full second: for example, eight-tenths of a second: (+ + + + + + + +);
  one-and-two-tenths seconds: (+ + + + + + + + + +   + +)

If you cannot time the pause, write *pause* in double brackets if it occurs
within a speaker's turn, and *gap* within double brackets if it occurs between
different speakers' turns:

(2) M: Okay here's °one° What's the capital o- ((pause)) What's
         the capital of Burkina Faso
     R: Wha-
         ((gap))
     M: [Burki-
     E: [Where the hell is °that°

How do I notate a silent nod of the head?

Simply write *nods* in double brackets. The same goes for other gestures,
including pointing, smiling, etc.:

(3) S: Who told you=don't tell me=Karen
     E: Mmm ((nods))
     S: ((smiles)) okay

Is there any way of indicating that someone has breathed in or out?

Yes. Most of the time you don't need to indicate it, because it is a background activity. But an audible breath, in or out, should be marked. Breath
is indicated by one or more 'h's, as follows:

- breathing out: followed by a dash.

(4) He was (0.6) hhh- no I s'pose not

- breathing in: preceded by a dot.

(5) Erm (0.4) .hhhh try the other (1.1) way roun-

- breath sounds associated with sobbing, laughing, being out of
  breath: in brackets.

(6) Then (hhh) he said wha(h)t ti(h)me d'you ca(hh)ll this (hhh)

Dealing with complexity

What do I do if two or more people are talking at once?

There are several aspects to this. If two people start at the same time, give them separate lines, beginning with a double opening square bracket:

(7) W: [[Take it if y-
       E: [[I mean (.) no I

Where one person begins when someone else is already speaking, there are two transcription methods:

Method 1: use a single opening square bracket before the new speaker's words, aligned vertically with another at the appropriate point in the established speaker's line (example 8). If two people interrupt in close succession, do the same again with a third line (example 9).

(8) R: so we didn't have to [wait long
      T: [no we didn't

(9) S: would you [li-(.) like o-orange or ap[ple
      M: [we've got
      E: [yes please

Method 2 (less commonly used): put a double oblique line // into the established speaker's line at the point of interruption, and start the new speaker on the next line (example 10). If two people interrupt in close succession, the first speaker beneath relates to the first set of lines, and the second to the second set (example 11):

(10) R: so we didn't have to // wait long
       T: no we didn't

(11) S: would you // li-(.) like o-orange or ap//ple
       M: we've got
       E: yes please

Where one person finishes while the other continues speaking:

Method 1: use a closing square bracket in both lines:

(12) T: till it cam- (0.5) we [weren't all that] all that s-sure
       G: [but did you]

Method 2: use an asterisk to indicate where in the continuing speech the simultaneous speech ended:

(13) T: till it cam- (0.5) we // weren't all that* all that s-sure
       G: but did you

If someone starts speaking immediately another has finished, is there any way of showing this?

Yes. This is called **latching**. Use an *equals* sign at the end of the first component and the beginning of the second (example 14). If two people latch at the same time, mark them both (example 15). Latching can also be marked within the turn of a single speaker, if one idea immediately follows another (example 16).

> (14)   A: before Sunday if you can=
>   K: =I'm really busy at the weekend

> (15)   R: so why didn't you after all that=
>   F: =[[yeah
>   G: =[[I was going to

> (16)   E: after y-you turned him down=why did you anyway

Dealing with obscurity and unusual pronunciations

What if I can't decipher what's being said?

Sometimes a speaker mumbles. Sometimes there are several people talking at once and one or more of them is virtually drowned out by the rest. Listen to it again. Listen to it yet again. Sit back and try to hear it as if for the first time. Imagine you are there: what is the speaker *likely* to say? Play it to someone else and see if they can decipher it. Do whatever you can to minimize the quantity of indecipherable speech. If it really is impossible, indicate that the utterance is there by putting empty single brackets for the appropriate duration (example 17). Alternatively, put 'indecipherable' in double brackets (example 18). It is also quite common to use an asterisk for each indecipherable syllable (example 19).

> (17)   W: and just as he's (0.2) he's about to [run off the guy c-come=
>   T: [oh God (   )]
>   W: = comes o]ver and

> (18)   W: and just as he's (0.2) he's about to [run off the guy c-come=
>   T: [oh God (indecipherable)]
>   W: = comes o]ver and

> (19)   W: and just as he's (0.2) he's about to [run off the guy c-come=
>   T: [oh God (*   *   *   )]
>   W: = comes o]ver and

It may be that you know what was said but not who said it. In this case, put empty single brackets in the margin:

(20)   R: for a few minutes till=
( ):   =huh you'll be luc-

If you are able to have a guess about what has been said, put your guess inside single brackets – this indicates that you have some doubt about it:

(21)   R: taken [it over again
E: [(likely to be)

If you can hear the sounds but cannot work out what the words are, the convention is to make an orthographic representation of them inside single brackets. It is not standard to use phonetic script (but see below):

(22)   D: (mekka bunit cor)

How can I show that a word has been started but not finished?

Use a hyphen at the point where the word ends (example 23). Note that because of English spelling it will not always be clear what the sound was that was uttered. If it matters, used phonetic script (see below). This notation works for slips of the tongue too (example 24).

(23)   P: hurt him an- and hit his head on the ste- on the top of
the steering wheel
(24)   F: there'll be pi- mist patches and some drizzle in the east

How can I show an unusual pronunciation of a word?

Because orthographic transcription was invented by sociologists, not linguists, it lacks some of the features that linguists are accustomed to employing for the close transcription of speech. Although phonetic script would be by far the best way to depict any pronunciation that could not be adequately indicated by conventional spelling, it is not often used. There are several ways of coping with the need to indicate a pronunciation more exactly. You can use conventional spelling and indicate, in double brackets, the relevant feature (example 25), or use conventional spelling to approximate the pronunciation (example 26).

(25)   D: he's a real bastard ((northern pronunciation))
(26)   R: you need to move in really sloooooly

Alternatively, skirt the issue in the main transcription, and use phonetic transcription when discussing the item in the analysis, or use phonetic script anyway, either instead of, or as well as, an orthographic representation. In the latter case, write the phonetic transcription immediately above the spelled version (example 27).

$$\{gɔrə\}$$
(27)   P: an. then (.) y. you just got to go

As always, it's important to clearly mark where a phonetic transcription begins and ends, otherwise the reader will not be able to tell if 'raid' is *raid* or *ride,* etc. But bear in mind that in orthographic transcription square brackets have another use, so you will need to find a way of indicating that this is phonetic transcription and not an overlap (you might need both at the same time anyway). It doesn't matter how you choose to indicate phonetic script, as long as it is explained in the key: you could use curly brackets, as in example 27. If you are word processing, but do not have phonetic symbols available, write them by hand in a contrasting colour – in this case square brackets could be used, because their function will be clearly different, or you could get away without using brackets at all.

How can I show that a word has been stretched out?

Use a colon immediately after the lengthened sound. The more colons you use, the longer the sound:

(28)   S: we- well it was (.) eno: : : : : rmous

If someone coughs or sneezes, should I include it?

Yes. Write *cough* or *sneeze* in double brackets:

(29)   T: oh God ((cough)) tha- ((cough)) Go- could I h-have
             ((cough)) that wa- wa((cough))ter

Use of conventional punctuation

Do I use a question mark to indicate a question?

No, not automatically. In orthographic transcription many of the standard punctuation symbols are used, but they have specific meanings, relating to intonation (see below). The question mark is used to indicate a rising intonation, irrespective of whether it is at the end of a question (it would, for example, be used at the end of many statements in American English). Any question *not* having a rising intonation at the end (and that is quite a proportion) will not have a question mark after it.

Dealing with pitch, emphasis, speed and volume

How can I indicate standard intonation patterns?

The intonation of speech is not represented in orthographic transcription with anything like the accuracy that a phonologist would expect. If you want to give greater detail, do a separate transcription of the relevant extract, using one of the standard systems of intonation transcription for phonology (see, for example, Clark and Yallop 1990: 303–7, Kreidler 1989, ch. 10, Roach 1991, chs. 15 to 19 and, for an overview, Malmkjaer 1991: 230–6). As indicated above, punctuation symbols are used for transcribing some of the specific intonation patterns of English. Although each represents the sort of pattern that we associate with it when it is punctuating ordinary text, the application of the symbols is much more rigid, and they must be reserved for their defined purpose, as follows:

- a **falling tone** is marked with a full stop (period). To indicate a particularly noticeable fall, put a downward arrow immediately before it begins:

(30)   R: There was ↓ nothing there.

- a **fall–rise** pattern, as when listing, or continuing at the end of a clause, is marked with a comma:

(31)   K: I had (.) um (0.7) a ball, (.) a cricket bat, an (.) tha. (0.4) um a ball and a cricket bat.

- a **rise** is marked with a question mark. For a weaker rise, put a comma instead of a dot at the bottom: ⸮ and for a particularly noticeable rise, use an upward arrow immediately before it begins:

(32)   F: Well would you ↑ like to be left behind?

- **animated tone**, as in an exclamation, is indicated by an exclamation mark.

For changes in pitch not associated with these familiar intonation patterns, see below.

How do I indicate pitch features?

Pitch movement is closely tied up with intrinsic (word-, phrase-) and emphatic stress. In addition, it often requires the stretching of the syllable so that there is time to achieve the effect. Because of this interrelationship it is possible to mark pitch features by underlining parts of the stretched syllable. The rules are quite subtle: basically, the underlined item is higher in pitch than what surrounds it, so underlining the pitch-carrying vowel itself raises it, and underlining anything *after* the pitch-carrying vowel indicates that that vowel is lower than what follows. Thus:

- a **drop in pitch** is marked by underlining the letter immediately before the colon that indicates the stretch. To indicate a prolonged drop, extend the line backwards, that is, towards the beginning of the word.

(33) G: It wasn't pounds it was do: llars
     R: What d'you mean do: : llars.

- a **rise in pitch** is indicated by underlining the colon following the vowel. A lengthened version is achieved by extending the underlining forwards, towards the end of the word:

(34) L: a sto: : : rage container?

- a **rise and fall** can be shown by underlining the point of the highest pitch, implying that what comes before and afterwards is lower:

(35) T: ((sarcastically)) Oh yeah it was rea: : : : : : : : lly good

- a **fall and rise** cannot be shown using these tools, so use an arrow to indicate the fall (see example 30).

How do I show that something has been emphasized?

Underline the relevant words, and combine this, as appropriate, with indicators of how the emphasis has been achieved, e.g. a falling tone (see example 30) or a change in volume (see below). If it is associated with a marked change in pitch, you cannot show emphasis independently of that, because underlining is intrinsic to it already.

How do I show that the volume has changed?

Use capital letters to show loudness, and a degree sign (superscript circle) either side of a quiet passage. Indicate whispering by writing *whispered* in double brackets:

(36) H: Mummy look there's FIVE!
     R: °don- (.) make so much [noise°
     H: [(((whispered)) Mum[my there's=
     R: [°yes I know°
     H: = ↓ five!

How do I show that the speaker has changed speed?

A faster passage is enclosed in inverted angle brackets, or, to put it another way, in 'arrow heads' with their points inwards (example 37). There is not normally any need for specific symbols to indicate a slower speed of delivery. If someone speaks slowly, they must either be extending the words (in which case use colons to show the 'stretch') or leaving gaps between the words (shown by the symbols for pauses).

(37)   K: yes (0.5) if you like (0.1) cooking = › if you do like
            cooking it's ‹ (0.3) well it's no problem then

External events

Supposing a fire engine goes past, or the phone rings?

The purpose of the transcription is to record everything that is part of the conversation. This means that an extraneous noise that is ignored by the participants does not need transcribing, but anything which provokes or indicates a reaction should be. If in doubt, put it in. Notate it with a description in double brackets, e.g. ((telephone rings)). You should follow this up with a later entry ((telephone stops ringing)) unless it is clear from the context that this is the case. There is a special convention for notating applause, using upper and lower case Xs for loud and soft respectively, as in example 38 (Atkinson and Heritage 1984, p. xv):

(38)   Audience: xxXXXXXXXXXXXXXxxx

Layout problems

What do I do when I get to the end of my line, if I want to show that the same speaker has continued, even though someone intervened during the line?

The problem here is that there is an intervening line for the second speaker. To show that there is no break in the first speaker's utterance, use the latching symbol =

(39)   W: tha- was [it? (.)y]eah we ha- we had eighteen of=
       R: [yeah]
       W: =them here a- all at once

How can I draw the reader's attention to something?

Put a horizontal arrow in the margin, to the left of the speaker's name/initial. Alternatively, use a large dot. Only mark things that are central to your discussion, and remember to refer to them in your commentary.

(40) E: Leave that will you?
  →K: Wh- ↓what

(41) E: Leave that will you?
  ●K: Wh- ↓what

What if I don't want to transcribe everything, and need to show that I have omitted bits?

You are more likely to need to do this when you are quoting from your transcription in the discussion than when doing the transcription itself, because by omitting things you are expressing an opinion about the relative importance of different parts of the whole. Show that you have missed out bits of a speaker's turn by using a horizontal sequence of dots:

(42) L: and I said . . . don't just don't try it

Use a vertical line of dots to indicate that turns have been missed out. Give the line numbers to make it clear what quantity of material is missing.

(43) 123 F: so he go- .hhh goes um what's that! and she
  ·
  ·
  ·
  131 F: so an he goes what's that an she says (0.3) it's your
       birthday pre(hh)sent

Other problems

What do I do if I want to mark something for which I don't know the convention in transcription?

Invent a symbol that is not going to be confused with anything else, and indicate clearly in the key what it stands for.

How should I present the actual taped material?

To assess a piece of your work properly, the marker will need to listen to a sample of the original material, to satisfy him/herself that it has been adequately transcribed. Doing this for everyone in the class is a time-consuming affair, and you can help the assessor to look favourably upon you by making the job as easy as possible. For guidance on this, see the final paragraph of Chapter 1.

For further transcription conventions, see Atkinson and Heritage (1984: ix–xvii), who cover the transcription of gaze-direction, for example, and individual papers themselves, many of which contain a key at the end (for example, Jefferson 1989: 193–6). For guidance on the transcription of spoken data for computer analysis, see Leech *et al.* (1995).

|19|

Using computers to study texts

CHRIS BUTLER

The computer is capable of processing vast amounts of material in a very short time, and with total accuracy. It can do in a few moments some things that it would take a human being many days or even weeks to do. Furthermore, the computer can produce information from texts in a form which reveals patterns that a human reader would probably never even notice. The kinds of linguistic analysis which computers can do easily are, however, still rather limited (see later).

Corpora and other computer-readable textual materials

A corpus (the usual plural is **corpora**) is a set of texts which has been put together for some purpose, usually (though not necessarily) in computer-readable form. A corpus may consist of written texts, transcriptions of spoken material, or both. In addition to specially compiled corpora, many single texts (often literary) and sets of texts (for example, the output of a particular poet) are available in computer-readable form. To study a corpus, you need special analytical tools. The following sections review the scope and availability of both the corpora and the tools.

Why you might want to study texts using a computer

Until computers made it possible, there were many questions about large texts that simply could not be answered without enormous effort. Imagine you wanted to know which of Jane Austen's novels contained most references to Bath, or how often Dickens began sentences with *and* or *but*, or whether Shakespeare more often used the word *fair* to refer to the appearance of men or women. To count these without a computer would be tedious and inaccurate, yet *with* one, enormously large corpora can be checked, with total accuracy, in hardly any time at all. Stubbs (1997) describes previous work in which he found support for the hypothesis that it is not uncommon for words to carry both female and pejorative connotations. He did this by demonstrating that in a 200-million-word corpus *little* occurs most often with *girl*, and that when it occurs with *man*, it is in phrases like *ridiculous little man*. In another analysis he was able to demonstrate that the word *care* has changed its connotations during this century. He concludes:

> Although the facts about *care* and *little* may seem obvious in retrospect, they are discoverable only via work on large corpora, and are not open to unaided introspection. And, if you are interested in a systematic and thoroughly documented study of cultural transmission, reproduction and change, then such studies are necessary.
>
> (Stubbs 1997: 114)

Some of the other applications of computers in text analysis are described and illustrated later in this chapter.

Compiling your own corpus: potential problems

- To create a corpus, you need to convert very large amounts of material to computer-readable form. This can be done using a scanner, but the results are by no means 100 per cent accurate, and need careful proof-reading.
- It is illegal to put copyright material (that is, almost all published works) into a computer corpus without permission.
- Spoken data, if that is what you want in your corpus, must first be collected and transcribed before it can go onto the computer.
- It is difficult to ensure that your corpus is truly representative of the type(s) of language you want to study.

Because of these difficulties you should consider using an existing corpus, as long as it will provide the data you require in the format you need.

Corpora and other texts of English available for academic use

Table 19.1 gives details of some of the corpora available from ICAME (the International Computer Archive of Modern English) in Bergen, Norway. Other corpora of English include the following (a more comprehensive list can be found in McEnery and Wilson 1996: 181–7).

- The **Bank of English**, containing several hundred million words of written and spoken English, collected at the University of Birmingham, and used for the well-known COBUILD series of dictionaries and grammars.

Table 19.1 Some corpora available from ICAME

Name	Language type (all English)	Size (words)	Spoken or written	Composition
Brown	American	1 million	written	500 samples, 2000 wds each, from 15 genres
Lancaster-Oslo-Bergen (LOB)	British	1 million	written	as for Brown
London-Lund	British	c.0.5 million	spoken	87 samples each 5000 wds; conversation, commentary, etc.
Melbourne-Surrey	Australian	100 000	written	newspaper texts
Kolhapur	Indian	1 million	written	printed texts
Helsinki	Old, Middle, Early Modern	1.5 million	written	242 texts
IBM/Lancaster Spoken English Corpus	English (British)	c.52 000	spoken (formal)	mostly from the BBC

- The **British National Corpus** (100 million words), involving Oxford University Press, Longman, Chambers, the British Library and the Universities of Oxford and Lancaster. The material is from a wide range of styles of written and spoken British English, and each word is grammatically tagged (see below). A set of corpus-processing tools has been developed in association with the corpus.
- The **Longman/Lancaster English Language Corpus**, containing 30 million words of twentieth-century English written texts, mainly British and American.
- The **International Corpus of English (ICE)**, consisting of 1 million words of spoken and written English (500 texts of about 2000 words each, produced in 1990 to 1996) from each of about a dozen countries where English is a first or second language. The British part of the corpus is due to be completed in Spring 1998. Meanwhile, a version may be consulted at the Survey of English Usage at University College London. Other components will become available later. The corpus is being tagged for word class, and every sentence will be parsed (see below).
- The **International Corpus of Learners' English** is part of ICE, kept at the University of Louvain, Belguim. It contains over a million words of written English produced by learners of English with 11 different native-language backgrounds.

- The **Association for Computational Linguistics Data Collection Initiative (USA) CD-ROM** contains *Wall Street Journal* texts, the *Collins English Dictionary* and the Penn treebank of parsed sentences (when a sentence is **parsed** it is annotated for its phrase and sentence structure).
- Computer archives such as those at the University of Bergen and the University of Oxford also contain large quantities of other, chiefly literary, material (such as novels and collections of plays and poems), much of which is readily available for non-commercial use by academics. Increasingly, textual material is also available for downloading from the Internet.

How to get hold of a corpus

Much of the material on the Internet can be obtained free of charge. Corpora and other materials on CD-ROM or other media can cost quite a lot, although some archives (like the Oxford Text Archive) make material available for little more than the cost of copying and postage. Your first port of call if you want to make use of corpora, or other textual material in computer-readable form, should be the computer centre at your institution, which may already hold it or be willing to obtain it.

Types of corpus annotation

Some corpora consist of just plain text. Most, however, contain additional information, which can be of various kinds. The simplest form of annotation involves embedding **text references** into the text. For instance, for the text of a play the user of the corpus is likely to need details of the author and title of the play, and an indication of where each act and scene begins, and maybe even where the characters start and finish speaking. For the beginning of Shakespeare's *All's Well That Ends Well*, a very simple version of this might look as shown in Fig. 19.1.

```
<A Shakespeare>
<P All's Well that Ends Well>
<Z 1>
<S 1>
<C Countess>

In delivering my son from me I bury a second husband.

[etc.]
```

Fig 19.1 Text references

The text references in the Figure are signalled as such by enclosing them in angle brackets, and A has been used to stand for author, P for play, Z for act, S for scene and C for character speaking.

An additional kind of annotation is **word-class tagging**, in which each word has attached to it a label showing the class of word to which it belongs (such as noun, verb, adjective, adverb, preposition, conjunction and so on, or more specific categories such as proper noun, common count noun, auxiliary verb and so on). An example, from the LOB corpus of written English, is given in Fig. 19.2.

hospitality_**NN** is_**BEZ** an_**AT** excellent_**JJ** virtue_**NN**,_, but_**CC** not_**XNOT**
when_**WRB** the_**ATI** guests_**NNS** have_**HV** to_**TO** sleep_**VB** in_**IN** rows_**NNS** in_**IN**
the_**ATI** cellar_**NN**!_!

Fig 19.2 Part of a corpus with word-class tagging

In the Figure the tag **NN** indicates a singular count noun, **BEZ** the third person singular of BE, **AT** the indefinite article, **JJ** an adjective, and so on. As mentioned earlier, texts can even be tagged with information on the syntactic structure of the phrases and sentences (that is, they can be **parsed**).

Linguistic analyses that can be done using computers and how to do them

It isn't sufficient *just* to have a corpus, because that is only the raw material. You need a program that will tell the computer what to look for:

- **wordlists:** If you are interested in knowing which words occur most frequently in the text(s), you need a text-analysis program that tells the computer to count up the occurrence of each word form and then to list them in descending or ascending order of frequency, or alphabetically, say. Fig. 19.3 shows the first 25 words in an alphabetical word list and in a list of the most frequently occurring words for Thomas Hardy's novel *Far from the Madding Crowd*, produced by means of the WordSmith Tools program (see below).
- **concordances:** You might want to know what sorts of words tend to occur in the immediate environment of a given word; this requires a concordancing program. You choose your key word, and the program searches for all the occurrences of it, and displays and/or prints them with your preferred amount of context (for example, one line or one sentence). Different orderings are also possible. Fig. 19.4 shows a concordance of the word *red* from Hardy's *Far from the Madding Crowd*,

WORD	FREQ.		WORD	FREQ.	
1. A	3710	(2.91%)	1. THE	7650	(5.73%)
2. A'MOST	1		2. AND	4152	(3.11%)
3. A'S	1		3. A	3845	(2.88%)
4. A'TERNOON	1		4. OF	3744	(2.81%)
5. AARON	1		5. TO	3575	(2.68%)
6. ABANDON	1		6. IN	2336	(1.75%)
7. ABANDONED	1		7. WAS	1958	(1.47%)
8. ABANDONMENT	2		8. I	1630	(1.22%)
9. ABASEMENT	1		9. IT	1511	(1.13%)
10. ABASHED	4		10. THAT	1480	(1.11%)
11. ABATED	1		11. HER	1461	(1.09%)
12. ABBEY	1		12. HE	1361	(1.02%)
13. ABEDNEGO	1		13. YOU	1361	(1.02%)
14. ABEL	1		14. SHE	1226	(0.92%)
15. ABIDE	2		15. AS	1180	(0.88%)
16. ABIDING	2		16. HAD	1142	(0.86%)
17. ABLE	29	(0.02%)	17. HIS	1137	(0.85%)
18. ABNORMAL	7		18. SAID	980	(0.73%)
19. ABOARD	1		19. FOR	979	(0.73%)
20. ABOAT	1		20. WITH	969	(0.73%)
21. ABODE	1		21. AT	937	(0.70%)
22. ABOUNDING	1		22. NOT	828	(0.62%)
23. ABOUT	252	(0.20%)	23. BE	796	(0.60%)
24. ABOVE	40	(0.03%)	24. IS	741	(0.56%)
25. ABRADED	2		25. ON	734	(0.55%)

Fig 19.3 Alphabetical and frequency-ordered words lists in *Far from the Madding Crowd*

again produced using WordSmith Tools. The concordance has been sorted according to the alphabetical order of the word to the right of the search word. The actual appearance of this concordance on the screen would be slightly different: the search word (*red*) would be picked out in one colour and the word to the right in a different colour. Further investigation of the occurrences of this word, using a larger context, reveals interesting connections with the characters in the novel.

In addition, some programs allow the user to study other features of texts:

- the **distribution** of words or sets of words through the various parts of the text(s): Fig. 19.5 shows the distribution of the name of the character *Troy* in *Far from the Madding Crowd* (again produced by WordSmith Tools). The horizontal bar represents the book, and each vertical line is an occurrence of the word. We can see from this that there are only two mentions of this character's name in the first third or so of the book.
- the **collocations** which particular words or sets of words enter into (that

1. y Ball out of breath, his mouth	red	and open, like the bell of a
2. t visible burnt rayless, like a	red	and flameless fire shining ov
3. ms. In the midst of these shone	red	and distinct the figure of Se
4. panting like a robin, her face	red	and moist from her exertions
5. his eyes, which were vermilion-	red	and bleared by gazing into it
6. and clinging to her hair, were	red	and yellow leaves which had c
7. spring waggon, picked out with	red,	and containing boughs and fl
8. re marked with great splotches,	red	as arterial blood, others wer
9. tight warm hide of rich Indian	red,	as absolutely uniform from e
10. silent awhile. He regarded the	red	berries between them over and
11. nted holly bush, now laden with	red	berries. Seeing his advance t
12. usual into the furnace with his	red,	bleared eyes. From the bedro
13. heba was unusually excited, her	red	cheeks and lips contrasting l
14. art of the circle, covered with	red	cloth, and floored with a pie
15. a sergeant, and good looking a	red	coat with blue facings? miss
16. ne upon the bright gown and his	red	coat my! how handsome they lo
17. l, his face turning to an angry	red.	Coggan twirled his eye, edge
18. th a single pane, though which	red,	comfortable rays now stretch
19. the snow, till it shone in the	red	eastern light with the polish
20. t, and to see how strangely the	red	feather of her hat shone in t
21. ed and hornless blue flocks and	red	flocks, buff flocks and brown
22. lly, some of the natural, rusty	red	having returned to his face.
23. ssment. She became more or less	red	in the cheek, the blood waver
24. The man was Sergeant Troy. His	red	jacket was loosely thrown on,
25., save the foremost, who wore a	red	jacket, and advanced with his
26. bled ropes of black hair over a	red	jacket. Oak knew her instantl
27. ness of aged men, and the rusty-	red	leaves of the beeches were hu
28. he close compression of her two	red	lips, with which she had acco
29. e keenly pointed corners of her	red	mouth when, with parted lips,
30. he saw a dim spot of artificial	red	moving round the shoulder of
31. few minutes she noticed the fat	red	nape of Coggan's neck among t
32. do we'll have another. A large	red	seal was duly affixed. Bathsh
33. astening itself, till the large	red	seal became as a blot of bloo
34. preceding day, at the insistent	red	seal: me, he said aloud. The
35. ily, if not quite, an enlarging	red	spot rising in each cheek. Ca
36. The sun went down almost blood-	red	that night, and a livid cloud
37. eturned Liddy promptly: rose is	red,	the violet blue, Carnation's
38. d Betelgueux shone with a fiery	red.	To persons standing alone on
39. d. A young cavalry soldier in a	red	uniform, with the three chevr
40. g waggon with the blue body and	red	wheels, and wash it very clea
41. heat, as if they were knots of	red	worms, and above shone imagin
42. ntly. I, said Boldwood, growing	red.	You needn't stay here a minu

Fig 19.4 A concordance

MADCROW2.TXT
304 hits in 133,456 words

2.3 per 1,000 words

Fig 19.5 Distribution of Troy in *Far from the Madding Crowd*

is, the other words with which they associate): Fig. 19.6 takes the words that occur in the immediate environment of *red* (that is, 1, 2, 3, 4 or 5 words to the left or right of it) and shows how often each one is found in each position.

1.	RED	42	0 0 0 0 0	-	0 0 0 0 0
2.	THE	24	3 3 1 4 3	-	1 1 4 4 0
3.	AND	22	1 1 1 1 2	-	7 5 1 2 1
4.	OF	15	2 2 3 2 1	-	0 3 0 0 2
5.	A	14	2 1 0 2 5	-	0 0 0 2 2
6.	WITH	14	1 0 2 1 3	-	0 3 2 2 0
7.	HIS	9	1 0 0 1 3	-	0 0 2 1 1
8.	HER	8	0 0 1 2 2	-	0 0 1 2 0
9.	WERE	6	1 0 1 1 1	-	0 0 0 0 2
10.	SHONE	5	0 1 1 0 1	-	0 0 0 1 1
11.	TO	5	1 1 1 0 0	-	1 0 1 0 0
12.	BLUE	4	0 0 2 0 0	-	0 0 2 0 0
13.	IN	4	0 0 0 2 0	-	1 0 1 0 0
14.	WAS	4	0 2 0 0 0	-	0 2 0 0 0
15.	WHICH	4	0 0 1 0 1	-	0 0 1 1 0
16	AS	3	0 0 0 0 0	-	2 0 1 0 0
17.	BLOOD	3	0 0 0 0 1	-	0 0 1 0 1
18.	EYES	3	0 1 0 0 0	-	0 1 0 0 1
19.	FACE	3	1 0 0 0 1	-	0 0 0 0 1
20.	FLOCKS	3	0 0 0 1 0	-	1 0 1 0 0
21.	FROM	3	0 0 0 0 0	-	0 0 2 1 0
22.	JACKET	3	0 0 0 0 0	-	3 0 0 0 0
23.	LIKE	3	1 0 0 1 0	-	0 0 1 0 0
24.	LIPS	3	0 0 0 0 0	-	1 0 1 0 1
25.	OUT	3	1 0 0 1 0	-	0 0 0 0 1
26.	OVER	3	0 0 0 1 0	-	0 0 0 1 1
27.	SEAL	3	0 0 0 0 0	-	3 0 0 0 0
28.	SHE	3	1 1 0 0 0	-	0 0 0 1 0

Fig 19.6 Collocations

- **key words** which, by comparison with another body of text taken as a norm, appear surprisingly frequently.

Programs that are available for text analysis

- **WordSmith Tools** is a recent, reasonably user-friendly software package for text analysis. It does all the things mentioned above and more, and is available from Oxford University Press. Examples have been given in Figs. 19.3 to 19.6.
- **MicroConcord** is also available from Oxford University Press, and is in many ways the forerunner of WordSmith Tools. It was intended to be

suitable for use not only by language researchers but also teachers who wanted to use word lists and concordances for 'data-driven learning' in the language classroom.

- **Oxford Concordance Program (OCP)** is available from Oxford University Press, the PC version being called **Micro-OCP**. OCP is very flexible, but rather slow, as it requires all the basic analysis (splitting up into words and so on) to be performed every time the program is run.
- **TACT**, a package written at the University of Toronto, operates in two stages: production of a database from a given text, and subsequent (fast) use of the database for particular analyses, without further reference to the original text. TACT will also produce collocational analyses with measures of statistical significance. There may be problems with computer memory if large texts are to be analysed.
- **WordCruncher**, developed at Brigham Young University and now distributed by Electronic Text Corporation, consists of a program for indexing texts, and one for generating concordances and so on from them. WordCruncher is powerful, but there is only one possible sort order and there are memory limitations.

Other applications of computers in relation to texts

The following are among the most successful and interesting applications of computer-based textual studies.

Stylistics

Computers can provide large amounts of information on statistical patterns of linguistic items in texts, and so can, if wisely used, be helpful in studying the style of both literary and non-literary texts. Examples of such applications include: work on semantic fields and imagery; investigations of the linguistic behaviour of particular characters in, say, a novel; and studies of the chronological development of an author's style, or of a genre. Computers have also been useful in attempts to settle questions of disputed authorship (of Elizabethan plays, for example), by comparing linguistic features of the disputed text with those of texts known to be by particular authors.

Dictionary making

Computers are now widely used in the production of dictionaries. The first dictionary for which the computer was used at all stages of production was the Collins COBUILD English Language Dictionary, which is based on the concordancing of a very large amount of text from what is now known as the Bank of English (see above).

Computer-assisted language learning (CALL)

The computer-assisted analysis of vocabulary and grammar is helpful in the design of language learning materials. Recently there has been an upsurge of interest in **data-driven language learning**, which exploits computer-generated concordances of authentic texts as a resource for classroom use.

Computer-based help with writing tasks

Computers can be helpful at all stages in the writing of a piece of text (such as an essay or laboratory report). At the stage where the writer is planning the text, **dialogue** programs can help to generate ideas, **outliners** can aid in the organisation of material, and **note-taking** tools allow the jotting down of material for later use. **Word processing** programs facilitate the composition process itself, and **spell checkers** and **grammar checkers** can be used either during composition, or to improve the end product.

Computer-based generation and 'comprehension' of texts

Computers can be used to create texts which approximate to natural human linguistic production, and also to extract information from texts which have been produced by human beings. This area, often called **Natural Language Processing (NLP)**, is part of the discipline of Artificial Intelligence (AI). At present it is much easier for a computer to produce or analyse *written* text than spoken, though much progress has been made in speech synthesis and analysis. The practical usefulness of such work, particularly in relation to spoken language, is considerable (for talking books for the blind, computers that can by accessed by telephone callers and so forth).

Textbooks

- **Barnbrook (1996)** is a general introduction to the use of computers in the study of language, covering the selection and capture of data for analysis, the production and use of word lists, concordances and collocational analyses, and an introductory treatment of Natural Language Processing and its applications. There is a useful chapter which discusses a number of case studies.

- **Roach (1992)** is a set of introductory readings for students of linguistics, phonetics and related disciplines, with chapters on the use of corpora to answer interesting questions about English, speech analysis and recognition, parsing and generation of language, machine translation and CALL.
- **Butler (1992)** gives an overview of the use of computers in the study of written texts, at a rather higher general level than Roach (1992). It contains chapters on tools and techniques, parsing, language generation, corpus linguistics, machine translation, stylistics, dictionaries, CALL, writing tools, and textual editing.
- **McEnery and Wilson (1996)** is a much more detailed treatment of corpus linguistics than any of the books mentioned above. It deals with the definition of a corpus, questions of representativeness, quantitative techniques of analysis, the uses of corpus linguistics, and Natural Language Processing applications.
- The emphasis in **Stubbs (1996)** is on text in relation to issues of cultural and societal importance. The second half of the book presents a number of illuminating corpus-based analyses.
- **Leech *et al.* (1995)** is a practical book on how to transcribe spoken English for the computer, what you can do with spoken corpora and what problems can arise.

|20|

The Data Protection Act

What is the Data Protection Act?

The Data Protection Act was introduced in the UK in 1984 in response to the increasing use of computers to store and distribute information about individuals. If you are not a UK resident there is still likely to be some equivalent law in your country. You should be able to find out about this via your local or university library.

What is it for?

The purpose of the British Data Protection Act is to protect the rights of people whose information is stored on computer. This is achieved by two basic means. Anyone who stores data on individuals must *only store what they actually need*, and must *register as a data user*, saying what the information will be used for.

What rights do I have if information is stored about me?

The law does not give the individual the right to control what is done with information stored about him- or herself, but it is possible to request a copy of what details are being held and/or distributed.

How does the information get there in the first place?

In most cases, individuals have given the information quite willingly, know what it will be used for, and have no cause for concern about it. For example, when you apply for a mortgage you divulge information about your income and expenditure. The mortgage company will have undertaken not to give that information to anyone else without your permission (you may have a box to tick on the form to control whether it goes, say, to their sister insurance company), and it will have registered as a Data User, stating the purposes for which the information will be used.

What does the Act actually do?

The problems that the Act is designed to address are mainly as follows:

- gathering data for one purpose and then using it for another, without the permission of the individual involved. This is controlled by the register, which monitors what the information is used for. If you were researching the effects of advertising language on TV viewers and, as part of this, asked your subjects what products they bought, it would be illegal to sell that information to a marketing company, because you gathered the data for another purpose and your informants provided it on that understanding.
- the storing of information that is incorrect – for example, if you move into a house previously occupied by someone who defaulted on credit payments, you might find that your address is blacklisted and you can't get credit clearance yourself. This is dealt with by individuals having the right to see the records that are kept on them by any Data User.

How does it affect academic research?

The Act was not designed with academic researchers in mind, but it can affect them. For example, if you were doing some case studies and you kept computer files with personal information in, then you might need to register.

Without question, the easiest and most sensible way to avoid needing to even think about the Act is to keep any personal information about your research subjects on paper. It is only information on computer that is subject to the Act. However, if you put the information onto computer solely as part of the word-processing of your work, that is, just for presentational purposes, it is not subject to registration.

There are some special provisions for data that is 'for historical, statistical or research purposes'. These permit data to be kept indefinitely (not normally allowed) and also allow researchers to use data for research that wasn't collected for that purpose. Data can be held for research purposes, provided that it is not used for anything else and the identity of individuals cannot be worked out from the write-up.

Confidentiality is standard practice in research. One way to ensure the anonymity of subjects is not to mention names at all, and to confine the personal details to groupings (e.g. ten unemployed men and ten pregnant women). In case studies it is common to alter the name and any details which are not vital to the interpretation of the results.

Registration

How do I know if I have data that requires me to register?

The following details may help you to decide whether you need to register. The Act applies only if:

- the people are still living
- they are individuals, not companies and organizations
- the data enables them to be identified
- the data includes statements of fact (as opposed to opinion).

Data Users can be exempt from registration for three basic reasons:

- the information isn't important enough, for example personal and family information (such as a family tree) held on a home computer; payment information used to keep the books straight, and not for marketing; mailing lists and club membership lists (though here, individuals have the right to object to their details being kept this way)
- the data is public by law, such as the Electoral Roll
- the data is too important to national security for individuals to be allowed to control what happens to it, as in the case of files on terrorists.

The official line is that you shouldn't assume that your data is exempt until you have read all the small print of the Act. You only need one little bit of your data *not* to be exempt for registration to be necessary. It is a criminal offence not to register if you need to and to do anything with the data other than what it has been registered for.

What do I do if I need to register?

If you need to register, get a registration pack, including form DPR1, from the Post Office. There is a fee of £22 to pay when you register. The form will ask what data you will have, what you will need it for, how you will get it, who you will disclose it to and where abroad it might be sent to. The rules for registered Data Users include:

- not having more detail than you need for the purpose
- ensuring that the information is accurate and up-to-date
- not keeping it longer than it is needed
- making the information properly secure, so that no-one else can access it

- supplying, in response to an individual's written request and payment of a set fee, a copy of the information about them.

Important note

This description of the Data Protection Act is intended for guidance only. If you are unsure whether you need to register, you must go to a fuller and more authoritative source than this. The Data Protection Registrar's Guideline series is available from most libraries and is free from the DPA Office, tel: 01625 545745. Other useful publications include Cornwell and Staunton (1985) and Sizer and Newman (1984).

|21|

How to reference

Basics

It is crucial to your work that you reference your sources correctly. This chapter aims to answer your questions about why and how to reference.

What is the point of referencing?

The point of referencing is that the reader is able to trace an idea or piece of information right back to its source. The conventions of referencing are such that it should always be possible to do this. The writer is leaving a 'trail', and this trail must be clear all the way back. Doing this is important for three reasons:

- One of the major ways in which all researchers come across important new information is by reading about it in another source. Without full references, it would be impossible to track the information down.
- When your project is marked, your assessors are looking to see that you understand the material you are writing about. If you make reference to, or quote, some work that they do not know (which is not uncommon), or if you back up an apparently wacky idea with a quote or reference, it will be necessary for them to check it. Unless you give the full details, including the page number, it may be impossible – and certainly very time-consuming – for them to find it. As pointed out in Chapter 1, the golden rule of project writing is not to annoy your assessor, and incomplete referencing is a sure-fire way to make yourself extremely unpopular.
- You do not want to be accused of plagiarism, that is, of passing someone else's ideas off as your own (see Chapter 22).

The basic procedure

This can be illustrated with an example from Wardhaugh (1993: 109).

> (1) The 'tip of the tongue' phenomenon (see Brown and McNeill, 1966) is an instance of this last kind of failure to bring an item immediately and completely out of long-term memory.

By referring to Brown and McNeill's paper, Wardhaugh is giving you, the reader, information about where to look for further details. The short reference given in the text (example 1) is backed up by a full reference in the alphabetical list of references at the back of Wardhaugh's book (example 2). This provides you with all you need to locate the original work, and to read for yourself what they did.

> (2) Brown, R., and McNeill, D. 1966. The 'tip of the tongue' phenomenon. *Journal of Verbal Learning and Verbal Behavior 5*, 325–37.

But what if I haven't seen the original, just a reference to it or quote from it somewhere else?

When writers have not had access to the original source themselves, they adopt the convention of **citing** or giving a **secondary quote**. Both of these are explained later on. It is sufficient at this point to illustrate how you proceed even in these circumstances. Aitchison (1994: 32) uses a quote from a medical writer called Thomson, which she has found in a paper by John Marshall. She writes:

> (3) As a medical writer suggests at the beginning of the century: 'After some brain shock, a person may be able to speak, but the wrong word often vexatiously comes to his lips, just as if ... shelves had become badly jumbled' (Thomson, 1907, quoted in Marshall, 1977, p. 479).

Aitchison shows us in a footnote where *she* found the quote (on page 479 in Marshall's paper), and tells us what reference to look up in that paper if we want to find the original (Thomson, 1907). In her references section at the back of the book, she gives the details of Marshall's paper, but not of Thomson's; but these in turn can be found in Marshall (1977).

Is there such a thing as referencing at third hand?

Yes. If you used Aitchison's passage in example 3 above as a quote, you would be quoting Aitchison quoting Marshall quoting Thomson. However, it is not a good idea to get so far removed from the original; so, generally speaking, it is preferable to avoid third-hand quoting and to keep second-hand quoting to a minimum. The way to achieve this is to trace the original source wherever possible, and draw from that instead. The only works that you should be quoting or citing second-hand are those which your library does not have, and which you have not had an opportunity to order from another library.

What is the difference between a 'references' list and a 'bibliography'?

These terms do tend to get used interchangeably in some contexts, but there is a difference. A list of references gives details of the books and articles that have been mentioned in a text. It should contain all of them, and should *not* contain anything you have read or looked at but not mentioned. A bibliography is a list of books and articles put together for some other purpose, usually to help researchers and/or as recommended reading for study. All of this means that the list of sources at the end of your project should be called *References*.

How do I make sure I have managed to list all and only the sources I have mentioned?

One of your jobs as a writer is to ensure that your reference list is complete and accurate. In order to make sure that you have not omitted a reference, make a print-out of the list, and then work through the text, ticking off on the print-out every reference as you come across it. If you find a reference in the text that ought to be on the list and isn't, then add it. Remember that you do not need to list secondary sources, that is, works that you have mentioned via another source, provided that you have clearly indicated what that other source is (see above). If at the end of the process there is any reference on the list that has not been ticked, then there is no mention of it in the text, and it should be removed. If you have a search facility on your word-processing program, you can type in the first few letters of a name from the reference list and search for it. If the first occurrence that the search comes up with is in the reference list itself, then there is no mention in the text and the entry should be deleted. This procedure cannot be used to find out if a reference in the text is *missing* from the list.

What is the best way to keep track of what references I need to put in the list?

There are various methods, two of which are given below. Whichever one you use, though, remember one golden rule: *Every time you use a book or article, keep a note of the complete details that you will need for referencing purposes.*

METHOD 1

Construct the reference list as you go. The advantage of this approach is that you have one less job to do at the end. There are a couple of disadvantages, though. First, as your work goes through different stages, you are likely to edit out passages containing references. It is not always easy to remember whether there are other mentions of those works in your project, and so you might not be sure whether or not to delete them from the reference list. Second, you may find that it breaks your flow to keep moving to the reference list when you are in the middle of writing.

METHOD 2

When you have finished writing, do a *very* careful read, identifying all the references at that stage, and building up the list. The advantage of this is that, if you are careful enough, you will end up with a list of all and only the references mentioned. The disadvantage is that you have to be quite disciplined to comb the text for *only* references. It is tempting to combine this job with a final read-through, or a proofread for typing errors, and this division of your attention is quite likely to make you less efficient on all of the tasks. If you have a search facility on your word-processor, and you have been careful always to put the dates for your references in brackets, you can do a search for the opening bracket and find the references that way. Alternatively, as you write, highlight each reference (on screen, or with highlighter pen, according to your medium). Then they will be easy to find later. If you use this method, be careful to write down the full reference information somewhere *before* the book goes back to the library, just in case it is not there when you go back to find it. You cannot rely on a library catalogue to give you all the information you need for a reference list: very often no place of publication is given, and no titles, author details or page numbers will be given for the papers in edited collections.

What is the difference between 'cited in' and 'quoted in'?

Many students muddle these two terms, probably because they have not really understood what they mean. When you **quote** something, you give the words as they appear in the original. Indicate this by putting inverted commas around the quote if it is less than two lines long, or by indenting the quote, with a line-space above and below (for one example of this, see p. 88 in this book). In both cases, write the author, date and page in brackets immediately after it. If you want to reproduce a quote that you have found in another work (as Aitchison has done in example 3 above), then you indicate this, as she has done, by writing the original author's name followed by *quoted in* and then your source, including the page number.

When you **cite** something, you *mention* it. There is no quotation involved. If you want to mention a source that you have found in another work, then you say *cited in*. For example, if you read in Wardhaugh (1993) about Brown and McNeill's (1966) experiment (see example 1 above), then you might write:

> (4)   The 'tip of the tongue' phenomenon can be investigated experimentally, as Brown and MacNeill (1966, cited in Wardhaugh 1993: 109) have demonstrated.

Is there only one way of referencing correctly?

No. There are two major systems, the **Harvard** and the **Humane**, and within each you may spot minor variations.

What is the basic difference between the Harvard and the Humane systems?

The distinction between Harvard and Humane has traditionally been associated with the major division between the science (including the social sciences) and the arts subjects, though the Harvard system is now tending to be used in both. As linguistics spans the sciences and arts, both systems can be found in older publications, but it is rare to find Humane referencing in recent books and journals. If you are studying a subject like English literature as well as linguistics, you may well find that you are required to use both systems. Accept this gracefully, and be careful to use whichever is required in each piece of work. Take particular care not to mix them, otherwise you will be using neither!

As to format, the Harvard system refers to works by their author(s) and date in the text, with full references at the end, alphabetically by author surname. The Humane system uses footnote numbers in the text, and gives the references, in numerical order (that is, in the order of their occurrence), at the foot of each page or at the end. In what follows, the guidelines relate to the Harvard system. A summary of how to reference in the Humane system is provided later in the chapter.

The Harvard system

How do I refer to a book?

In the text, give the author's name followed by date of publication (example 5). Where appropriate, give page numbers too (example 6).

(5)   Wardhaugh (1993).

(6)   Wardhaugh (1993: 64–8)

In the reference list, give the author's name, initial(s), date in brackets (although note that, in some versions of this system, the date is not in brackets, and it is followed by a colon; in others, there are neither brackets nor a colon) and title in italics, followed by a full stop, place of publication followed by a colon, publisher and full stop:

(7)   Wardhaugh, R. (1993) *Investigating language*. Oxford: Blackwell.

What if the book is an edited collection of papers by other people?

In the text, proceed as above. In the reference list, give the author's name, initial(s), '(ed.)' or '(eds.)', and then as above:

(8)   Giglioli, P.P. (ed.) (1972) *Language and social context*. Harmondsworth: Penguin.

What if there are two authors?

In the text, give both, linked by 'and' (example 9) and *in the reference list*, give both, with initials (example 10). If they are editors, put '(eds.)' before the date (example 11).

(9)   Graddol and Swann (1989)

(10)   Graddol, D. and Swann, J. (1989) *Gender voices*. Oxford: Blackwell.

(11)   Carruthers, P. and Smith, P.K. (eds.) (1996) *Theories of theory of mind*. Cambridge: Cambridge University Press.

What if there are three or more authors?

In the text, either give the first author, followed by '*et al.*', then the date (example 12), or, on the first occurrence of the reference, give all the names, and after that use '*et al.*' as above (example 13):

(12)   Bates *et al.* (1988)

(13)   Bates, Bretherton and Snyder (1988) . . . Bates *et al.* (1988)

In the reference list, give all the authors with their initials, linking them with a comma until the last two, which are linked with 'and':

> (14) Bates, E., Bretherton, I. and Snyder, L. (1988) *From first words to grammar*. Cambridge: Cambridge University Press.

How is a paper in an edited book notated?

In the text, give the author of the paper and the date of the edited book. *Do not* mention the editor(s) of the book here:

> (15) Smith (1996)

In the reference list, give the author with the initial(s), date, title of paper (*not* in italics; in some versions of this system the title of a paper is put in inverted commas) followed by a full stop. Then write 'In', followed by the book details, as described above. Finally, give the page numbers of the paper, preceded by a comma (or, in some versions, a colon, or a comma and 'p.' or 'pp.') and followed by a full stop:

> (16) Smith, P.K. (1996) Language and the evolution of mind-reading. In Carruthers, P. and Smith, P.K. (eds.) (1996) *Theories of theory of mind*. Cambridge: Cambridge University Press, 344–54.

What are the conventions for a paper in a journal?

In the text, as above. *In the reference list*, give the author(s) with initials, date, title of paper (*not* in italics; in some versions of this system the title is put in inverted commas), full stop. Then give the title of the journal, in italics, volume number, part number in brackets if appropriate, and pages, preceded by a comma (or, in some versions, by a colon, or a comma and 'p.' or 'pp.') and followed by a full stop:

> (17) Brakke, K.E. and Savage-Rumbaugh, E.S. (1995) The development of language skills in bonobo and chimpanzee – I. Comprehension. *Language and Communication* 15(2), 121–48.

Where do I find the information I need?

In a book, the details are in the first few pages at the front. Be careful to copy the authors' names and the book or paper title correctly. The date of publication will normally be on the same left hand page as the ISBN number and the British Library or Library of Congress (or other national library) cataloguing data. It is not usually difficult to spot the publisher (but beware of giving the printer or typesetter by mistake). However, it is sometimes difficult to work out the *place* of publication. If there is an address for the publisher, give the town and, if American, the state as well. If there are several addresses, give the top one, or the one associated with editorial as opposed to marketing concerns. Some large publishing houses publish simultaneously in two countries (such as the UK and the US): if you can't tell which country the book was probably commissioned in, give both places.

In a journal, the name of the journal and the volume number and part *should* be printed somewhere on the article as a header or footer. If they are not, and you have the whole journal in your hand, look in the front, or on the back cover. If you have only a photocopy, you obviously needed to write down the details when you made the copy. If you didn't, you have a problem, so remember to do that in future! One way to get the information if you can't remember where the article came from and there is no indication on it is to check through the reference lists of publications that might mention it, especially (if applicable) the one that first alerted you to its existence.

If a book has been reprinted or revised, which date do I use?

Inside a book all sorts of information is given and only some of it is relevant to academic referencing needs. The basic rule is to give the earliest date for the text in its current form. When a new **edition** of a book is produced, material is added and the page numbers end up different, so it is important that you indicate which edition you have used, and give the correct date for that edition. Indicate an edition by putting '(*n*th edition)' after the title, where *n* stands for the edition number (e.g. 3rd, 4th). However, when a book is **reprinted**, or comes out in **paperback**, the material is not altered, so you should not make any reference to reprint or paperback dates. Sometimes there is a date given for a **reprint with revisions**. In this case, give the reprint date, and in the reference, put '(revised edition)' after the title.

What if the date of publication is different from the copyright date?

Use the publication date, unless there is evidence to the contrary in the reference lists of others. If there is a large discrepancy it will probably be because the work has been reissued, in which case the 'copyright' date coincides with the original date of publication. In the case of key papers which end up in a 'reader', it can be useful to indicate the original publication date as well – see the section 'What if . . .?' below.

Are there any special conventions for referencing more than one work by the same person?

Practice varies on this. It is common simply to see the name repeated on line after line where there are a lot of references to one person's work. That is the practice adopted in this book. However, another option is to replace the name by a long dash after its first occurrence:

(18)   Trudgill, P. (1974) *The social differentiation of English in Norwich*. Cambridge: Cambridge University Press.
—— (1978) *Sociolinguistic patterns in British English* London: Arnold.
—— (1983) *On dialect*. Oxford: Blackwell.

What should I do if I have referred to more than one work by the same person published in the same year?

As it would be confusing to have two or more works all referred to as, say, Crystal (1988), the convention is to label them a, b, c, and so on. You should use these letters both in the main text and in the reference list, and ensure that you always use the same letter for the same one. Note that the use of letters is *local* to the piece of writing in question, so only use them if *you* have referred to several works from the same year. If you find letters in someone else's references, because *they* have encountered this problem, *do not* adopt the letter as part of the reference unless you actually need it. In other words, you should never have in your reference list a date with a letter after it unless there is at least one other work by that author with that date, also with a (different) letter after it. Look at the entries for Crystal (1988) in this book to see how this operates. Note also that there is nothing intrinsic in the publication that is referred to as 'a' that means it *had* to be 'a'. Someone else might list it as 'b' with another publication as 'a'.

What if there is more than one author with the same surname?

In the reference list, give the authors in alphabetical order of their forenames or initials. In the text, because authors are referred to by surname only, there is the potential for confusion if both authors have published in the same year. The best way round this is to add the initial in the text reference, for example G. Cook (1992), so that the reader knows which Cook (1992) reference you mean. In this book we only narrowly missed having this problem with the names Brown, Carroll, Chomsky, Clark, Cook, Ellis, Wells and White.

If an author has co-authored with others, which order do the works go in on the reference list?

To illustrate how to do this, we'll use some made-up authors, so that we can imagine various permutations. We'll call the first author *Penelope Wilkinson*. First put *all* the single-authored work by that person, in order of year; then sort the co-authored works alphabetically by the second author's name, and list them in that order. Works by the same two authors are in date order:

> (19) Wilkinson, P. (1986) . . .
> Wilkinson, P. (1989) . . .
> Wilkinson, P. (1994) . . .
> Wilkinson, P. and Armitage, S. (1988) . . .
> Wilkinson, P. and Cooper, M. (1983) . . .
> Wilkinson, P. and Cooper, M. (1991) . . .

If a two-author team has also written with a third person, put the three-author work last, even if it is of an earlier date. If there is more than one work by the same three-author team, put them in date order:

> (20) Wilkinson, P. and Armitage, S. (1988) . . .
> Wilkinson, P. and Cooper, M. (1983) . . .
> Wilkinson, P. and Cooper, M. (1991) . . .
> Wilkinson, P., Cooper, M. and Bryant. Q. (1984) . . .
> Wilkinson, P., Cooper, M. and Bryant, Q. (1991) . . .
> Wilkinson, P., Cooper, M. and Caradine, K. (1997) . . .
> Wilkinson, P., Cooper, M., Collins, R. and Bryant, Q. (1989) . . .

In other words, clear up all the works by the author on his/her own before doing the two-author works. Clear up everything by each two-author team, including works with extra authors, before moving onto the next two-author team. Remember that the *order* in which the authors' names appear on a book or paper is extremely important and you must not change it. So, in the final line of example 20, Bryant is listed after Collins, and it is Collins's name that determines the position of the reference, below the publication with Caradine.

What are the conventions for punctuation in reference lists?

These do vary considerably; however, as long as you are consistent, it doesn't matter too much which conventions you use, unless you are preparing something for publication, when you should check with the author's notes issued by the publisher. Certain conventions, however, are fairly standard. Follow each initial by a full stop; follow names in a list of authors by a comma, except the penultimate (which is linked to the final one with 'and'); put the date of publication in brackets; use a full stop after abbreviations such as 'ed.' (for *editor*); use a colon after the place of publication (and put the place of publication *before* the publisher); and use italics for book and journal titles.

Amongst the additional conventions that we have adopted in this book are: using a colon before the page numbers; using lower case letters in book and paper titles, except the first word and proper names; and not using italics or inverted commas for paper titles.

What should I do if I can't print italics or I am writing by hand?

Wherever italics would occur (in reference lists and also in the main text), it is acceptable to use underlining.

Is it possible to put into the reference list a work that has not yet been published?

Yes. If you have had sight of a paper or book that is currently being printed but hasn't yet appeared, write *forthcoming* or *in press* where you would otherwise write the date and, if it is a paper and the page numbers are not available, omit them. It is also possible to refer to a work that is at an earlier stage. Do this in the same way as above, but replacing *forthcoming* or *in press* with *in preparation*. Beware of using these labels when you have found the reference in another source. A work that was *forthcoming, in press* or *in preparation* in 1994 is probably published by now, so you need to try and find its publication date.

What if . . .?

In this section we refer you to titles in the reference section at the back of this book, to check on the conventions for less common details. Look up the work we suggest, to see how we have referenced it.

- A modern reissue of an older work: Boas (1911/1966).
- A modern edition (prepared by someone else) of a classic work: Carroll (1865/1971).
- A reprint of a classic paper in a 'reader': Searle (1965).

The Humane system

In this referencing system, a superscript number in the text points the reader to a footnote or endnote containing the reference information.

Thus, *in the text*, place a superscript number adjacent to the word that precedes the reference you wish to make:

> (21) Messages in language fall into three *situation types*: states, events and actions.[18] These situation types are . . .

In the footnote or endnote, adopt the following procedures.

For a book

Give the initial(s), author(s), title in italics, place of publication, publisher and date together in brackets, and page(s) relevant to the point you are making, if any:

> (22) [18]D. Graddol and J. Swann, *Gender Voices* (Oxford, Blackwell, 1989), p. 77.

If you have to refer to it again, you use a shortened form, with just the surnames, a shortened title if it isn't short enough already, and the page:

> (23) [20]Graddol and Swann, *Gender Voices*, p. 54.

It is also possible to refer to the last work you have mentioned with *op. cit.* (short for *opera citato* – 'in the work cited'), or *ibid.* (short for *ibidem* – 'in the same place'). However, these terms are used much less frequently than they used to be. If you do use them, do so only in the final draft, as they *must* refer to the immediately preceding reference. As references often get moved around, added or removed in the course of a rewrite, you could end up with an *ibid.* or *op. cit.* referring back to the wrong work if you put it in too soon.

For an edited book

Proceed as above, but add 'ed.,' after the author name(s).

For a paper in an edited volume

Give the initial(s), author(s), title in inverted commas, 'in', editor's name, comma, '(ed.)', title of book in italics, place of publication, publisher and date together in brackets, and page(s) relevant to the point you are making, if any (*not* the page range for the entire paper) (example 24). Use a short reference for later mentions (example 25). There are no rules for what the title gets shortened to, provided a reader will be entirely sure which work you are referring to.

(24) [41]G.R. Guy, 'Language and Social Class', in F.J.Newmark, (ed.) *Linguistics: The Cambridge Survey IV – Language: The Sociocultural Context* (Cambridge, Cambridge University Press, 1988), pp. 60–1.

(25) [45]Guy, 'Social Class', p. 63.

For a paper in a journal

Give the initial(s), author(s), title in inverted commas, journal name in italics, volume number, date in brackets and page(s) relevant to the point you are making, if any (*not* the page range for the entire paper) (example 26). Use a short reference for later mentions (example 27):

(26) [3]N. Alm, J.L. Arnott and A.F. Newell, 'Discourse Analysis and Pragmatics in the Design of a Conversation Prosthesis', *Journal of Medical Engineering and Technology,* 13/2 (1989), p. 12.

(27) [12]Alm *et al.,* 'Prosthesis', p. 11.

The use of punctuation

This varies somewhat between users of the Humane system. The Arnold guidelines, from which the above information has been taken, require the capitalization of every initial letter in titles, full stops at the end of the entire reference, and commas in the places illustrated in the examples above.

|22|

Plagiarism and how to avoid it

What is plagiarism?

Plagiarism is the *theft* of other people's words and ideas. Plagiarism happens when you claim (or *appear* to claim) that an idea, or the expression of it, is your own when in fact it is someone else's. **Deliberate plagiarism** usually takes the form of either getting someone else to write your essay for you and then saying it's yours, or copying chunks of text out of a book with the deliberate intent of deceiving the reader into thinking they are in your own words. **Accidental plagiarism,** which most institutions are obliged to penalize equally heavily, is achieved by oversight and/or lack of skill in manipulating information. Here are some examples of how it can happen:

- You make notes from a book, copying out lots of relevant passages and then, when you come to write the essay, you copy your notes into it, forgetting that they were copied in the first place.
- You use a book which covers exactly the area you are dealing with; you are aware that you mustn't copy it out, so you deftly rephrase little bits, by replacing 'small' with 'little', 'major differences' by 'main differences' and by swapping over the order of two halves of a sentence. *You* think that this is now legitimate, but your assessors do not.
- You use entirely your own words, but you don't acknowledge the source of your information.
- You draw from notes you made or were given for some previous course of study (like school notes, for example), without realizing that these were copied or adapted from some other source.

A reader will assume that any idea not referenced is your own, and that any passage not in quote marks is in your own words. This is a contract of trust which you must respect.

How to avoid accidental plagiarism: some strategies

Expect to acknowledge everything you've got from a source other than your own head. The things that don't need referencing are your own ideas and common or uncontroversial knowledge (*English is a Germanic language,* for example). If in doubt, err on the side of *over*-referencing, until you get the knack. Having too many references in a text breaks up the flow of your writing, but that is the lesser of two evils. To avoid too much repetition, you may be able to say at the beginning of a section or paragraph: *The following is a summary of information given in Smith (1994).* Note, however, that it is *not* sufficient to give one vague reference to your source somewhere, and then draw directly from it for page after page.

Rather than just summarizing what you are reading for the sake of it, make notes relevant to the task in hand and identify the major points that relate to your purpose. Make the notes under headings; you can then write out your own version based on those points. When making notes, use your own words wherever possible. *Never* copy anything out without putting it in inverted commas and putting a page reference next to it. Always keep the full reference details for any source you draw on, as you will need them later. These details should be integral to your notes, so that you can easily see where an idea or quote has come from.

Where your source text gives examples of a phenomenon under discussion, try to think of some examples of your own (or look them up in a dictionary or another book). This is in any case a good way of ensuring that you understand what you are writing about. However, if you are in doubt about whether your example is valid (e.g. where the examples have been drawn from a particular source that you cannot access), quote the ones you have been given and acknowledge them appropriately. If there is any terminology you don't understand, look it up, don't just copy it out.

An exercise in using published sources, creating a sophisticated account and avoiding plagiarism

Accidental plagiarism, correct referencing and the use of a variety of sources in your account are inextricably linked. The one most common reason why students end up accidentally plagiarizing is because they find it impossible to express the information they have read in a new way. There are two major causes of this problem. One is using only one source. Reading about something in only one place can beguile you into thinking that this is the only way to see the issue, and that there is nothing else to say and no other way to say it. In fact, it is a mistake to assume that all books will tell you the same thing, so it is always a good idea to look up the same information in more than one place. The second cause is needing about the same quantity of information as the source provides you with.

You are more likely to avoid plagiarism if the source has twenty pages and you only need five lines, or if you need to write twenty pages and the source only gives five lines.

In this exercise, Part 1 demonstrates the problems of drawing from only one source and suggests some ways of finding a new approach to the material. Part 2 challenges you to use two sources to create a tension, giving you an opportunity to take sides or act as referee. Part 3 shows how to add extra information and references to a point you have already established. Although this study will make sense if you just read the commentaries, it will make more impact on your skills if you do the exercises for each section before moving on.

The theme

For the purposes of this exercise, imagine you need to write a section of an essay on the way that English expresses comparatives and superlatives and how it used to do this in the past. This is not a very complicated subject, and most books deal with it in a few sentences. So will you, but how do you avoid simply reproducing the sentences in a book word for word?

1. Using one source only

EXERCISE

Read the extract from Barber (1993: 274) given in Fig. 22.1 and then write a paragraph on the subject, in your own words. Try to apply the guidelines on how to avoid plagiarism (see above). When you have finished, read the commentary below.

COMMENTARY

This is actually an extremely difficult task, because using only one source gives you very little room to manoeuvre. The referencing can look rather silly if you are acknowledging the same page of the same work all the time. You may have felt under-confident about inventing your own examples, in case there were not valid ones. You may have found it very difficult to express things in your own words. Remember that it is still plagiarism if you change the odd word but leave the text effectively the same. Example 1 illustrates a 'rewrite' that would consitute plagiarism, because the under-lined changes to the original are only superficial ones:

> (1)   Once, -er and -est were used much more <u>than they are</u> today, and in Early Modern English <u>forms could be found</u> like ancien-test, famousest, patienter, perfecter and shamefuller.

Changes in grammar

In grammar we can see the continuation, in small ways, of the long-term historical trend in English from synthetic to analytic, from a system that relies on inflections to one that relies on word-order and grammatical words. An example is the comparison of adjectives, where *more* and *most* are spreading at the expense of the endings *-er* and *-est*. At one time, *-er* and *-est* were used much more widely than today, and in Early Modern English you meet forms like *ancientest, famousest, patienter, perfecter*, and *shamefuller*. In the first half of the present century, adjectives of more than two syllables always had *more* and *most* ('more notorious, most notorious'), while adjectives of one syllable normally had *-er* and *-est* ('ruder, rudest'). Adjectives of two syllables varied, some being compared one way ('more famous, most famous') and some the other ('commoner, commonest'). In this group of two-syllabled adjectives there has been a tendency in recent years for *-er* and *-est* to be replaced by *more* and *most*, and it is now quite normal to say 'more common, most common', and similarly with *cloudy, cruel, fussy, pleasant, quiet*, and *simple*. Recently, moreover, *more* and *most* have been spreading to adjectives of one syllable, and it is not at all uncommon to hear expressions like 'John is more keen than Robert' and 'It was more crude than I expected'.

Fig 22.1 Barber, C. (1993) *The English language: a historical introduction.* Cambridge: CUP, 274.

You need a strategy that enables you to break out of the narrow restrictions imposed by the source text. One possibility is to approach the subject from a different direction:

(2) Within living memory the expression of some comparatives and superlatives has changed . . .

Another is to present some of the facts in list form:

(3) . . . Until relatively recently, the basic rules were as follows:

- polysyllabic adjectives (more than two syllables): add *more* (comparative) and *most* (superlative), e.g. *more beautiful, most beautiful; more interesting, most interesting.*
- monosyllabic adjectives: add *-er* (comparative) and *-est* (superlative), e.g. *richer, richest; bluer, bluest.*
- disyllabic adjectives could take either form, e.g. *most famous, commonest* (Barber 1993: 274).

It can help to use phrases like 'according to', to distance yourself from the author, making it clear that this is only one view and that others might exist:

(4) According to Barber (1993: 274), a study of the forms used in Early Modern English through to the present day indicates that a change has been in progress. He believes that there has been a decrease in the tolerance for *-er* (comparative) and *-est* (superlative), which were once acceptable endings on even polysyllabic words (e.g. *ancienter, ancientest; famouser, famousest*) but which have gradually been replaced by *more* and *most* (e.g. *more ancient, most ancient; more famous, most famous*). This change happened earliest on the longest words. By the early 20th century the preferences were:

- polysyllabic adjectives (more than two syllables): add *more* (comparative) and *most* (superlative), e.g. *more beautiful, most beautiful; more interesting, most interesting*.
- monosyllabic adjectives: add *-er* (comparative) and *-est* (superlative), e.g. *richer, richest; bluer, bluest*.
- disyllabic adjectives: either form, e.g. *most famous, commonest*.

Barber claims that the transition is now almost complete, with the *-er* and *-est* endings apparently being edged out of the picture entirely, as even monosyllabic words form their comparative and superlative with *more* and *most* (e.g. *The star is more bright than it was yesterday, but it will be most bright tomorrow*).

II. Using two sources and any arising

EXERCISE

Read the extracts from Strang (1970: 58 and 138) in Figs. 22.2 and 22.3. Write a new account, incorporating the information from both Barber and Strang: note that the relevant extract from Barber (1964) has also been provided for you (Fig. 22.4). When you have finished, read the commentary below.

COMMENTARY

The thing you should have noticed is that Strang (1970) and Barber (1993) do not hold entirely the same position. It is extremely good news for you when writers disagree. Firstly, you can demonstrate that you noticed their doing so. Observe how much reservation Strang (1970) expresses on p. 58 about Barber's claims. This can be highlighted by foregrounding the disagreement as a theme.

§41 It is very much more difficult to show how synchronic variation in grammar provides a model for variation through time. A recent book on *Linguistic Change in Present-day English* (Barber, 1964) has substantial sections on pronunciation (33–76), and vocabulary and meaning (77–128), but a much shorter one on grammar (129–45). About the developments mentioned in the chapter on *Grammatical Changes* some people might have reservations – for instance, under the heading 'loss of inflections' Barber discusses the distribution of *who* and *whom*, though uncertainties in this area of usage can clearly be traced back to the time of Shakespeare, and sequences like *he gave it to my brother and I*, though many will feel this is non-standard (i.e., not a change in the variety of English under discussion). Barber thinks there is an increasing use of *more, most*, rather than *-er, -est*, in comparison, in keeping with a trend which again goes back at least four hundred years; he may be right, but we lack precise numerical information on the subject.

Fig 22.2 Strang, B. (1970) *A history of English*. London and New York: Routledge, 58. Reproduced with permission of Routledge Ltd.

The roles of adjectives and nouns were perhaps less sharply distinguished than now; such uses as *better than he* (= better men), *full of poor* (= poor people), and, with a determiner, *in many's eyes*, now require a nominal head. This is related to the growth of the prop-word as a noun-place filler, an aspect of the general sense that there are places that ought to be filled by certain form-classes or certain clause-elements.

Double comparatives and superlatives were perfectly acceptable at the beginning of the period (*more properer, most handsomest*), though they came under corrective treatment in the 18c. In certain cases where the forms of comparison had, for phonological reasons, come to be irregular, such as *late, latter, last*, new analogical forms, *later, latest*, had been developed before II, but they were quite recent, and were alternatives in free variation with the historic forms. It is only more recently that the two sets have been differentiated.

Fig 22.3 Strang, B. (1970) *A history of English*. London and New York: Routledge, 138. Reproduced with permission of Routledge Ltd.

The continued loss of inflexions, and their replacement by syntactic devices, is also seen in the comparative and superlative of adjectives, where forms with *-er* and *-est* are being replaced by forms with *more* and *most*. Here we see the continuation of a trend of long standing: Milton wrote *elegantest*, *famousest*, and *sheepishest*, and Archbishop Laud *notoriousest*, where we should write *most elegant*, and so on. To-day, adjectives with three or more syllables are normally compared with *more* and *most* (*beautiful, more beautiful, most beautiful*); monosyllabic adjectives, on the other hand, are normally compared with *-er* and *-est* (*bright, brighter, brightest*). The adjectives with two syllables are divided, some usually being compared one way, the others the other; and it is in this dissyllabic group that the change is most noticeable, adjectives formerly taking *-er* and *-est* tending to go over to *more* and *most*. A word where this is especially noticeable is *common*; twenty or thirty years ago, *commoner* and *commonest* were normal, but nowadays nearly everybody says *more common, most common*. Indeed, I recently borrowed from a university library a book written in the nineteen-thirties by a distinguished literary scholar: in one place, the word *commonest* occurred; this had been vigorously crossed out by some borrower (presumably a student), who had written in the margin "most common!!!" Another example is heard in B.B.C. weather-forecasts, which frequently say that it will be *more cloudy*, instead of *cloudier*. Other adjectives that I have heard with *more* or *most* include *fussy, quiet, cruel, subtle, clever, profound, simple*, and *pleasant*; all these, I think, were normally compared with *-er* and *-est* before the War. I have also been struck by the frequency of forms like *more well-informed* and *most well-dressed*, where people would formerly have said *better-informed* and *best-dressed*. Recently there have been many cases of *more* and *most* spreading even to monosyllabic adjectives; examples I have noticed in educated speech and writing include *more crude, more plain*, and *more keen*. In Miss Iris Murdoch's well-known novel, *The Bell*, occurs the remarkable phrase *one of the most good people that he knew*.

Fig 22.4 Barber, C. (1964) *Linguistic change in present-day English*. London: Oliver and Boyd, 131–2.

But first, notice that Strang is referring to an earlier work by Barber, not to Barber (1993). So direct reference to Barber (1964) may be appropriate. In Barber (1964) the tone is very different from that in Barber (1993). In the former, he is much more personal. He lists examples that he has encountered. He refers to 'twenty or thirty years ago' (p. 131): remember that he is counting from *then*, not now, so he means the 1930s and 1940s. (The moral is, always check when a book was written.) But is the *sentiment* the same in the two books? You must not assume that it is without checking. An author is at liberty to change his mind in the course of 30 years. In fact, it can be seen that Barber *does* still hold the same opinion in 1993 as in 1964. So that too can be incorporated, by giving both dates:

(5) Barber (1964, 1993) claims that the transition is now almost complete, with the *-er* and *-est* endings apparently being edged out of the picture entirely, as even monosyllabic words form their comparative and superlative with *more* and *most* (e.g. *The star is more bright than it was yesterday, but it will be most bright tomorrow*). Barber (1964) cites examples that he has observed, including *more crude, more plain* and *more keen* (p. 132). Strang (1970), however, is more cautious about the final stages of this change:

> Barber thinks there is an increasing use of *more, most*, rather than *-er, -est*, in comparison, in keeping with a trend which . . . goes back at least 400 years; he may be right, but we lack precise numerical information on the subject (p. 58).

Note how a quote of more than two lines is indented and starts a new line, instead of being in the running text with quote marks round. As the page reference could indicate citation rather than quotation, the indentation is the only way in which this passage is marked as a quote, so it must be clear.

Once you have identified a disagreement, you can join in! Who do you think is right? Why? How could the conflict be resolved? Adding your views when you have explained those of others is a very good way of making your mark. You are able to speak with authority because you have clearly understood both sides of the argument. Here are some examples of how one might state a position:

(6) As Strang (1970) points out, it is probably too early to say whether the trend will continue to its logical conclusion.

(7) With the perspective of those extra 25 years since Strang was writing, it is possible to see that the trend Barber describes has actually slowed down: although people do say *more keen, most keen, more plain, most plain* today, they also continue to use the *-er* and *-est* forms *keener, keenest, plainer, plainest*. This is, perhaps, not something that Barber would have predicted in 1964.

(8)   It is probably fair to say that there is no one correct solution to this conundrum. In the post-war period English has diversified, as places other than Britain, particularly America and Australia, have become influential in setting trends. There is never any guarantee that a change, once begun, will continue in the same direction, as Aitchison (1991: 52 ff.) illustrates with the case of post-vocalic *r* in New York English, studied by Labov. It is perfectly conceivable that, in a hundred years, the changes in comparative and superlative forms will have reversed, so that *famousest* and *perfecter* (Barber 1993: 274) are as common as they were in Early Modern English.

Note that a reference to Aitchison (1991) has appeared in this example. This illustrates how, as you develop an argument, you may be reminded of something you read elsewhere, which turns out to be relevant to your point. We have not reproduced the text from Aitchison (1991) here, as it is rather long, but in essence she describes how post-vocalic *r* disappeared from British and some east-coast American English by the end of the eighteenth century, with the *r*-less pronunciation continuing to spread into other parts of the US well into the 1930s. But by the 1950s and 1960s the change had reversed, with post-vocalic *r* considered higher-status, a trend headed by the class-conscious lower middle class in New York, as Labov's research of the 1970s demonstrated (see Chapter 7 in this book for more details).

III. Incorporating other information into what you've already written

Once you have found a good source or two, and are satisfied (a) that they give the information you want and (b) that you can avoid plagiarizing, you may get on and write. But that doesn't mean that you can't incorporate other information and references at even quite a late stage.

EXERCISE

Read the extracts from Pyles and Algeo (1993: 186) and Crystal (1995: 199) in Figs. 22.5 and 22.6, and try to add references to them in relevant places. You can either add them to your own version or to one of the examples given above. Then read the commentary.

COMMENTARY

Neither of these extracts provides sufficient new material to justify a complete rewrite. But there are opportunities to indicate that you can see how

---

ADJECTIVES

Inflections provide one of the ways in which the quality expressed by an adjective (p. 211) can be compared. The comparison can be to the same degree, to a higher degree, or to a lower degree.

- The base form of the adjective is called the *absolute* form: *big, happy*.

The inflections identify two steps in the expression of a higher degree.

- Adding *-er* produces the *comparative* form: *bigger, happier*.
- Adding *-est* produces the *superlative* form: *biggest, happiest*.

There are no inflectional ways of expressing the same or lower degrees in English. These notions are expressed syntactically, using *as... as* (for the same degree: *X is as big as Y*) and *less* or *least* for lower degrees (*X is less interested than Y, Z is the least interested of all*).

There is also a syntactic (often called a *periphrastic*) way of expressing higher degree, through the use of *more* (for the comparative) and *most* (for the superlative): *A is more beautiful than B* and *C is the most beautiful of all*.

Fig 22.5 Crystal, D. (1995) *Encyclopaedia of the English language*. Cambridge: CUP, 199. Reproduced with permission of Cambridge University Press.

their standpoint and/or illustrations relate to what you already have. Pyles and Algeo (1993) refers to the preference for avoiding *-er, -est* with polysyllabic words as a 'stylistic objection' which 'had somewhat less force in the early Modern English period' (p. 186). This way of putting things is quite elegant, so a quote might be in order. In the example below, we have underlined the passage that has been added:

(9) According to Barber (1993: 274), a study of the forms used in Early Modern English through to the present day indicates that a change has been in progress. This <u>has entailed the development of a 'stylistic objection to affixing the endings [*-er* (comparative)</u>

Adjectives and adverbs continued to form comparatives with *-er* and superlatives with *-est*, but increasingly they used **analytical comparison** with *mo(e)* (a semantic equivalent of *more*, though not comparative in form), *more*, and *most*, which had occurred as early as Old English times. The present stylistic objection to affixing the endings to polysyllables had somewhat less force in the early Modern English period, when forms like *eminenter*, *impudentest*, and *beautifullest* are not particularly hard to find, nor, for that matter, are monosyllables with *more* and *most*, like *more near*, *more fast*, *most poor*, and *most foul*. As was true in earlier times also, a good many instances of **double comparison** like *more fitter*, *more better*, *more fairer*, *most worst*, *most stillest*, and (probably the best-known example) *most unkindest* occur in early Modern English. The general rule was that comparison could be made with the ending or with the modifying word or, for emphasis, with both.

Fig 22.6 Pyles and Algeo (1993: 186)

and *-est* (superlative)] to polysyllables' (Pyles and Algeo 1993: 186), such that forms that used to be acceptable (e.g. *ancienter*, *ancientest; famouser, famousest*) have gradually been replaced by forms with *more* and *most* (e.g. *more ancient, most ancient; more famous, most famous*). . .

Note how a clarification of the forms under discussion has been added within the quote by enclosing it in square brackets. This indicates that it is not part of the original quote, where the immediate context made the focus clear.

Pyles and Algeo also say something else very interesting. They claim that in Early Modern English it was not unusual to find monosyllables with *more* and *most*! This is quite contrary to Barber's hypothesis that the trend towards these forms has taken 400 years. And in the light of this new evidence, Strang seems positively *timid* in her non-committal stance. This means you can make even more of a meal of the disagreements and, subsequently, of your own views on the matter. Rather than supporting any one opinion too wholeheartedly, treat everyone with scepticism! Example 10 demonstrates how this can be done, the new text slotting onto the end of that given in example 5.

(10) Such prudence on Strang's part is certainly wise, if Pyles and Algeo's (1993: 186) claim, that monosyllables with *more* and *most* were quite common in Early Modern English, is to be believed. If they are right, then Barber may be mistaken when he says that there has been a change since Early Modern English *towards* these forms. On the other hand, such evidence may simply serve to remind us that no language changes either

all at once or in only one direction, as Aitchison (1991: 52 ff.) illustrates with the case of post-vocalic *r* in New York English, studied by Labov. Perhaps trends are *only* trends, and it is not necessary to believe in a time when a form *never* existed in order to identify a shift towards its increasing popularity.

Now look at Crystal's (1995) comments (p. 199). He is not being *prescriptive*, so we have no reason to doubt that he intends to simply describe English as it is today. His account of the rules for today looks very similar to Barber's for the first half of the century! What does that mean? There is potentially quite a lot of mileage in identifying all the possible interpretations of this correspondence. It could be that Crystal has an exceedingly old-fashioned view and/or he hasn't noticed the forms that Barber describes. Alternatively, it could be that the trend stopped in the first half of the century and Barber's examples are just 'noise'; that Barber was wrong about how things were then, but the description is correct for today; that Barber's basic idea is right, but the speed of change is much slower than he assumed; that Crystal knows about the forms that Barber describes but he doesn't think they're important; or that the changes Barber reported in the 1960s have reversed (and Barber hasn't noticed, so he's just reproduced his 1960s findings in his 1993 book). The point is, of course, we don't know which is right. We can't know. That means we are free to argue whichever one we like, provided we can justify our preference:

> (11)   A different challenge to Barber's view comes from Crystal (1995), who describes the *current* rules for the formation of comparative and superlative forms in virtually the same way as Barber gives for the first half of this century. There are many possible explanations for this. One of the most plausible is that the speed of change is slower than Barber suggests. Another is that the system for expressing these forms has reached a steady state: perhaps the 'stylistic objections' (Pyles and Algeo 1993: 186) that have powered the change for so long have lost their momentum for some reason.

Crystal says that, in disyllabic words, 'the choice is often made on stylistic grounds' (p. 199), which is reminiscent of what Pyles and Algeo said. That parallel can be highlighted. In example 12, the information that has been added is underlined.

> (12)   . . .There are many possible explanations for this. One of the most plausible is that the speed of change is slower than Barber suggests. Another is that the system for expressing these forms has reached a steady state: perhaps the 'stylistic objections' (Pyles and Algeo 1993: 186) that have powered the change for so long have lost their momentum for some reason. Those very stylistic considerations might even be responsible for maintaining

the steady state. Crystal (1995) suggests that it is our preferences in rhythm and lexical context which determine which form we choose in disyllabic words (p. 199).

SUMMARY

Having begun with one text which it was difficult to avoid simply copying or paraphrasing, we now have an account which draws together information from several sources, contrasts opposing views and provides a forum for personal opinions that are not simply plucked out of the air, but are firmly based in the possibilities provided (explicitly or implicitly) in the literature. Here is one possible outcome, based on the examples given above. It ends with a list of references in the format described in Chapter 21. This list is an essential feature of academic writing, and must be both complete and accurate.

(13) According to Barber (1993: 274), study of the forms used in Early Modern English through to the present day indicates that a change has been in progress. This has entailed the development of a 'stylistic objection to affixing the endings [-*er* (comparative) and -*est* (superlative)] to polysyllables' (Pyles and Algeo 1993: 186), such that once-acceptable forms (e.g. *ancienter, ancientest; famouser, famousest*) have gradually been replaced by forms with *more* and *most* (e.g. *more ancient, most ancient; more famous, most famous*). This change happened earliest on the longest words. By the early twentieth century the preferences were:

- polysyllabic adjectives (more than two syllables): add *more* (comparative) and *most* (superlative), e.g. *more beautiful, most beautiful; more interesting, most interesting.*
- monosyllabic adjectives: add -*er* (comparative) and -*est* (superlative), e.g. *richer, richest; bluer, bluest.*
- disyllabic adjectives: either form, e.g. *most famous, commonest.*

According to Barber (1964, 1993) the transition is now nearing completion, with the -*er* and -*est* endings apparently being edged out of the picture entirely, as even monosyllabic words form their comparative and superlative forms with *more* and *most*. Barber (1964) cites examples that he has observed, including *more crude, more plain* and *more keen* (p. 132). Strang (1970), however, is more cautious about the final stages of this change:

> Barber thinks there is an increasing use of *more, most,* rather than -*er,* -*est,* in comparison, in keeping with a trend which . . . goes back at least four hundred years; he may be right, but we lack precise numerical information on the subject. (p. 58).

Such prudence on Strang's part is certainly wise, if Pyles and Algeo's (1993: 186) claim, that monosyllables with *more* and *most* were quite common in Early Modern English, is to be believed. If they are right, then Barber may be mistaken when he says that there has been a change since Early Modern English *towards* these forms. On the other hand, such evidence may simply serve to remind us that no language changes either all at once or in only one direction, as Aitchison (1991: 52 ff.) illustrates with the case of post-vocalic *r* in New York English, studied by Labov. Perhaps trends are *only* trends, and it is not necessary to believe in a time when a form *never* existed in order to identify a shift towards its increasing popularity.

A different challenge to Barber's view comes from Crystal (1995), who describes the *current* rules for the formation of comparative and superlative forms in virtually the same way as Barber gives for the first half of this century. There are many possible explanations for this. One of the most plausible is that the speed of change is slower than Barber suggests. Another is that the system for expressing these forms has reached a steady state: perhaps the 'stylistic objections' (Pyles and Algeo 1993: 186), that have powered the change for so long, have lost their momentum for some reason. Those very stylistic considerations might even be responsible for maintaining the steady state. Crystal (1995) suggests that it is our preferences in rhythm and lexical context which determine which form we choose in disyllabic words (p. 199).

REFERENCES

Aitchison, J. (1991) *Language change: progress or decay?* (2nd edition). Cambridge: Cambridge University Press.

Barber, C. (1964) *Linguistic change in present-day English.* London: Oliver & Boyd.

Barber, C. (1993) *The English language: a historical introduction.* Cambridge: Cambridge University Press.

Crystal, D. (1995) *The Cambridge encyclopaedia of the English language.* Cambridge: Cambridge University Press.

Pyles, T. and Algeo, J. (1993) *The origins and development of the English language* (4th edition). New York: Harcourt Brace Jovanovich.

Strang, B. (1970) *A history of English.* London and New York: Routledge.

Of course, everyone's finished product will be different; indeed, that is the whole point. You can be sure, if you approach your work like this, that it will be individual as well as sophisticated and informative. Precisely because your own ideas, interpretations and conclusions are integrated with the information from your (fully acknowledged) sources, you can be sure that no-one will be able to accuse you of plagiarism.

|23|

Statistics

CHRIS BUTLER

This chapter is not intended to teach you how to do statistics. There are some very good books on this subject and you should use them. As a guide, many of them are briefly described below. Rather, we aim here to help those who are rather intimidated by the idea of statistics, and so to bridge the gap between where many students feel they are, and the level at which most of the books start. The chapter is organized as a series of questions which should help to take the mystery out of the subject and prepare you for the specialist books. Where statistical tests are named, the recommended books will provide you with the procedural information that you need in order to use them.

Why use statistics?

Statistical techniques are relevant for linguists because some linguistic research requires a quantitative treatment, and because it is difficult otherwise to understand and evaluate the published research that uses statistics. Not all research on language requires a knowledge of statistics. For example, studies of the formal nature of language ignore variability by focusing on:

> an ideal speaker-listener, in a completely homogeneous speech-community, who knows its language perfectly and is unaffected by such grammatically irrelevant conditions as memory limitations, distractions, shifts of attention and interest, and errors (random or characteristic) in applying his knowledge of the language in actual performance. (Chomsky 1965: 3)

In fact, any type of linguistic study that does not need to measure variability, that is, differences in people's linguistic behaviour or in the patterns of language itself, does not need to use statistics directly. However, as soon as we focus on variability there is a role for statistics in a surprisingly large range of areas, so a basic knowledge of statistics is an essential part of the toolbox of the well-rounded linguist. Although it is only 'scientific' studies that will formulate and check hypotheses in a rigorous way, simple descriptive statistics (graphs, averages, frequency, range and so on) can be useful in a much wider range of linguistic studies.

What can statistics do?

Statistics can describe data, assess the degree of confidence we can have that a small set of results is representative of what we would get from a larger population of the same type, check whether a hypothesis is valid when it proposes a certain relationship between two or more sets of data, and investigate, in an open-ended way, relationships between different variables. A **variable** is any property whose value may vary (such as gender, age, test score or reaction time). **Data,** in the narrow context of statistical work, are the observations we make. There are three important kinds of data, measured in different ways:

- **Truly quantitative data**: measurable on a scale with equal intervals (e.g. time; the number of sentences remembered correctly in a recall test; the number of interruptions in a given amount of conversation).
- **Ordinal data**: not measurable on a scale with equal intervals, but able to be ranked in terms of *more* and *less* (such as politeness, acceptability of a grammatical structure or aesthetic appeal of an accent).
- **Nominal data**: not quantitative at all (except in the sense that you can count the *frequencies* for nominal variables), and organized into named types (such as ethnic group, native language, gender, word class or tense of a verb).

How do we use statistics to describe data?

Imagine that a cohort of 100 language students has just completed a translation from French to English, and each has received a mark out of 20 for it. It would be hard to see any pattern in the data just by looking at the list of marks, but there are three things that you could do to get an overview of the profile. You could look at the **distribution** of the data to see if there were lots of high values, lots of low values, or more scores in the middle than at the two extremes. You would find this out by creating a frequency table for the data, showing how many students got each score, and by drawing graphs (histograms, frequency polygons, and so on) to create a visual representation of the distribution of scores.

You could also calculate the **average** scores for your data. There are three types of average. The **mean** is the ordinary arithmetic average, and is really only suitable for truly quantitative data. You calculate it by adding up all the scores and dividing by the number of scores. The **median** is the middle value, when all the scores are arranged in ascending or descending order. It is suitable for ordinal data, or for data where there is heavy *skewing* of the distribution (that is, where a high proportion of the scores lies to one side of the middle range). The **mode** is simply the most frequent value, and is rarely of much use.

You could determine the **degree of spread** or **variability** in the data. There are several measures for this:

- The **mean deviation** is the mean (average) of the distances of each observation from the mean. You calculate this by finding the difference between each score and the mean, adding all the differences together and dividing by the number of scores. The mean deviation is easy to interpret, but you can't use it for any further tests.

- The **standard deviation** is another way of calculating distance from the mean, but rather more complex. You calculate it by finding the difference between each score and the mean, squaring the results, adding the squares together, dividing by the number of scores minus 1, and then taking the square root. This procedure means that the figure produced is not so transparent or easy to interpret. However, it can be used as part of the input in further calculations. The standard deviation is a suitable calculation only for truly quantitative data.

- The **quartile deviation** is suitable for ordinal data, and is a way of measuring the spread between the first and third quartiles (i.e. the middle 50 per cent of the scores). You calculate it by arranging the scores in ascending or descending order, as for the median, but dividing them into four parts, not two. Take the lower of the two quartile values and subtract it from the other. Then divide the result by two.

Determining the degree of confidence one can have in generalizing from a sample

If you test a sample out of a larger population, you can only draw conclusions about the larger population if you are confident that the sample is truly representative. For example, if you analysed 1000 words of a Dickens novel, how sure could you be that the results reflected the pattern in Dickens's work as a whole?

By knowing the **z-distribution** (for large samples) or the **t-distribution** (for small samples), it is possible to use the **mean**, the **sample size** and the **standard deviation** in a calculation that will tell you with, say, 95 per cent confidence, a range within which the mean score of the whole population would fall if you ran the study on all of them. The limits of this range are called **confidence limits**. As an example, if you knew the mean score and standard deviation for a group of, say, 30 students on a particular test, you could work out the range within which you could be 95 per cent sure that the mean would lie for the whole population of students from which the group was drawn.

You can also calculate confidence limits for the proportions of observations with a particular property. For example, you might measure the proportion of nouns in a sample of words taken by random sampling from a text. Knowing this proportion, and also the sample size, you could then calculate the range within which, with 95 per cent confidence, you could expect the proportion of nouns to total words in the whole text to lie.

Statistics and hypotheses

What is a hypothesis, and how do you test it?

A hypothesis is simply a guess about the relationship between two or more variables. Your hypothesis will probably be based on what you already know about the phenomenon of interest, including what other researchers have found out about it. A hypothesis must be testable: that is, it must be possible to predict what the results of a test would look like if the hypothesis was supported and if it was not. Here are some example hypotheses:

- In a given stretch of dialogue between males and females who are native speakers of English, the number of interruptions per unit of time will be higher for the male than for the female speakers.
- Vowels before voiced final consonants in monosyllabic English words are longer than those before the corresponding voiceless consonant.
- Students taught French by means of a particular video-based course will perform better on a language test than students taught by purely audio-based methods.

How do you know if your hypothesis was right?

Taking the third example above, let's assume that the video-taught group have a mean (average) test score of 62 per cent, whereas the mean score for the audio-taught group is 58 per cent. Has this 'proved' the hypothesis? For various reasons, one would need to be rather cautious:

- The result only indicates a superiority for the individuals in one of the two *sample groups* that have actually been tested. Would the same superiority be found if all students of French taught by these methods were tested, or, as is more feasible, if two more sample groups were selected and tested? There is, inevitably, inherent variability in the population, so we might reasonably expect that any repeat of the experiment would give slightly different results. But how different? Would there still be a superiority for the video-taught group, or might the scores be more even?

- The fact that the difference between the two mean scores (62 and 58) *looks* small, warns us that another test might not confirm the existence of any 'real' difference. But where does a small difference end and a large one begin? How can we know when a result has meaning and when it doesn't? Is 62 as against 58 a large enough difference or not? What if it was 62 and 61? Or 62 and 52?

These questions can be answered mathematically using statistics. Statistical tests can tell us whether two scores are **significantly** different, that is, highly unlikely to be the product of chance variation. They can tell us how large the difference between two scores has to be for it to be considered supportive of the hypothesis. The calculations take into account the number of subjects, number and type of test items and the precise expectations of the hypothesis itself.

Note that you can never definitively *prove* a hypothesis to be correct unless you have examined all of the potential data (that is, from the whole population), rather than just a sample of it, and it is rarely possible to do this. The reason for this caution is that there is always a possibility that the outcome observed is the consequence of having used an oddly unrepresentative sample.

How is a hypothesis tested statistically?

First you must state the **null** and **alternative** hypotheses. The **null hypothesis** is that of *no difference*: it states that, as regards the specific property under investigation, there is no difference between the two populations from which your samples are drawn. The **alternative hypothesis** is normally the one that you want to support: it states that there is a difference between the two populations for the specific property under investigation. An alternative hypothesis can be either **directional** or **non-directional**. A **directional** hypothesis predicts the direction of the difference (for example, students taught by video perform better on the test than those taught by audio techniques; males interrupt more than females). A **non-directional** hypothesis predicts a difference but not the direction (for example, males and females differ in the range of vocabulary they use in a particular descriptive test, but there is no prediction of which group will have the larger range). You need to know whether you have a directional or a non-directional hypothesis, in order to correctly interpret the result of your statistical calculation (see below).

Next, select a suitable **significance level**. Put simply, this is the margin of error or chance that you are willing to tolerate. In most linguistic research, a significance level of 5 per cent is good enough. This means that any *significant* difference that you find between your samples has a greater than

95 per cent chance of reflecting a genuine difference of the same kind in the population from which they are drawn.

Then select an appropriate **test of significance**. Three factors guide the selection of the test. One is the kind of data you have. If you have truly quantitative data, and various other conditions are met, then you can use a **parametric** test. Parametric tests for comparing two samples include the **z**- and **t-tests**, the latter being for small samples. If you have ordinal or nominal data, then you need **non-parametric** tests. These include the **Mann-Whitney, Wilcoxon, sign and chi-square** tests.

The second factor is the shape of the data distribution. For some parametric tests, such as the **t-test**, if the samples are small, then the data must be **normally distributed**. Normal distribution is defined by a precise mathematical formula. If the data are not normally distributed, a **non-parametric** test should be used instead.

The third factor is the type of research design. Different tests are required for **independent** and for **correlated (repeated measures/matched pairs)** designs (see below).

When you carry out a statistical test, you end up with a figure, which is known as the **test statistic**. On its own this will not tell you anything. It has to be compared with the **critical value**. This is a figure that you will find in published tables (most of the books reviewed below contain such tables). Where you look on the tables depends on the significance level (see above), and whether the hypothesis is directional or not. According to whether the test statistic is bigger or smaller than the critical value (remember to check which – bigger or smaller – it needs to be in the test you are using), you will be able to state whether the difference you found between your samples is **significant** at the level you have chosen; that is, whether it is a large enough difference to allow you to reject the null hypothesis in favour of the alternative hypothesis.

Choosing statistical tests

What is the relationship between the statistical tests you choose and the overall research design?

There is a close relationship. You cannot choose the right statistical test unless you know what your research design is. There are, broadly speaking, two types of research design, which can be easily illustrated with reference to human subjects:

- **Independent designs**: two (or more) different groups of subjects do a task under different conditions. Example: two different groups of students learn French by different techniques.

- **Correlated designs**: where the results in the different conditions are interrelated, because the subjects are the same people, or very similar people. There are two subtypes of correlated design. In a **repeated measures** design the same group of subjects does both or all conditions of the test (thus, whatever an individual brings to one test, he or she brings to them all). Clearly, this design cannot be used for certain types of research, where doing the task once would spoil it for the next time. In a **matched pairs** design, each individual subject in one group is matched with a subject in the other group, on any factors that the research suggests might otherwise influence the results.

Is there any way of getting something more open-ended out of statistics?

Although any particular test needs to be quite tightly controlled, so that you can be as sure as possible that the differences you observe really are due to the factor you are interested in, the results of one test may well suggest further hypotheses that can be investigated. This means that the whole process is actually open-ended.

There is a set of techniques known as **multivariate** analyses, which can be used for isolating patterns in data sets which have been classified according to a number of different variables. A good example is found in the work of Biber (such as Biber 1988, 1989, 1992) on text typology. Here he submits a wide range of text samples to a large number of linguistic analyses, and then searches, using multivariate analyses, for associations between clusters of linguistic properties and textual dimensions. Some important multivariate techniques include **factor analysis, cluster analysis, principal component analysis** and **multidimensional scaling**. For more detail on these, see Woods, Fletcher and Hughes (1986) or Hatch and Lazaraton (1991).

What other techniques are commonly used?

- **Correlation**: this is used when you want to know whether high values for one variable tend to go with high values, or low values, for a second variable. Example: scores on a recall test and age of the subject.
- **Multiple regression**: this is used to predict values for one variable, given values for another.
- **Analysis of variance**: this is used to test differences in the means of more than two samples.

For other, more advanced techniques see Hatch and Lazaraton (1991) and other recommended books.

Gaining confidence

How does one get to feel confident about using statistical techniques?

There are no easy answers to this. Some people feel generally much more confident about mathematics than others do. Nevertheless, there are some practical ways to help oneself. Attend a taught course on basic statistics for linguists, preferably one that requires you to try out what you learn in a practical way. Read an introductory text on the subject, and only then graduate to anything harder. Table 23.1 below should help you identify what you need. Take note of the results and analysis sections in published research, identifying what the authors have compared with what, why and how. Perhaps try running their figures through the same procedures yourself, and see if your results match theirs.

Many researchers design their work around one or two simple statistical tests and stick to them. Provided that you are sure that a certain test is going to be the appropriate one for your data, there is no need to learn how to use any others. Over a period of time, you will add new tests to your repertoire; this 'trickle-feed' method is one way to become confident about how to apply a test and when.

Textbooks

Statistics is an enormous subject which can get as complicated as you like. The books available vary tremendously according to their primary purpose. There are books for advanced mathematicians (beginners are advised to leave these alone), others for researchers and students who have a substantial background in statistical work, and yet others for people who need leading gently by the hand. Many linguists fall into the last category! It is worth using a book written *for* linguists if possible, rather than a general one, or one intended for some other subject area, because the examples will be relevant, will make sense to you, and may give you ideas for your own research. Also, aspects of statistics that are not applicable to linguistics will not be there to distract or confuse you.

All the same, Table 23.1 includes a few books not aimed at the linguist, as well as some that are.

Table 23.1 Useful texts for statistics (see page xiv for key to levels)

Book	Level	Notes on Content/Style
Anshen 1978	2	introduction, incl. basic techniques & reasons for using statistics in linguistics; exercises
Butler 1985	3	for maths-shy linguists; basic techniques; intended to be worked through: dipping in means reading relevant earlier sections

Book	Level	Notes on Content/Style
Castle 1977	2	excellent format, with interesting medical examples; no index; could be dipped into; take care adopting tests to linguistic data
Clarke and Cooke 1992	3	no linguistic examples; clear accounts of basic concepts and tests; useful for checking you have got the right test
Coolican 1995	2–3	user-friendly, aimed at psychologists; interesting examples, well illustrated; may occasionally over-simplify complex issues
Hatch and Lazaraton 1991	4	comprehensive, covering research design and statistics for applied linguists; examples are from real studies; not for beginners
Robson 1973	1–2	clear and friendly guide, test by test, with step-by-step worked examples
Rowntree 1981	1–2	for real beginners; wordy and over-general; hard to dip into
Woods *et al.* 1986	4	detailed, with examples from linguistic research; headings assume you know what you're looking for; not for beginners

Key to the most common algebraic symbols used in basic statistics

The secret is, treat symbols as your friends: they tell you unambiguously and succinctly what to do to get a valid answer to your calculations. The point of using letters and symbols is that one statement will cope with lots of different individual calculations. To convert a string of symbols into a sum, you simply work out what number each symbol stands for in your case, and replace the symbols with the numbers. The intimidating thing about them is that they look so foreign; but it's just a code. The key to them appears in Table 23.2.

Table 23.2 The most commonly used algebraic symbols

Symbol	Explanation
x	Any single value or score
y	Another single value or score
N	Number of results or subjects
Σ	This is 'sigma' and it means 'Sum of', so Σx means 'add together all the values of x'
x^2	x squared, i.e. multiplied by itself. Example: if $x = 3$, then $x^2 = 9$

continued overleaf

Table 23.2 (*continued*)

Symbol	Explanation
$\sqrt{x}$	square root of x, i.e. the number which, multiplied by itself, gives x. Example: if $x = 64$, then $\sqrt{x} = 8$ (use a calculator with a square root button)
x or x/y y	divide x by y, i.e. the same as $x \div y$. Example: $\frac{3}{4} = (3 \div 4) = 0.75$
$\frac{\Sigma x}{N} = \bar{x}$ or $\Sigma x/N = \bar{x}$ or $\frac{\Sigma fx}{N} = \bar{x}$ or $\Sigma fx/N = \bar{x}$	all the values of x, added together, and divided by the number of values, giving an answer called 'x bar' ($\bar{x}$), which represents the **mean** (see earlier). For example, if x is the score on a word memory recall test, scores might be: Subject 1: $x = 15$; Subject 2: $x = 9$; Subject 3: $x = 13$; Subject 4: $x = 12$. Then: $\Sigma x = 15 + 9 + 13 + 12 = 49$ and: $\bar{x} = \Sigma x/N = (49 \div 4) = 12.25$
$(\dots)$	putting brackets round something means 'do the sum inside first'. Example: $33 \div (6+5) = 33 \div 11 = 3$. Doing the sum in a different order may change the result: $(33 \div 6) + 5 = 5.5 + 5 = 10.5$
$\lvert \dots \rvert$	whether the outcome is positive or negative, treat it as positive, so, for example, $\lvert x - \bar{x} \rvert$ means 'subtract the **mean** ($\bar{x}$) from each value (x) and make the result positive if it isn't already'. Example: if $x = 5$ and $\bar{x} = 6.1$, then the result is $+1.1$ (not -1.1).
σ	standard deviation (of a *population*)
f	frequency
df	number of degrees of freedom (e.g. number of cells in a frequency table that can vary without changing the row or column total).
χ	Chi. Used in the chi-square test
E	Expected frequency
O	Observed frequency
p	probability (of getting a given result by chance)
ρ	(rho) Spearman's correlation coefficient
s	standard deviation (of a *sample*) (used in the calculation itself)
sd	standard deviation (of a *sample*) (sometimes used when referring to it in a graph, table or commentary).
s^2	variance in a sample
$<$ $>$	'smaller than' and 'bigger than', e.g. $x < 12$ means: *the value of x is smaller than 12*
$\leq$ $\geq$	'smaller than or equal to' and 'bigger than or equal to'
t, z, U, W, etc.	Letters may relate to the value of the *test statistic* of specific tests, e.g. t (the test statistic of the t-test), z (the test statistic of the z-test), U (the test statistic of the Mann-Whitney U-test), W (the test statistic of the Wilcoxon signed-ranks test). You can get an idea of what these letters stand for by studying or using the relevant test.

|24|

Using an abstracting journal

What are abstracting journals?

Every year an enormous number of articles are published in journals, because that is the main forum in which academics present their research. Abstracting journals are important because few people have the time to check every journal as it comes out, and they are therefore in danger of missing things relevant to their work. Furthermore, there are not many libraries that take all the journals that might be of use.

What do they do, and how?

Abstracting journals provide an invaluable service for researchers. They are a short-cut to the articles of most interest. A team of abstracters (usually volunteers) shares out the responsibility for checking through the journals, and they then send in short summaries (abstracts) of what each paper addresses, including experimental results. Often the author has supplied an abstract at the front of the article; if not, the abstracter writes one. The abstracts are then put together into a volume, with an index of keywords or subjects and an author index; they have a reference number, so you can move from the indices to the abstract itself easily. Once you have read the abstract, you can use the full reference that is provided to locate the article itself, if it seems relevant to your needs.

What makes a good abstracting journal?

The best abstracting journals are the ones that survey the greatest possible range of journals within that field. You are most reliant on abstracting journals when they cover publications that your library doesn't hold, for how else will you ever know what is in them? (Most articles not available locally should be obtainable via inter-library loan.) It also helps if they aim to cover a fairly broad field. You may be researching in semantics, but find a relevant article from the field of historical linguistics or child language. A good abstracting journal appears frequently (several times a year) and is up-to-date (articles are abstracted within a few months of their publication). Some abstracting journals produce a cumulative index at the end of each year. This enables you to check a greater body of material in one go.

What abstracting journals are available?

- **Linguistics and Language Behavior Abstracts (LLBA)** This is the biggest and the best. It appears four times a year, and covers all the major areas of linguistics plus some other areas on the periphery.
- **Linguistics Abstracts** is smaller volume published in the UK, covering the most important linguistics journals, although not always uniformly.
- **Language Teaching Abstracts** is dedicated to the language-teaching part of the field. This is clearly more specialist and does not aim to offer the same scope. Particularly useful about this publication is the fact that each issue also contains an article giving an overview of a subfield of the research. It is worth checking back issues to see if anything relevant to your work has been surveyed there.
- **Linguistics Abstracts on Line** is an Internet service from Blackwell, accessed via http: //www.blackwellpublishers.co.uk/labs. This is a commercial service, so it costs money to use it. However, it should not cost *you* anything. Your library may have a subscription, in which case they can provide you with the password to access the service. If the service is not available in your library, approach the subject librarian about it, or ask staff in your department to request subscription.

The abstracting journals for other disciplines may also contain abstracts of some linguistic work, so think carefully about which areas border on your subject of study.

What to do

The information in abstracting journals can be accessed via author, journal or keywords. Find the most recent edition first, and work backwards through the earlier ones as far as you feel you need to. In this way your research will be as up-to-date as possible. A recent article will mention older ones in its reference list, which gives you another way to find out about them. The reverse, of course, is not true!

If you know already who the major researchers in the field are, use the author index to see what articles of theirs have been abstracted in that edition. If you are very clear about which journals are of interest, go to the journal index. Otherwise, use the keyword index. First, clarify in your own mind what you are looking for. Envisage the sort of paper that you are hoping to locate, and work out what keywords might have been provided by the abstracter for the subject index. For example, if you are looking for experimental reports on children's colour terminology, then you might try *colour, vocabulary, lexicon, child (language), development,* and so on. It can, admittedly, be hit-and-miss, but you only need to get one keyword right in order to find the article. Remember that keywords have two roles: to lead the interested reader to the article, and to deter everyone else – you don't want to have to check lots of irrelevant abstracts because a keyword is too general. Therefore, keywords tend to be quite specific, often 'technical'. In the LLBA (see above) there are general headings in bold type, with sub-headings beneath. This is not always easy to handle as a reader, because you need to guess which major heading is most likely to carry the more specific keywords you want.

When you have found your keyword, author or journal name in the relevant index, note down the reference number(s). The abstracts are in numerical order, usually in the same volume as the index, but if you are using a cumulative index they may be in an earlier volume. Read the abstract and decide whether the paper it summarizes is relevant to you. Whether it is or not, keep a note of which abstracts you have read, so that you don't waste time another day looking them up again. Remember to write down which abstracting journal you used, and which issue you got the information from; the reference numbers are unique, but it saves time to know which one to go to.

If the abstract is relevant, make a *careful* note of the full reference. You can then check in your library catalogue whether the journal is on site. If it isn't, you will need to look further afield (use Internet links to other libraries) and if necessary request it via the inter-library loan service. On an ILL request form you will have to state clearly where you got the reference from, so don't lose your note of this. Remember: reading the abstract *is not a substitute* for reading the article itself if you are intending to refer to the research. A brief summary cannot give you sufficient detail for your purposes, so you must read the full account in context.

|25|

Handy hints on writing good academic English

Before you write

Model your style on what you read

A general awareness of what academic writing looks like will help you to adopt that style yourself. The best models are journal articles and subject-specialist books, but most introductory textbooks also use a suitable style.

Write a plan

This will keep your ideas organized. Start off by dividing the work into an introduction, between three and six major sections and a conclusion. Then plan a breakdown of each section, itemizing what will go in it. If you allot to each section and sub-section an approximate number of words you will have almost total control over keeping to your word limit. By using a plan you are much less likely to wander off the point or say anything twice. For big pieces of work, keep a separate sheet of paper for each chapter or section, and jot down your ideas, references and any other material on it. Then, when you come to write, all the information is already in the right place.

Know your weaknesses

Take a careful look at your previous marked work and write a list of the problems with structure or presentation that have been highlighted in it. If there are any that you don't understand, ask the tutor in question. Identify strategies for avoiding these problems in the future, such as keeping a list of any words you have spelt incorrectly. Most people have only a few words that they always get wrong. Write the correct spelling of each on a sheet of paper and stick it on the wall above your desk. Don't worry about memorizing the correct spelling, but do try to remember which words are on the list, so that you look at it when you need to!

As you are writing

Develop and sustain a sense of audience

Be aware of who you are writing for, and why. Remember that you are writing in order to explain your research, so you need to say *why* you did what you did (why it was an interesting research question, for example) and be explicit about the issues and your procedures. You are writing for assessment purposes, so make sure you demonstrate that you know what you are talking about. If in doubt, err on the side of being too explicit: assessors will tend to assume, if you explain something inadequately, that you do not understand it properly. Your work may be read by a second internal assessor and/or an external examiner, so do not make references to information that they are not party to (such as institution-specific titles like a module name or residence hall, or activities or running jokes from within a lecture course) unless you clearly contextualize them.

As your assessors are knowledgeable about the general field you can make certain assumptions about what they will understand, particularly when it comes to peripheral information. For example, it is acceptable to make a passing reference to Chomsky when writing about something in which his ideas are not central. However, no-one, including your assessors, knows about *everything*, so if you are making reference to work or ideas that are not commonly known about, give all the details necessary to make your account comprehensible.

Use the technology

If possible, word-process from the start. This means you can alter things and still have a clean copy. It also means you can run spellchecks and use thesaurus and dictionary facilities at any stage.

Mark problems for later checking

You may feel that stopping to check a spelling or to rephrase an awkward sentence will break your flow when you are writing the first draft. If so, simply mark any problem by underlining or asterisking it. Then, later, you can easily return to the right place and find a better alternative. The same technique can be used if you have a fact or a reference to check: just write *check* beside it and carry on, coming back to it when you have finished.

Use a dictionary and thesaurus

Do not be reticent about using a dictionary. Even the best writers have to do it. There is no shame in not knowing the meaning of, or how to spell, a word, providing you know that you don't know, and look it up! Where terminology is concerned, use a specialist dictionary or a subject textbook with a glossary. Use a thesaurus to widen your vocabulary: this can increase the accuracy with which you express yourself, as well as making your prose more stylish.

Copy correctly

When quoting, citing or otherwise taking information from another source, pay attention to the form. In a quote, copy the punctuation and spelling correctly. Take particular care with proper names.

Use headings

In keeping with your plan (see above) use headings in your work. These can save words, and make it much easier for you, and your assessor, to follow the structure of your work.

Write summaries

In a lengthy piece of work, and especially in data analysis, it is often helpful to provide a one- or two-sentence summary at the end of each section. This helps both the writer and the reader to retain a focus and sense of the structure of the whole piece of work.

Draft it and craft it

Don't be beguiled into thinking that everyone else gets it right first time. Drafting and rewriting is part and parcel of the process. The best writing is carefully crafted, which is an absorbing and rewarding aspect of the work. Stand back from your draft and ask yourself whether you could make it flow better, say something more succinctly or draw out the points in a more appropriate way.

After you have written

Proof-read

Leave enough time to put your work aside and then come back to it with a fresh eye. Try to read it as someone would who was seeing it for the first time. Check that the argument and ideas are clear and that there are no problems with the grammar or spelling. If it is too late to change typed or word-processed work, make neat, legible corrections by hand.

The uses of apostrophes

Most people who use apostrophes incorrectly do so because no-one has ever explained the rules to them. So here they are. The apostrophe has *two* major functions. One is to indicate that one or more letters are missing. The other is to indicate possession.

Omission of one or more letters

This accounts for *can't, don't, won't,* for *ha'penny, o'clock,* and for abbreviations like *M'day, S'hampton,* etc. Importantly, it also accounts for the word *it's,* which therefore means *it is* (**not** the possessive form of *it*).

Possession

There are several parts to the pattern:

- **Singular nouns that do not end in s already** take an apostrophe + *s* to form the possessive form. Examples include: *the dog's bone, Michael's concern, a professor's priority, this curate's bicycle.*
- **Singular nouns that end in s** either take an apostrophe at the end of the word, or apostrophe + s. Examples include: *the class' assignment* or *the class's assignment, Her Royal Highness' schedule* or *Her Royal Highness's schedule, Mr Jones' complaint* or *Mr Jones's complaint.*
- **Plural nouns that already have an s** (that is, most of them) take an apostrophe at the end. Examples include: *three horses' heads* and *twenty boys' results.*
- **Plural nouns that do not end in an s** take apostrophe *s*. Examples include: *the children's games* and *the women's semi-finals.*
- *Pronouns*: The possessives of pronouns do *not* take apostrophes. *His, hers* and *its* are all examples of possessive pronouns. Remember that *it's* means 'it is', while *its* means 'belonging to it'.

For more information about the use of the apostrophe, see the *Oxford Guide to the English Language* (1984: 29–30).

Using punctuation

Using punctuation correctly is important not only on stylistic grounds, but because you may end up saying something you didn't mean otherwise. Common problems include the following.

Commas where full stops should be

In speech we tend to chain sentences together without stopping for breath, but in academic writing sentences must be separated by full stops. For example, *The subjects sat at separate tables, they read the text for ten minutes.* This should read *The subjects sat at separate tables. They read the text for ten minutes.* Alternatively, the two parts should be linked with *and*.

Full stops where commas should be

In this case, only half a sentence has been written before the full stop comes. This tends to occur where a dependent clause (a clause that needs another one) has been stranded. An example is: *Although the subjects had several minutes to prepare themselves.* Here, *although* has been treated as if it means *however*, whereas it actually needs an answering clause: *although this . . . (nevertheless) that.* Example: *Although the subjects had several minutes to prepare themselves, they seemed flustered when the stimulus presentation began.*

Another common cause is using a verb in non-finite form, as in: *The reason being clear.* In academic writing, there needs to be a finite verb in the main clause of every sentence, as in: *The reason is clear.*

Semi-colons for colons

The **colon** (:) is little used these days, but it still has one important function. It introduces items. This means that when you write a list, a colon needs to precede it. A list may define (e.g. *There are three primary colours: red, blue and green*) or it may illustrate (e.g. *The stationery shop sold various things: pens, paper, diaries, etc.*). Avoid using the semi-colon for these purposes.

The **semi-colon** (;) is also rarely used. It acts as a weaker version of the full stop, and the clause which follows it may contain a finite verb (e.g. *Eight subjects failed to complete the task; four others left early*), but need not (e.g. *He glanced round the room; what to do now?*).

Other common problems

Subjectivity

It is not customary in academic writing to use the first person or to make personal comments (e.g. *After interviewing my subjects I transcribed the tapes,* or *I found this book very interesting*). In particular, avoid undermining your case by self-deprecating comments such as *This was all I could find out about the subject* or *Here is one explanation for the phenomenon, but knowing me it's probably wrong.*

Referencing

There are clear conventions for referencing, which are laid out in Chapter 21. Poor referencing will be interpreted as indicative of carelessness or ignorance, and can lead to charges of plagiarism (see Chapter 22).

Use of i.e. and e.g.

i.e. means *that is,* as in: *I filled him in on the situation, i.e. I explained what had happened.* **E.g.** means *for example,* as in: *If you have anything for the sale, e.g. old clothes or toys, please bring them.* Some people feel that *i.e.* and *e.g.* should not be used in prose writing, and your tutors may prefer that you avoid them. The important thing is that if you do use them, you know which is which and employ them appropriately.

References

Aijmer, K. (1996) *Conversational routines in English*. London and New York: Longman.

Aitchison, J. (1989) *The articulate mammal* (3rd edition). London: Unwin Hyman.

Aitchison, J. (1991) *Language change: progress or decay?* (2nd edition). Cambridge: Cambridge University Press.

Aitchison, J. (1992) *Teach yourself linguistics*. London: Hodder & Stoughton.

Aitchison, J. (1994) *Words in the mind* (2nd edition). Oxford: Blackwell.

Alderson, C. (1997) Models of language. Whose? What for? What use? In Ryan, A. and Wray, A. (eds.) *Evolving models of language: papers from the annual meeting of the British Association for Applied Linguistics 1996*. Clevedon: Multilingual Matters, 1–22.

Anderson, S. (1988) Morphological theory. In Newmeyer, F. (ed.) *Linguistic theory: foundations. Linguistics: the Cambridge survey*, vol. 1. Cambridge: Cambridge University Press, 146–91.

Anshen, F. (1978) *Statistics for linguists*. Rowley, Mass.: Newbury Press.

Appel, R., and Muysken, P. (1987) *Language Contact and Bilingualism*. London: Arnold.

Asher, R.E. (ed.) (1994) *The encyclopedia of language and linguistics* (10 vols). Oxford: Pergamon Press.

Atkinson, J.M. and Heritage, J. (eds.) (1984) *Structures of social action*. Cambridge: Cambridge University Press.

Atkinson, M., Kilby, D. and Roca, I. (1988) *Foundations of general linguistics* (2nd edition). London: Unwin Hyman.

Austin, J.L. (1961) Performative utterances. In Austin, J.L. *Philosophical papers* (ed. by Urmson, J.O. and Warnock, G.J., 3rd edition, 1979). Oxford: Oxford University Press. Reprinted in Martinich, A.P. (ed.) (1996) *The philosophy of language* (3rd edition). New York: Oxford University Press, 120–9.

Austin, J.L. (1962) *How to do things with words*. Oxford: Oxford University Press.

Ayers, D.M. (1965) *English words from Latin and Greek elements*. Tucson, Ariz.: University of Arizona Press.

Bachman, L.F. (1990) *Fundamental considerations in language testing*. Oxford: Oxford University Press.

Bachman, L.F. and Palmer, A.S. (1996) *Language testing in practice*. Oxford: Oxford University Press.

Bailey, K. (1981) *Methods of social research* (2nd edition). New York: Macmillan.

Bailey, K.M. and Nunan, D. (eds.) (1996) *Voices from the language classroom*. Cambridge: Cambridge University Press.

Baker, C. (1993) *Foundations of bilingual education and bilingualism*. Clevedon: Multilingual Matters.

Baker, C.L. (1995) *English syntax* (2nd edition). Cambridge, Mass.: MIT Press.

Barber, C. (1964) *Linguistic change in present-day English*. London: Oliver & Boyd.

Barber, C. (1972) *The story of language* (revised edition). London: Pan.

Barber, C. (1993) *The English language: a historical introduction*. Cambridge: Cambridge University Press.

Barber, C. (1997) *Early Modern English* (2nd edition). Edinburgh: Edinburgh University Press.

Barfield, O. (1953) *History of English words*. London: Faber & Faber.

Barnbrook, G. (1996) *Language and computers: a practical introduction to the computer analysis of language*. Edinburgh: Edinburgh University Press.

Baron, J. (1973) Phonemic stage not necessary for reading. *Quarterly Journal of Experimental Psychology* 25, 241–6.

Baugh, A.C. and Cable, T. (1993) *A history of the English language* (4th edition). London: Routledge.

Beattie, G.W. (1982a) Why is Mrs Thatcher interrupted so often? *Nature* 300, 744–7.

Beattie, G.W. (1982b) Thatcher and Callaghan compared. *Semiotica* 39, 93–114.

Beattie, G.W. (1983) *Talk: an analysis of speech and non-verbal behaviour in conversation*. Buckingham: Open University Press.

Bennett-Kastor, T. (1988) *Analyzing children's language: methods and theories*. Oxford: Blackwell.

Bergvall, V.L., Bing, J.M. and Freed, A.F. (eds.) (1996) *Rethinking language and gender research: theory and practice*. London and New York: Longman.

Berko-Gleason, J. (1975) Fathers and other strangers: men's speech to young children. In Dato, D. (ed.) *Developmental psycholinguistics: theory and applications*. Washington: Georgetown University Press.

Berlin, B. and Kay, P. (1969) *Basic color terms: their universality and evolution*. Berkeley and Los Angeles: University of California Press.

Biber, D. (1988) *Variation across speech and writing*. Cambridge: Cambridge University Press.

Biber, D. (1989) A typology of English texts. *Linguistics* 27, 3–43.

Biber, D. (1992) On the complexity of discourse complexity: a multidimensional analysis. *Discourse Processes* 15, 133–63.

Blake, N.F. (ed.) (1992) *1066–1476 Cambridge history of the English language*, vol. 2. Cambridge: Cambridge University Press.

Blake, N.F. (1996) *A history of the English language*. Basingstoke: Macmillan.

Blakemore, D. (1992) *Understanding utterances*. Oxford: Blackwell.

Bloor, T. and Bloor, M. (1995) *The functional analysis of English: a Hallidayan approach*. London: Arnold.

Boas, F. (1911/1966) *Introduction to the handbook of American Indian languages*. Lincoln, Nebr.: Nebraska Press. Originally in the *Handbook of American Indian languages* (4 vols.). Washington DC: Government Printing Office, 1911.

Bolinger, D. (1981) *Aspects of language* (3rd edition). New York: Harcourt Brace Jovanovich.

Bornstein, D.D. (1976) *Readings in the theory of grammar: from the 17th to the 20th century.* Cambridge, Mass: Winthrop.

Borsley, R.D. (1991) *Syntactic theory: a unified approach.* London: Edward Arnold.

Bradley, H. (1916) Shakespeare's English. In Bradley, H. *Shakespeare's England.* Oxford: Oxford University Press.

Bridges, R. (1913) *A tract on the present state of English pronunciation.* Oxford: Clarendon Press.

Bright, W. (ed.) (1992) *International encyclopedia of linguistics* (4 vols.). Oxford: Oxford University Press.

Brook, G.L. (1957) *English sound changes.* Manchester: Manchester University Press.

Brook, G.L. (1978) *English dialects* (3rd edition). London: André Deutsch.

Brouwer, D., Gerritsen, M. and de Haan, D. (1979) Speech differences between men and women: on the wrong track? *Language and Society* 8, 33–50.

Brown, G. (1977) *Listening to spoken English.* London and New York: Longman.

Brown, R. (1973) *A first language: the early stages.* Cambridge, Mass: Harvard University Press.

Brown, R. and McNeill, D. (1966) The 'tip of the tongue' phenomenon. *Journal of Verbal Learning and Verbal Behavior* 5, 325–37.

Burchfield, R. (1985) *The English language.* Oxford: Oxford University Press.

Burchfield, R. (ed.) (1994) *English in Britain and overseas. Cambridge history of the English language,* vol. 5. Cambridge: Cambridge University Press.

Burke, P. and Porter, R. (1987) *The social history of language.* Cambridge: Cambridge University Press.

Burke, P. and Porter, R. (eds.) (1991) *Language, self and society.* Cambridge: Polity Press.

Burnley, D. (1992) *The history of the English language: a source book.* London: Longman.

Burstall, C., Jamieson, M., Cohen, S. and Hargreaves, M. (1974) *Primary French in the balance.* Windsor: NFER.

Burton-Roberts, N. (1986) *Analysing sentences.* London: Longman.

Butler, C.S. (ed.) (1992) *Computers and written texts.* Oxford: Blackwell.

Butler, C.S. (1985) *Statistics for linguistics.* Oxford: Blackwell.

Caldas-Coulthard, C.M. and Coulthard, M. (1996) *Texts and practices: readings in critical discourse.* London: Routledge.

Cameron, D. (1995) *Verbal hygiene.* London: Routledge.

Cameron, K. (1961) *English placenames.* London: Batsford.

Cameron, K. (1965) *Scandinavian settlement in the territory of the five boroughs: the place-name evidence.* University of Nottingham, Inaugural Lecture, 4/3/65.

Caplan, D. (1987) *Neurolinguistics and linguistic aphasiology: an introduction.* Cambridge: Cambridge University Press.

Caron, J. (1992) *An introduction to psycholinguistics* (trans. Tim Powell). Hemel Hempstead: Harvester Wheatsheaf.

Carroll, B.J. and Hall, P.J. (1985) *Make your own English language tests.* Oxford: Pergamon.

Carroll, J.B. (ed.) (1956) *Language, thought and reality: selected writings of Benjamin Lee Whorf* . Cambridge, Mass.: MIT Press.

Carroll, J.B. (1975) *The teaching of French as a foreign language in eight countries*. Stockholm: Almqvist & Wiksell International; New York and London: John Wiley.

Carroll, J.B., Davies, P. and Richman, B. (1971) *Word frequency book*. Boston: Houghton Mifflin; New York: American Heritage.

Carroll, L. (1865/1971) *Alice through the looking glass*. London: Macmillan.

Carter, R. (ed.) (1982) *Language and literature*. London: Allen & Unwin.

Carter, R. (1987) *Vocabulary*. London: Allen & Unwin.

Carter, R. and Nash, W. (1990) *Seeing through language*. Oxford: Blackwell.

Carter, R. and Simpson, P. (1989) *Language, discourse and literature*. London: Allen & Unwin.

Castle, W.M. (1977) *Statistics in small doses* (2nd edition). New York: Churchill Livingstone.

Cavalli-Sforza, L.L. (1991) Genes, peoples and languages. *Scientific American* Nov. 1991, 72–8.

Chambers, A. and Trudgill, P. (1980) *Dialectology*. Cambridge: Cambridge University Press.

Cheshire, J. (1978) Present tense verbs in Reading English. In Trudgill, P. (ed.), *Sociolinguistic patterns in British English*. London: Edward Arnold, 52–68.

Cheshire, J. (1982) *Variation in an English dialect*. Cambridge: Cambridge University Press.

Chiaro, D. (1992) *The language of jokes: analysing verbal play*. London: Routledge.

Chierchia, G. and McConnell-Ginet, S. (1990) *An introduction to semantics*. Cambridge: Cambridge University Press.

Chilton, P. (ed.) (1985) *Language and the nuclear arms debate: nukespeak today*. London: Pinter/Cassell Academic.

Chomsky, C. (1969) *The acquisition of syntax in children from 5 to 10*. Cambridge, Mass.: MIT Press.

Chomsky, N. (1957) *Syntactic structures*. The Hague: Mouton.

Chomsky, N. (1965) *Aspects of the theory of syntax*. Cambridge, Mass.: MIT Press.

Clark, E.V. (1993) *The lexicon in acquisition*. Cambridge: Cambridge University Press.

Clark, H.H. and Clark, E.V. (1977) *Psychology and language: an introduction to psycholinguistics*. New York: Harcourt Brace Jovanovitch.

Clark, J. and Yallop, C. (1990) *An introduction to phonetics and phonology*. Oxford: Blackwell.

Clark, J.L. (1987) *Curriculum renewal in school foreign language learning*. Oxford: Oxford University Press.

Clarke, G.M. and Cooke, D. (1992) *A basic course in statistics* (3rd edition). London: Edward Arnold.

Clifton, C. Jr. and Ferreira, F. (1989) Ambiguity in context. *Language and Cognitive Processes* 4 (3/4), Special Issue (SI), 77–103.

Coates, J. (1993) *Women, men and language* (2nd edition). Harlow: Longman.

Coates, J. (1996) *Women talk*. Oxford: Blackwell.

Coates, J. and Cameron, D. (eds.) (1989) *Women in their speech communities*. London: Longman.

Coates, R. (1987) Lexical morphology. In Lyons, J., Coates, R., Deuchar, M. and Gazdar, G. (eds.) *New horizons in linguistics 2*. London: Penguin, 103–21.

Collins Cobuild (1991) *English guides 1: prepositions*. London: Harper Collins.

Collins Cobuild (1996) *Grammar patterns 1: verbs.* London: Harper Collins.

Coltheart, M., Curtis, B., Atkins, P. and Haller, M. (1993) Models of reading aloud: dual-route and parallel-distributed-processing approaches. *Psychological Review* 100, 589–608.

Coltheart, M., Patterson, K.E. and Marshall, J.C. (eds.) (1987) *Deep dyslexia* (2nd edition). London: Routledge & Kegan Paul.

Cook, G. (1992) *The discourse of advertising.* London: Routledge.

Cook, V. (1993) *Linguistics and second language acquisition.* Basingstoke: Macmillan.

Cook, V. (1996) *Second language learning and teaching* (2nd edition). London: Arnold.

Cook, V. (1997) *Inside language.* London: Arnold.

Cook, V.J. and Newson, M. (1996) *Chomsky's universal grammar* (2nd edition). Oxford: Blackwell.

Coolican, H. (1995) *Introduction to research methods and statistics in psychology.* London: Hodder & Stoughton.

Cornwell, R. and Staunton, M. (1985) *Data protection: putting the record straight.* London: National Council for Civil Liberties.

Coulmas, F. (1981) *Conversational routine.* The Hague: Mouton.

Coulthard, M. (1985) *An Introduction to Discourse Analysis* (2nd edition). London: Longman.

Coupland, N., Coupland, J. and Giles, H. (1991) *Language, society and the elderly.* Oxford: Blackwell.

Cromer, R.F. (1991) *Language and thought in normal and handicapped children.* Oxford: Blackwell.

Cruttenden, A. (1974) An experiment involving comprehension of intonation in children from 7 to 10. *Journal of Child Language* 1, 221–31.

Cruttenden, A. (1979) *Language in infancy and childhood.* Manchester: Manchester University Press.

Crystal, D. (1982) *Profiling linguistic disability.* London: Edward Arnold.

Crystal, D. (1986) *Listen to your child: a parent's guide to children's language.* Harmondsworth: Penguin.

Crystal, D. (1987) *Child language, learning and linguistics: an overview for the teaching and therapeutic professions* (2nd edition). London: Arnold.

Crystal, D. (1988a) *The English language.* London: Penguin.

Crystal, D. (1988b) *Rediscover grammar.* London: Longman.

Crystal, D. (1995) *The Cambridge encyclopedia of the English language.* Cambridge: Cambridge University Press.

Crystal, D. (1996) *A dictionary of linguistics and phonetics* (4th edition). Oxford: Blackwell.

Crystal, D. (1997a) *The Cambridge encyclopedia of language* (2nd edition). Cambridge: Cambridge University Press.

Crystal, D. (1997b) *Global English.* Cambridge: Cambridge University Press.

Crystal, D., Fletcher, P. and Garman, M. (1989) *The grammatical analysis of language disability: a procedure for assessment and remediation* (2nd edition). London: Whurr Publishers.

Cummings, M. and Simmons, R. (1983) *The language of literature.* Oxford: Pergamon.

Cutler, A. (1982) *Slips of the tongue and language production.* Berlin: Mouton.

DES (1975) *A language for life.* Report of the Committee of Inquiry appointed by the Secretary of State for Education and Science under the Chairmanship of Sir Alan Bullock, FBA. Department of Education and Science, London: HMSO.

DFE (1995) *English in the National Curriculum*. Department for Education, London: HMSO.

Data Protection Registrar (1987) *Guidelines 1–8*. Wilmslow: Office of the Data Protection Registrar.

De Villiers, J.G. and de Villiers, P.A. (1973) A cross-sectional study of the acquisition of grammatical morphemes. *Journal of Psycholinguistic Research* 2, 267–78.

De Villiers, J.G. and de Villiers, P.A. (1978) *Language acquisition*. Cambridge, Mass.: Harvard University Press.

Dickson, P. and Cumming, A. (eds.) (1996) *Profiles of language education in 25 countries*. Slough: NFER.

Dictionary of South African English (1996). Oxford: Oxford University Press.

Dorian, N. C. (1981) *Language death: the life cycle of a Scottish Gaelic dialect*. Philadelphia: University of Pennsylvania Press.

Downes, W. (1984) *Language and society*. London: Fontana.

Drew, P. (1994) Conversation analysis. In Asher, R.E. (ed.) *The encyclopedia of language and linguistics,* vol. 2. Oxford: Pergamon, 749–54.

Drew, P. and Heritage, J. (eds.) (1992) *Talk at work*. Cambridge: Cambridge University Press.

Dromi, E. (1987) *Early lexical development*. Cambridge: Cambridge University Press.

Edelsky, C. (1976) The acquisition of communicative competence: recognition of linguistic correlates of sex roles. *Merril-Palmer Quarterly* 22, 47–59.

Eggins, S. (1994) *An introduction to systemic functional linguistics*. London: Pinter.

Eggins, S. and Slade, D. (1997) *Analysing casual conversation*. London: Cassell.

Ehrman, M.E. (1996) *Understanding second language learning difficulties*. Thousand Oaks, Calif.: Sage.

Ekwall, E. (1923) *English place-names in* -ing. Lund: C.W.K. Gleerup; Oxford: Oxford University Press.

Ekwall, E. (1925) The Scandinavian element. In Mawer, A. and Stenton, F.M. (eds.), *Introduction to the survey of English placenames*. Cambridge: Cambridge University Press, 55–92.

Ekwall, E. (1928) *English river-names*. Oxford: Clarendon Press.

Elliot, A.J. (1981) *Child language*. Cambridge: Cambridge University Press.

Ellis, A.W. (1993) *Reading, writing and dyslexia: a cognitive analysis* (2nd edition). Hove: Lawrence Erlbaum Associates.

Ellis, G. and Sinclair, B. (1989) *Learning to learn English*. Cambridge: Cambridge University Press.

Ellis, R. (1994) *The study of second language acquisition*. Oxford: Oxford University Press.

Eysenck, M.W. and Keane, M.T. (1995) *Cognitive psychology* (3rd edition). Hove: Lawrence Erlbaum Associates.

Faerch, C. and Kasper, G. (eds.) (1987) *Introspection in second language research*. Clevedon, Avon: Multilingual Matters.

Fairclough, N. (1989) *Language and power*. Harlow: Longman.

Fairclough, N. (1995) *Critical discourse analysis*. London: Longman.

Farb, P. (1973) *Word play*. Sevenoaks: Hodder & Stoughton.

Farringdon, J. (ed.) (1996) *Analysing for authorship: a guide to the CUSUM technique*. Cardiff: University of Wales Press.

Fasold, R. (1984) *The sociolinguistics of society*. Oxford: Blackwell.

Fasold, R. (1990) *The sociolinguistics of language: introduction to sociolinguistics,* vol. 2. Oxford: Blackwell.

Fischer, J.L. (1958) Social influences on the choice of a linguistic variant. *Word* 14, 47–56.

Fisher, J.H. and Bornstein, D. (1974) *In forme of speche is chaunge: readings in the history of the English language*. Englewood Cliffs, NJ: Prentice-Hall.

Fishman, J. (1971) *Advances in the sociology of language* vol.1. The Hague: Mouton.

Fishman, P.M. (1978) What do couples talk about when they're alone? In Butturff, D. and Epstein, E.L. (eds.) *Women's language and style*. Department of English, University of Akron.

Fletcher, P. (1985) *A child's learning of English*. Oxford: Basil Blackwell.

Fletcher, P. and Garman, M. (eds.) (1986) *Language acquisition* (2nd edition). Cambridge: Cambridge University Press.

Fletcher, P. and MacWhinney, B. (eds.) (1995) *The handbook of child language*. Oxford: Blackwell.

Fodor, J.A. (1983) *The modularity of mind*. Cambridge, Mass.: MIT Press.

Fodor, J.A., Bever, T.G. and Garrett, M.F. (1974) *The psychology of language*. New York: McGraw-Hill.

Foss, D.J. and Hakes, D.T. (1978) *Psycholinguistics*. Englewood Cliffs, NJ: Prentice-Hall.

Foster, S.H. (1990) *The communicative competence of young children*. London: Longman.

Fowler, R. (1991) *Language in the news: discourse and ideology in the press*. London: Routledge.

Fowles, B. and Glanz, M.E. (1977) Competence and talent in verbal riddle comprehension. *Journal of Child Language* 4, 433–52.

Frazier, L. and Rayner, K. (1982) Making and correcting errors during sentence comprehension: eye movements in the analysis of structurally ambiguous sentences. *Cognitive Psychology* 14, 178–210.

Freeborn, D. (1992) *From Old English to Standard English*. Basingstoke: Macmillan.

Freeborn, D. (1995) *A course book in English grammar: Standard English and the dialects*. Basingstoke: Macmillan.

Freeborn, D. (1996) *Style: text analysis and linguistic criticism*. Basingstoke: Macmillan.

Freeborn, D. with Langford, D. and French, P. (1993) *Varieties of English* (2nd edition). Basingstoke: Macmillan.

Fromkin, V.A. (1973) *Speech errors as linguistic evidence*. The Hague: Mouton.

Fromkin, V. and Rodman, R. (1993) *An introduction to language* (5th edition). Fort Worth, Tex.: Harcourt Brace Jovanovich.

Gamkrelidze, T.V. and Ivanov, V.V. (1990) The early history of Indo-European languages. *Scientific American* March 1990, 82–9.

Garman, M. (1990) *Psycholinguistics*. Cambridge: Cambridge University Press.

Garnham, A. (1985) *Psycholinguistics: central topics*. London and New York: Routledge.

Garrett, M.F. (1976) Syntactic processes in sentence production. In Wales, R. and Walder, E. (eds.) *New approaches to language mechanisms*. Amsterdam: North Holland, 231–55.

Garton, A. and Pratt, C. (1989) *Learning to be literate: the development of spoken and written language*. Oxford: Blackwell.

Giglioli, P.P. (ed.) (1972) *Language and social context*. Harmondsworth: Penguin.

Giles, H., Ball, S. and Fielding, G. (1975) Communication length as a behavioural index of accent prejudice. *International Journal of the Sociology of Language* 6, 73–81.

Giles, H. and St Clair, R. (eds.) (1979) *Language and social psychology.* Oxford: Blackwell.

Gilliéron, J. and Edmont, E. (1902–1910) *Atlas linguistique de la France.* Paris: Champion.

Gimson, A.C. (1962) *An introduction to the pronunciation of English.* London: Edward Arnold.

Gleitman, L. and Landau, B. (1994) *The acquisition of the lexicon.* Cambridge, Mass.: MIT Press.

Gombert, E. (1992) *Metalinguistic development.* Hemel Hempstead: Harvester Wheatsheaf.

Goodluck, H. (1991) *Language acquisition: a linguistic introduction.* Oxford: Blackwell.

Görlach, M. (1991) *Introduction to Early Modern English.* Cambridge: Cambridge University Press.

Graddol, D., Leith, D. and Swann, J. (1996) *English history, diversity and change.* London: Routledge.

Graddol, D. and Swann, J. (1989) *Gender voices.* Oxford: Blackwell.

Graesser, A.C., Singer, M. and Trabasso, T. (1994) Constructing inferences during narrative text comprehension. *Psychological Review* 101, 371–95.

Gray, M. (1984) *A dictionary of literary terms.* London: Longman.

Green, G.M. and Morgan, J.L. (1996) *Practical guide to syntactic analysis.* Stanford, Calif.: Center for the Study of Language and Information.

Greenbaum, S. (1991) *An introduction to English grammar.* London: Longman.

Greenberg, J.H. (1970) *The languages of Africa* (3rd edition). Bloomington, Ind.: Indiana University Press; The Hague: Mouton.

Greene, J. and Coulson, M. (1995) *Language understanding: current issues* (2nd edition). Buckingham: Open University Press.

Gregory, M. and Carroll, S. (1978) *Language and situation.* London: Routledge & Kegan Paul.

Grice, H.P. (1975) Logic and conversation. In Cole, P. and Morgan, J.L. (eds.) *Syntax and semantics,* vol. 3. New York: Academic Press. Reprinted in A.P. Martinich (ed.) (1996) *The philosophy of language* (3rd edition), New York: Oxford University Press, 156–67.

Griffiths, P.D. (1986) Constituent structure in text-copying. *York Papers in Linguistics* 12, 75–116.

Groom, B. (1934) *A short history of English words.* London: Macmillan.

Gruneberg, M. (1987) *Linkword: French.* London: Corgi.

Gruneberg, M. (1997) *Linkword* (CD-ROM). Nailsea, Avon: Edge Publishing.

Gumperz, J. (ed.) (1982) *Language and social identity.* Cambridge: Cambridge University Press.

Halliday, M.A.K. (1975) *Learning how to mean.* London: Edward Arnold.

Halliday, M.A.K. (1985) *An introduction to functional grammar.* London: Edward Arnold.

Halsall, E. (1968) *French as a second language: levels of attainment in three countries.* Hull: Institute of Education, University of Hull.

Harley, T.A. (1995) *The psychology of language: from data to theory.* Hove: Psychology Press.

Harris, J. (1993) *Introducing writing.* London: Penguin.

Hartmann, R. (ed.) (1996) *The English language in Europe.* Exeter: Intellect.

Hatch, E. and Lazaraton, A. (1991) *The research manual: design and statistics for applied linguistics.* Boston, Mass.: Heinle & Heinle.

Hawkins, E. and Perren, G.E. (eds.) (1978) *Intensive language teaching in schools.* London: CILT.

Hawkins, E. (1987) *Modern languages in the curriculum* (revised edition). Cambridge: Cambridge University Press.

Hawthorn, P. (1991) *The Usborne book of silly jokes.* London: Usborne.

Heath, C. (1992) The delivery and reception of diagnosis in the general practice consultation. In Drew, P. and Heritage, J. (eds.) 235–67.

Heath, S.B. (1983) *Ways with words.* Cambridge: Cambridge University Press.

Heaton, J. (1988) *Writing English language tests.* Harlow: Longman.

Heritage, J. (1989) Current developments in conversation analysis. In Roger, D. and Bull, P. (eds.) *Conversation: an interdisciplinary perspective.* Clevedon: Multilingual Matters, 21–47.

Hindmarsh, R. (1980) *Cambridge English lexicon: a graded word list for materials writers and course designers.* Cambridge: Cambridge University Press.

Hirsh-Pasek, K. and Golinkoff, R.M. (1996) *The origins of grammar: evidence from early language comprehension.* Cambridge, Mass.: MIT Press.

Hogg, R.M. (ed.) (1992) *The beginnings to 1066: Cambridge history of the English language,* vol. 1. Cambridge: Cambridge University Press.

Holmes, J. (1995) *Women, men and politeness.* London: Longman.

Hopper, R. (1991) Hold the phone. In Boden, D. and Zimmerman, D.H. (eds.) *Talk and social structure.* Cambridge: Polity Press, 217–31.

Horn, L.R. (1988) Pragmatic theory. In Newmeyer, F.J. (ed.) *Linguistics: the Cambridge survey,* vol. 1: *Linguistic theory: foundations,* 113–45.

Hotopf, W.N. (1983) Lexical slips of the pen and tongue: what they tell us about language production. In Butterworth, B. (ed.) *Language production,* vol. 2: *Development, writing and other language processes.* London: Academic Press, 147–99.

Houtkoop-Steenstra, H. (1991) Opening sequences in Dutch telephone conversations. In Boden, D. and Zimmerman, D.H. (eds.) *Talk and social structure.* Cambridge: Polity Press, 232–50.

Howatt, A.P.R. (1984) *A history of English language teaching.* Oxford: Oxford University Press.

Hudson, R.A. (1996) *Sociolinguistics* (2nd edition). Cambridge: Cambridge University Press.

Hughes, A. and Trudgill, P. (1996) *English accents and dialects: an introduction to social and regional varieties of British English* (3rd edition). London: Edward Arnold. (An accompanying cassette tape is also available.)

Hurford, J.R. (1994) *Grammar: a student's guide.* Cambridge: Cambridge University Press.

Hurford, J.R. and Heasley, B. (1983) *Semantics: a course book.* Cambridge: Cambridge University Press.

Hymes, D. (1971) On communicative competence. In Pride, J.B. and Holmes, J. (eds.) (1972) *Sociolinguistics.* Harmondsworth: Penguin.

Ingram, D. (1989) *First language acquisition: method, description and explanation.* Cambridge: Cambridge University Press.

Jackson, H. (1988) *Words and their meaning*. London: Longman.

Jackson, H. (1990) *Grammar and meaning: a semantic approach to English grammar*. London: Longman.

Jefferson, G. (1989) Preliminary notes on a possible metric which provides for a 'standard maximum' silence of approximately one second in conversation. In Roger, D. and Bull, P. (eds.) *Conversation*. Clevedon: Multilingual Matters, 166–96.

Johansson, S. and Hofland, K. (1989) *Frequency analysis of English vocabulary and grammar: based on the LOB corpus*, vol. 1. Oxford: Clarendon Press.

Johnson, S. and Meinhof, U. (eds.) (1996) *Language and masculinity*. Oxford: Blackwell.

Joyce, P. (1991) The people's English: language and class in England, *c.* 1840–1920. In Burke, P. and Porter, R. (eds.) *Language, self and society*. Cambridge: Polity Press, 154–90.

Kaufer, D., Hayes, J.R. and Flower, L.S. (1986) Composing written sentences. *Research in the teaching of English* 20, 121–40.

Keller, R. (1994) *On language change: the invisible hand in language*. London: Routledge.

Kess, J.E. (1992) *Psycholinguistics*. Amsterdam: John Benjamins.

Kökeritz, H. (1953) *Shakespeare's pronunciation*. New Haven: Yale University Press.

Kramarae, C. (1981) *Women and men speaking*. Rowley, Mass.: Newbury House.

Kramer, C. (1974) Stereotypes of women's speech: the word from cartoons. *Journal of Popular Culture* 8, 624–30.

Kramer, C. (1977) Perceptions of male and female speech. *Language and Speech* 20 (2), 151–61.

Krashen, S. and Terrell, T. (1983) *The natural approach*. Oxford: Pergamon.

Kreidler, C.W. (1989) *The pronunciation of English*. Oxford: Blackwell.

Kress, G. (1990) Critical discourse analysis. *Annual Review of Applied Linguistics* 11, 84–99.

Kress, G. (1994) *Learning to write* (2nd edition). London: Routledge.

Kucera, H. and Francis, W.N. (1967) *Computational analysis of present-day American English*. Providence: Brown University Press.

Kuiper, K. and Allan, W.S. (1996) *An introduction to English language*. Basingstoke: Macmillan.

Kurath, H. (1949) *A word geography of the eastern United States*. Ann Arbor: University of Michigan.

Labov, W. (1966) *The social stratification of English in New York City*. Washington DC: Georgetown University Press.

Labov, W. (1969) The logic of nonstandard English. *Georgetown Monographs on Language and Linguistics* 22, 1–31. Reprinted in Gigioli (1972), 179–215.

Labov, W. (1972) *Sociolinguistic patterns*. Philadelphia: University of Pennsylvania Press.

Lakoff, G. and Johnson, M. (1980) *Metaphors we live by*. Chicago: University of Chicago Press.

Lakoff, R. (1975) *Language and woman's place*. New York: Harper & Row.

Lambert, W., Gardner, R., Olton, R. and Tunstall, K. (1968) A study of the roles, attitudes and motivation in second language learning. In Fishman, J. (ed.) *Readings in the sociology of language*. The Hague: Mouton, 473–91.

Langford, D. (1994) *Analysing talk*. Basingstoke: Macmillan.

Larsen-Freeman, D. and Long, M.H. (1991) *An introduction to second language acquisition research*. Harlow: Longman.

Leech, G.N. (1969) *A linguistic guide to English poetry*. London: Longman.

Leech, G.N. (1992) *Introducing English grammar*. London: Penguin.

Leech, G.N., Deuchar, M. and Hoogenraad, R. (1982) *English grammar for today*. Basingstoke: Macmillan.

Leech, G.N., Myers, G. and Thomas, J. (eds.) (1995) *Spoken English on computer*. Harlow: Longman.

Leech, G.N. and Short, M. (1981) *Style in fiction: a linguistic guide to English fictional prose*. London: Longman.

Leith, D. (1983) *A social history of English*. London: Routledge.

Lesser, R. (1989) *Linguistic investigations of aphasia* (2nd edition). London: Cole & Whurr.

Levelt, W.J.M., Schriefers, H., Vorberg, D., Meyer, A.S., Pechmann, T. and Havinga, J. (1991) The time course of lexical access in speech production: a study of picture naming. *Psychological Review* 98, 615–18.

Levinson, S.C. (1983) *Pragmatics*. Cambridge: Cambridge University Press.

Lewis, T. (1991) *Pisspote's Progress*. Lichfield: Leomansley Press.

Lightbown, P. and Spada, N. (1993) *How languages are learned*. Oxford: Oxford University Press.

Lockwood, W.B. (1969) *Indo-European philology*. London: Hutchinson.

Lynn, J. and Jay, A. (eds.) (1987) *Yes Prime Minister*. London: BBC Books.

Malmkjaer, K. (ed.) (1991) *The linguistics encyclopedia*. London: Routledge.

Maltz, D. and Borker, R. (1982) A cultural approach to male–female miscommunication. In Gumperz, J. (ed.) *Language and social identity*. Cambridge: Cambridge University Press.

Marenbon, J. (1994) The new orthodoxy examined. In Brindley, S. (ed.) *Teaching English*. Milton Keynes: Open University, 16–24.

Marslen-Wilson, W. and Tyler, L. (1980) The temporal structure of spoken language understanding. *Cognition* 8, 1–71.

Mather, J.Y. and Speitel, H.H. (1975) *The linguistic atlas of Scotland*. London: Croom Helm.

McClelland, J.L. and Elman, J.L. (1986) The TRACE model of speech perception. *Cognitive Psychology* 18, 1–86.

McCloskey, J. (1988) Syntactic theory. In Newmeyer, F. (ed.) *Linguistics: the Cambridge survey*, vol. 1: *Linguistic theory: foundations*. Cambridge: Cambridge University Press, 18–59.

McCrum, R., Cran, W. and MacNeil, R. (1992) *The story of English* (revised edition). London: Faber/BBC Books.

McEnery, T. and Wilson, A. (1996) *Corpus linguistics*. Edinburgh: Edinburgh University Press.

McMahon, A. (1994) *Understanding language change*. Cambridge: Cambridge University Press.

McNamara, T. (1996) *Measuring second language performance*. London and New York: Longman.

McNeill, D. (1987) *Psycholinguistics: a new approach*. New York: Harper & Row.

McTear, M. (1985) *Children's conversation*. Oxford: Blackwell.

Meinhof, U. and Richardson, K. (eds.) (1994) *Text, discourse and context*. London: Longman.

Miles, T.R. and Miles, E. (1983) *Help for dyslexic children*. London: Routledge.

Mills, S. (ed.) (1995) *Language and gender: interdisciplinary perspectives*. Harlow: Longman.

Milroy, J. and Milroy, L. (1978) Belfast: change and variation in an urban vernacular. In Trudgill, P. (ed.) *Sociolinguistic patterns in British English*. London: Arnold, 19–36.

Milroy, L. (1987a) *Observing and analysing natural language*. Oxford: Blackwell.

Milroy, L. (1987b) *Language and social networks* (2nd edition). Oxford: Blackwell.

Milton, J. and Meara, P. (1995) How periods abroad affect vocabulary growth in a foreign language. *ITL Review of Applied Linguistics* 107/108, 17–34.

Minsky, M. (1988) *The society of mind*. New York: Touchstone.

Mitton, R. (1996) *English spelling and the computer*. London: Longman.

Mitzka, W. and Schmidt, L.E. (1953–1978) *Deutsche Wortatlas*. Giessen: Schmitz.

Montgomery, M. (1995) *An introduction to language and society* (2nd edition). London: Routledge.

Morton, J. (1979) Word recognition. In Morton, J. and Marshall, J. (eds.) *Psycholinguistics series 2: structures and processes*. London: Paul Elek, 107–56.

Mugglestone, L. (1995) *Talking proper: the use of accent as a social symbol*. Oxford: Oxford University Press.

Munby, J. (1978) *Communicative syllabus design*. Cambridge: Cambridge University Press.

Myers, L.M. and Hoffman, R.L. (1979) *The roots of modern English* (2nd edition). Boston and Toronto: Little, Brown.

Naiman, N., Fröhlich, M., Stern, H.H. and Todesco, A. (1978/1995) *The good language learner*. Toronto: Ontario Institute for Studies in Education 1978; Clevedon: Multilingual Matters 1995.

Nash, W. (1985) *The language of humour*. London: Longman.

Nash, W. (1990) *Language in popular fiction*. London: Routledge.

Nation, I.S.P. (ed.) (1986) *Vocabulary lists: words, affixes and stems* (revised edition). Victoria, New Zealand: English Language Institute, Victoria University of Wellington.

Nation, I.S.P. (1990) *Teaching and learning vocabulary*. Boston, Mass.: Heinle & Heinle.

Nattinger, J.R. and De Carrico, J.S. (1992) *Lexical phrases and language teaching*. Oxford: Oxford University Press.

Ni, W., Crain, A. and Shankweiler, D. (1996) Sidestepping garden paths: assessing the contributions of syntax, semantics and plausibility in resolving ambiguities. *Language and Cognitive Processes* 11(3), 283–334.

Nofsinger, R.E. (1991) *Everyday conversation*. Newbury Park: Sage.

O'Barr, W. and Atkins, B. (1980) 'Women's language' or 'powerless language'? In McConnell-Ginet, S., Borker, R. and Furman, N. (eds.) *Women and language in literature and society*. New York: Praeger, 93–110.

O'Donnell, W.R. and Todd, L. (1991) *Variety in contemporary English* (2nd edition). London: Harper Collins.

Obelkevich, J. (1987) Proverbs and social history. In Burke and Porter (1987), 43–72.

Olson, R.K. (1994) Language deficits in 'specific' reading ability. In Gernsbacher, M.A. (ed.) *Handbook of psycholinguistics*. San Diego: Academic Press, 895–916.

Onions, C.T. (ed.) (1966) *The Oxford dictionary of English etymology*. Oxford: Clarendon Press.

Oppenheim, A. (1966) *Questionnaire design and attitude measurement*. London: Heinemann.

Orton, H. (1962) *Survey of English dialects: introduction*. Leeds: Arnold.

Orton, H. *et al.* (1962–1971) *Survey of English dialects: the basic material* (4 volumes). London: Arnold.

Orton, H., Sanderson, S. and Widdowson, J. (1978) *The linguistic atlas of England*. London: Croom Helm.

Oxford guide to the English language (1984) Oxford: Oxford University Press.

Palmer, F.R. (1981) *Semantics* (2nd edition). Cambridge: Cambridge University Press.

Partridge, E. (1948) *Words at war, words at peace*. London: Frederick Muller.

Partridge, E. (1966) *Origins: a short etymological dictionary of modern English* (4th edition). London: Routledge & Kegan Paul.

Pawley, A. and Syder, F.H. (1983) Two puzzles for linguistic theory: nativelike selection and nativelike fluency. In Richards, J.C. and Schmidt, R.W. (eds.) *Language and Communication*. New York: Longman, 191–225.

Pederson, L. *et al.* (eds.) (1986) *The linguistic atlas of the Gulf States: a concordance of basic materials*. Ann Arbor: University Microfilm.

Perera, K. (1979) Reading and writing. In Cruttenden (1979), 130–60.

Perera, K. (1984) *Children's writing and reading: analysing classroom language*. Oxford: Blackwell.

Perera, K. (1986) Language acquisition and writing. In Fletcher and Garman, 494–518.

Pinker, S. (1994) *The language instinct*. London: Penguin.

Plaut, D.C. and Shallice, T. (1993) Deep dyslexia: a case study in connectionist neuropsychology. *Cognitive Neuropsychology* 10, 377–500.

Potter, S. (1975) *Language in the modern world* (revised edition). Harmondsworth: Penguin.

Preston, D. (1989) *Sociolinguistics and second language acquisition*. Oxford: Blackwell.

Prideaux, G.D. (1984) *Psycholinguistics: the experimental study of language*. London: Croom Helm.

Psathas, G. (1995) *Conversation analysis: the study of talk-in-interaction*. Thousand Oaks, Calif.; London: Sage.

Pyles, T. and Algeo, J. (1993) *The origins and development of the English language* (4th edition). New York: Harcourt Brace Jovanovich.

Quirk, R. and Greenbaum, S. (1973) *A university grammar of English*. Harlow: Longman.

Quirk, R. Greenbaum, S., Leech, G. and Svartvik, J. (1972) *A grammar of contemporary English*. London and New York: Longman.

Quirk, R., Greenbaum, S., Leech, G. and Svartvik, J. (1985) *A comprehensive grammar of the English language*. London: Longman.

Rayner, K. and Pollatsek, A. (1989) *The psychology of reading*. London: Prentice Hall.

Rayner, K. and Sereno, S.C. (1994) Eye movements in reading: psycholinguistic studies. In Gernsbacher, M.A. (ed.) *Handbook of psycholinguistics*. New York: Academic Press.

Rees, F. (1989) *Languages for a change: diversifying foreign language provision in schools*. Windsor: NFER-Nelson.

Reid, E. (1978) Social and stylistic variation in the speech of some Edinburgh schoolchildren. In Trudgill, P. (ed.) *Sociolinguistic patterns in British English*. London: Arnold, 158–71.

Renfrew, C. (1987) *Archaeology and language: the puzzle of Indo-European origins.* London: Penguin.

Renfrew, C. (1989) The origins of Indo-European languages. *Scientific American* October 1989, 82–90.

Renfrew, C. (1994) World linguistic diversity. *Scientific American* January 1994, 104–10.

Richards, J.C. and Lockhart, C. (1994) *Reflective teaching in second language classrooms.* Cambridge: Cambridge University Press.

Richards, J.C., Platt, J. and Platt, H. (1992) *Longman dictionary of language teaching and applied linguistics* (2nd edition). Harlow: Longman.

Roach, P. (1991) *English phonetics and phonology* (2nd edition). Cambridge: Cambridge University Press.

Roach, P. (ed.) (1992) *Computing in linguistics and phonetics.* London: Academic Press.

Robson, C. (1973) *Experiment, design and statistics in psychology.* Harmondsworth: Penguin.

Romaine, S. (1984) *The language of children and adolescents.* Oxford: Blackwell.

Romaine, S. (1995) *Bilingualism* (2nd edition). Oxford: Blackwell.

Room, A. (1982) *Dictionary of trade name origins.* London: Routledge & Kegan Paul.

Room, A. (1991) *NTC's dictionary of changes of meaning.* Chicago: National Textbook Company (previously Routledge & Kegan Paul 1986).

Room, A. (1992) *Brewer's dictionary of names: people, places, things.* London: Cassell.

Ross, P.E. (1991) Hard Words. *Scientific American* April 1991, 70–9.

Rowntree, D. (1981) *Statistics without tears: a primer for non-mathematicians.* Harmondsworth: Penguin.

Sachs, J.S. (1967) Recognition memory for syntactic and semantic aspects of connected discourse. *Perception and psychophysics* 2: 437–42.

Sacks, H. (1995) *Lectures on conversation,* vols. 1 and 2. Oxford: Blackwell.

Sadock, J.M. (1979) Figurative speech and linguistics. In Ortony, A. (ed.) *Metaphor and thought.* Cambridge: Cambridge University Press, 46–64.

Sadock, J.M. (1988) Speech act distinctions in grammar. In Newmeyer, F.J. (ed.) *Linguistics: the Cambridge survey,* vol. 2: *Linguistic theory: extensions and implications.* Cambridge: Cambridge University Press, 183–97.

Samuels, M.L. (1972) *Linguistic evolution.* Cambridge: Cambridge University Press.

Sandred, K.I. (1963) *English placenames in* -stead. Uppsala: Almqvist & Wiksell.

Saville-Troike, M. (1989) *The ethnography of communication* (2nd edition). Oxford: Blackwell.

Schiffrin, D. (1987) *Discourse markers.* Cambridge: Cambridge University Press.

Schiffrin, D. (1994) *Approaches to discourse.* Oxford: Blackwell.

Scrivener, J. (1994) *Learning teaching.* Oxford: Oxford University Press.

Searle, J.R. (1965) What is a Speech Act? In Black, M. (ed.) *Philosophy in America.* London: Allen & Unwin, 221–39. Reprinted in Martinich, A.P. (ed.) (1996) *The philosophy of language* (3rd edition). New York: Oxford University Press, 130–40.

Searle, J.R. (1969) *Speech acts.* Cambridge: Cambridge University Press.

Searle, J.R. (1975) Indirect speech acts. In Cole, P. and Morgan, J.L. (eds.) *Syntax and semantics,* vol. 3. New York: Academic Press. Reprinted in Martinich, A.P. (ed.) (1996) *The philosophy of language* (3rd edition). New York: Oxford University Press, 168–82.

Searle, J.R. (1976) The classification of illocutionary acts. *Language and Society 5,* 1–24.

Searle, J.R. (1979) A taxonomy of illocutionary acts. In Searle, J.R. *Expression and meaning.* New York: Cambridge University Press. Reprinted in Martinich, A.P. (ed.) (1996) *The philosophy of language* (3rd edition). New York: Oxford University Press, 141–55.

Seliger, H.W. and Shohamy, E. (1989) *Second language research methods.* London: Oxford University Press.

Selinker, L. (1972) Interlanguage. *International Review of Applied Linguistics* 10, 201–31.

Serjeantson, M.S. (1935) *A history of foreign words in English.* London: Routledge & Kegan Paul.

Shultz, T.R. and Horibe, F. (1974) Development of the appreciation of verbal jokes. *Developmental Psychology* 1(1), 13–20.

Shuy, R. (1993) *Language crimes: the use and abuse of language evidence in the courtroom.* Oxford: Blackwell.

Sinclair, J. (1991) *Corpus, concordance, collocation.* Oxford: Oxford University Press.

Singer, M. (1990) *Psychology of language: an introduction to sentence and discourse processes.* Hillsdale, NJ: Lawrence Erlbaum Associates.

Sizer, R. and Newman, P. (1984) *The Data Protection Act: a practical guide for managers and professionals incorporating an annotated copy of the Data Protection Act 1984.* Aldershot: Gower.

Skeat, W.W. (1911) *English dialects from the eighth century to the present.* Cambridge: Cambridge University Press. (Also Kraus Reprint Co., New York, 1973.)

Slobin, D. (1966) Grammatical transformations and sentence comprehension in childhood and adulthood. *Journal of Verbal Learning and Verbal Behavior* 5: 219–27.

Slobin, D. (1979) *Psycholinguistics* (2nd edition). Glenview, Ill.: Scott, Foresman & Co.

Smith, J. (1996) *An historical study of English.* London: Routledge.

Smith, N.V. (1973) *The acquisition of phonology: a case study.* Cambridge: Cambridge University Press.

Smith, P. (1985) *Language, the sexes and society.* Oxford: Blackwell.

Smith, P.T. (1986) The development of reading: acquisition of a cognitive skill. In Fletcher and Garman, 475–93.

Snow, C. (1986) Conversations with children. In Fletcher and Garman, 69–89.

Snowling, M.J. (1987) *Dyslexia: a cognitive development perspective.* Oxford: Blackwell.

Spada, N. and Fröhlich, M. (1995) *Communicative orientation of language teaching observation scheme: coding conventions and applications.* Sydney: National Centre for English Language Teaching and Research.

Spender, D. (1985) *Man made language* (2nd edition). London: Routledge & Kegan Paul.

Sperber, D. and Wilson, D. (1987) Precis of 'Relevance: communication and cognition'. *Brain and Behavioral Sciences* 10, 697–754. Reprinted in Geirsson, H. and Losonsky, M. (1996) *Readings in language and mind.* Cambridge, Mass.: Blackwell, 460–86.

Sperber, D. and Wilson, D. (1995) *Relevance: communication and cognition* (2nd edition). Oxford: Blackwell.

Stark, R.E. (1986) Prespeech segmental feature development. In Fletcher and Garman, 149–73.

Stevick, E. (1989) *Success with foreign languages*. Hemel Hempstead: Prentice Hall.

Stilwell Peccei, J. (1994) *Child language*. London: Routledge.

Stoppard, T. (1979) *Dogg's our pet*. London: Fraser & Dunlop.

Strang, B. (1970) *A history of English*. London and New York: Routledge.

Stubbs, M. (1993) *Discourse analysis*. Oxford: Blackwell.

Stubbs, M. (1995) Collocations and cultural connotations of common words. *Linguistics and Education* 7 (4), 379–90.

Stubbs, M. (1996) *Text and corpus analysis: computer-assisted studies of language and culture*. Oxford: Blackwell.

Stubbs, M. (1997) Whorf's children: critical comments on critical discourse analysis (CDA). In Ryan, A. and Wray, A. (eds.) *Evolving models of language: papers from the annual meeting of the British Association for Applied Linguistics 1996*. Clevedon: Multilingual Matters, 100–16.

Swan, M. and Smith, B. (1987) *Learner English: a teacher's guide to interference and other problems*. Cambridge: Cambridge University Press.

Swann, J. (1992) *Girls, boys and language*. Oxford: Blackwell.

Talbot, M. (1995) *Fictions at work: language and social practice in fiction*. London: Longman.

Tannen, D. (1991) *You just don't understand: women and men in conversation*. London: Virago Press.

Taylor, T.J. and Cameron, D. (1987) *Analysing conversation: rules and units in the structure of talk*. Oxford: Pergamon.

Thomas, L. (1993) *Beginning syntax*. Oxford: Blackwell.

Thorne, B. and Henley, N. (eds.) (1975) *Language and sex: difference and dominance*. Rowley, Mass.: Newbury House.

Tough, J. (1976) *Listening to children talking*. London: Ward Lock Educational.

Trask, R.L. (1993) *A dictionary of grammatical terms in linguistics*. London: Routledge.

Trask, R.L. (1995a) *Dictionary of phonetics and phonology*. London: Routledge.

Trask, R.L. (1995b) *Language: the basics*. London: Routledge.

Trott, K. (1996) *'Pink for girls, blue for boys': aspects of lexical development in children aged 4 to 9*. Misterton: The Language Press.

Trudgill, P. (1972) Sex, covert prestige and linguistic change in urban British English of Norwich. *Language in Society* 1, 179–95.

Trudgill, P. (1974) *The social differentiation of English in Norwich*. Cambridge: Cambridge University Press.

Trudgill, P. (ed.) (1978) *Sociolinguistic patterns in British English*. London: Arnold.

Trudgill, P. (1983) *On dialect*. Oxford: Blackwell.

Trudgill, P. (1994) *Dialects*. Routledge Language Workbooks. London: Routledge.

Trudgill, P. (1990) *The dialects of England*. Oxford: Blackwell.

Trudgill, P. (1995) *Sociolinguistics* (2nd revised edition). Harmondsworth: Penguin.

Trudgill, P. and Hannah, J. (1985) *International English: a guide to varieties of standard English* (2nd edition). London: Edward Arnold. (An accompanying cassette tape is also available.)

Tyler, L. K. and Marslen-Wilson, W.D. (1977) The on-line effects of semantic context on syntactic processing. *Journal of Verbal Learning and Verbal Behavior* 16, 683–92.

Upton, C. and Widdowson, J.D.A. (1996) *An atlas of English dialects*. Oxford: Oxford University Press.

Vallins, G.H. (1954) *Spelling*. London: André Deutsch.

Van Orden, G.C. (1987) A ROWS is a ROSE: spelling, sound and reading. *Memory and Cognition* 15, 181–98.

Verma, M. K. (1991) The Hindi speech community. In Alladina, S. and Edwards, V. (eds.) *Multilingualism in the British Isles,* vol. 2: *Africa, the Middle East and Asia*. Harlow: Longman, 103–14.

Wadler, A.D. (1948) *The origin of language*. New York: American Press for Art & Science.

Wakelin, M.F. (1977) *English dialects: an introduction* (revised edition). London: Athlone Press.

Wakelin, M.F. (1988) *The archaeology of English*. London: Batsford.

Wales, K. (1989) *A dictionary of stylistics*. London: Longman.

Wardhaugh, R. (1985) *How conversation works*. Oxford: Blackwell.

Wardhaugh, R. (1992) *An introduction to sociolinguistics* (2nd edition). Oxford: Basil Blackwell.

Wardhaugh, R. (1993) *Investigating language*. Oxford: Blackwell.

Webelhuth, G. (ed.) (1995) *Government and binding theory and the minimalist program*. Cambridge, Mass.: Blackwell.

Wells, G. (ed.) (1981) *Learning through interaction: the study of language development*. Cambridge: Cambridge University Press.

Wells, G. (1985) *Language development in the pre-school years*. Cambridge: Cambridge University Press.

Wells, G. (1986a) *The meaning makers: children learning language and using language to learn*. London: Hodder & Stoughton.

Wells, G. (1986b) Variation in child language. In Fletcher and Garman, 109–39.

Wells, J.C. (1982) Accents of English (3 volumes). Cambridge: Cambridge University Press.

Wells, J.C. and Colson, G. (1971) *Practical phonetics*. London: Pitman.

Wenden, A. (1987) *How to be a successful learner: insights and prescriptions from L2 learners*. In Wenden, A. and Rubin, J. (eds.), *Learner Strategies in Language Learning*. Englewood Cliffs, NJ: Prentice-Hall.

Wesche, M., Paribakht, T. and Reading, D. (1996) A comparative study of four ESL placement instruments. In Milanovic, M. and Saville, N. (eds.) *Selected papers from the 16th Language Testing Research Colloquium*. Cambridge: UCLCJ.

West, C. (1984) When the doctor is a 'lady': power status and gender in physician–patient encounters. *Symbolic Interaction* 7, 87–106.

West, M. (1953) *A general service list of English words*. Harlow: Longman.

White, J. (1986) The writing on the wall: beginning or end of a girl's career? *Women's Studies International Forum* 9(5), 561–74.

White, L. (1989) *Universal grammar and second language acquisition*. Amsterdam: John Benjamins.

Williams, J.M. (1975) *Origins of the English language: a social and linguistic history*. New York: Free Press; London: Collier Macmillan.

Woods, A., Fletcher, P. and Hughes, A. (1986) *Statistics in language studies*. Cambridge: Cambridge University Press.

Wray, A. (1990) The dual systems ('focusing') hypothesis: a right hemisphere account of language processing. *Speculations in Science and Technology* 13(1), 3–12.

Wray, A. (1992a) *The focusing hypothesis: the theory of left hemisphere lateralised language re-examined*. Amsterdam: John Benjamins.

Wray, A. (1992b) Restored pronunciation. In Knighton, T. and Fallows, D. (eds.) *Companion to medieval and renaissance music*. London: Dent, 292–9.

Wray, A. (1992c) Authentic pronunciation for early music. In Paynter, J., Howell, T., Orton, R. and Seymour, P. (eds.) *Companion to contemporary musical thought*. London: Routledge, 1051–64.

Wray, A. (1995) English pronunciation *c.*1500-*c.*1625. In Morehen, J. (ed.) *English choral practice 1400–1650*. Cambridge: Cambridge University Press, 90–108.

Wray, A. (1996) The occurrence of 'occurance' and 'alot' of other things 'aswell': patterns of errors in undergraduate English. In Blue, G. and Mitchell, R. (eds.) *Language and education: papers from the annual meeting of the British Association for Applied Linguistics 1995*. Clevedon: Multilingual Matters, 94–106.

Wrede, F. and Mitzka, W. (1926–1956) *Deutsche Sprachatlas*. Marburg: Elwert.

Young, D.J. (1984) *Introducing English grammar*. London: Hutchinson.

Zachrisson, R.E. (1909) *A contribution to the study of Anglo-Norman influence on English place-names*. Lund: Håkan Ohlsson.

Zachrisson, R.E. (1913) *Pronunciation of English vowels 1400–1700*. Gothenburg: Zachrisson.

Index

Numbers in italics indicate that at least one reference on that page is within a project.

DATE DUE

DEC 09 2005	
FEB 2 6 2006	
ILL: 2155 2998	due 8/14/06
MAY 0 1 2010	

GAYLORD   PRINTED IN U.S.A.